P9-CLF-760

American Presidential Elections

SUNY Series on the Presidency: Contemporary Issues
John Kenneth White, Editor

American Presidential Elections

Process, Policy, and Political Change

Edited by
Harvey L. Schantz

Andrew Carnegie Library
Livingstone College
701 W. Monroe St.
Salisbury, N.C. 28144

STATE UNIVERSITY OF NEW YORK PRESS

128204

Published by
State University of New York Press, Albany

© 1996 State University of New York

All rights reserved

Printed in the United States of America

No part of this book may be used or reproduced
in any manner whatsoever without written permission.
No part of this book may be stored in a retrieval system
or transmitted in any form or by any means including
electronic, electrostatic, magnetic tape, mechanical,
photocopying, recording, or otherwise without the prior
permission in writing of the publisher.

For information, address State University of New York Press,
State University Plaza, Albany, N.Y., 12246

Production by Cathleen Collins
Marketing by Bernadette LaManna

The following are reprinted by permission: Table 1.1 on page 30 by permission
of Elections Research Center. Table 2.1 on page 52 and table 2.9 on pages 74–75
by permission of National Journal, Inc. Copyright © 1992. All rights reserved.
Figure 4.3 on page 148 and Appendix pages 227–231 by permission of Congressional Quarterly Inc. Chapter 2 includes excerpts from *Democracy under Pressure: An Introduction to the American Political System,* Seventh Edition by Milton C. Cummings, Jr., and David Wise, copyright © 1993 by Harcourt, Brace and
Company, reprinted by permission of the publisher. Parts of chapter 3 originally
appeared in the Spring 1992 issue of *Polity,* Volume 24, No. 3. Reprinted with
permission.

Library of Congress Cataloging-in-Publication Data

American presidential elections : process, policy, and political
    change / edited by Harvey L. Schantz.
        p.   cm. — (SUNY series on the presidency, contemporary
    issues)
    Includes bibliographical references and index.
    ISBN 0–7914–2863–X (alk. paper). — ISBN 0–7914–2864–8 (pb : alk.
    paper)
    1. Presidents—United States—Election.   2. Presidents—United
States—Election—History.   I. Schantz, Harvey L., 1951–   .
II. Series: SUNY series on the presidency.
JK524.A75   1996
324.6'3'0973—dc20   95-18472
                                                                CIP

10 9 8 7 6 5 4 3 2 1

To Our Teachers

Contents

List of Figures   ix

List of Tables   xi

Acknowledgments   xiii

Introduction   1
HARVEY L. SCHANTZ

Chapter 1   The Presidential Selection Process   9
             HARVEY L. SCHANTZ

Chapter 2   Political Change Since the New Deal: The 1992
             Presidential Election in Historical Perspective   51
             MILTON C. CUMMINGS, JR.

Chapter 3   Sectionalism in Presidential Elections   93
             HARVEY L. SCHANTZ

Chapter 4   Alive! The Political Parties after the 1980–1992
             Presidential Elections   135
             GERALD M. POMPER

Chapter 5   Presidential Elections and Policy Change:
             How Much of a Connection Is There?   157
             DAVID R. MAYHEW

Chapter 6   Political Parties and Presidential Elections in
             the Postindustrial Era   189
             EVERETT CARLL LADD

Chapter 7   Conclusion   211
             HARVEY L. SCHANTZ

Appendix: Presidential Election Results, 1789–1992   227

Suggested Reading   233

About the Authors   243

Index   245

List of Figures

Figure 3.1. Sectional Mean Deviation from Jacksonian Democratic or Democratic Percentage of National Two-Party Vote, Presidential Elections, 1824–1852   101

Figure 3.2. Sectional Mean Deviation from Republican Percentage of National Two-Party Vote, Presidential Elections, 1856–1992   105

Figure 3.3. Sectional Mean Deviation from Jacksonian Democratic or Democratic Vote Swing, National Two-Part Vote, Presidential Elections, 1828–1852   112

Figure 3.4. Sectional Mean Deviation from Republican Vote Swing, National Two-Party Vote, Presidential Elections, 1860–1992   115

Figure 4.1. Realignment in Presidential Elections: Correlation of Democratic Vote in Successive Presidential Elections, 1956–1992   138

Figure 4.2. State Variation in the Democratic Presidential Vote, 1976–1992 (in Standard Deviations)   140

Figure 4.3. Party Unity in Congress, 1970–1993   148

Figure 6.1. Vote Switching in Presidential Elections, 1952–1980   194

Figure 6.2 Ticket Splitting: Proportion of All Voters Who Split Their Ballot in the Year's Presidential and Congressional Contests, 1952–1992   195

Figure 6.3 Party Identification, 1940–1994 (Gallup Poll)   196

Figure 6.4 Educational Attainment in America, 1970 and 1993   200

List of Tables

Table 1.1.   Voter Turnout in Presidential Elections, 1920–1992   30

Table 1.2.   Party Identification in the United States, 1952–1992 (University of Michigan Poll)   33

Table 1.3.   Political Party Success in Presidential Elections   36

Table 1.4.   Political Party Turnover in Presidential Elections   40

Table 2.1.   Those Who Voted in 1992: A Profile by Groups   52

Table 2.2.   The Democratic Percentage of the Total Vote for President: The South and the Rest of the United States Compared, 1932–1992   55

Table 2.3.   Democrats and Republicans Elected to the U.S. House of Representatives: The South and the Rest of the United States Compared, 1950–1994   58

Table 2.4.   Party Identification Among the American Electorate, 1940–1992 (Gallup Poll)   60

Table 2.5.   Democratic Voting Strength, by States, in 1988: States Ranked from Highest to Lowest Democratic Percentage of the Two-Party Vote for President in 1988   63

Table 2.6.   President Bush's Job Rating, 1989–1992   65

Table 2.7.   Annual Rates of Inflation and Unemployment in the United States, 1980–1992   66

Table 2.8.   Voter Support for Clinton, Bush, and Perot: The Gallup Poll's Three-Way Trial Heats Between March and Election Eve, 1992   68

Table 2.9.   How Groups Voted in 1992   74

Table 2.10.   Voters' "Family Financial Situation" Compared
              with Four Years Earlier, 1984–1992   81

Table 3.1.   Sectional Deviations from Jacksonian Democratic
              or Democratic Percentage of National Two-Party
              Vote, Presidential Elections, 1824–1852   100

Table 3.2.   Sectional Deviations from Republican Percentage
              of National Two-Party Vote, Presidential Elections,
              1856–1992   106

Table 3.3.   Sectional Deviations from Jacksonian Democratic
              or Democratic Vote Swing, National Two-Party Vote,
              Presidential Elections, 1828–1852   113

Table 3.4.   Sectional Deviations from Republican Vote
              Swing, National Two-Party Vote, Presidential
              Elections, 1860–1992   116

Table 4.1.   Correlation of Democratic Vote in Presidential
              Elections, 1976–1992   141

Table 6.1.   Partisan Identification of the American Public,
              1993 (Gallup Poll)   202

Appendix   Presidential Election Results, 1789–1992   227

Acknowledgments

I would most like to thank Milton Cummings, Everett Carll Ladd, David Mayhew, and Gerald Pomper. Each wrote his own chapter, presented his findings to an audience at my college, and contributed to the conceptualization of this book.

At the State University of New York, Plattsburgh, I would like to thank Martin Lubin, professor of political science, and David Mowry, professor of philosophy and director of the College Honors Program, for their counsel during the development of this book. Thanks too to Ms. Doris McKinstry, secretary of the Political Science Department, for preparing the manuscript. I am also grateful to Bernie Grabczewski of the Computing Support Center for the computer graphics. Financial aid for this project was provided by the SUNY Plattsburgh Distinguished Visiting Professors Fund.

At SUNY Press, I am grateful for the early and continuous support shown for this project by Clay Morgan, the political science editor, and Professor John Kenneth White, general editor of the SUNY Series on "The Presidency: Contemporary Issues."

Introduction

HARVEY L. SCHANTZ

In our nation's constitutional history, since 1789, there have been fifty-two presidential elections—three in the eighteenth century, twenty-five in the nineteenth century, and twenty-four so far in this century. These elections are among the most studied events in the American political system. Yet important questions concerning presidential elections remain, and older questions need fresh answers.

The studies in this book are guided by three basic questions. These are as follows:

- Are presidential elections a set of fifty-two discrete events, or are there patterns among them?
- Are these elections equal in importance, or are some contests more crucial than others?
- What are the relationships of presidential elections to the political parties, public policy, and society?

The authors of this book approach these questions from the perspective of an extended time dimension. Unlike many electoral studies, this book is concerned with the "population of elections," rather than the "population of individual voters."[1] This book compares and contrasts presidential elections in order to increase our understanding of their individual dynamics, sequences, and impact.

To carry out these goals, I have had the good fortune to collaborate with four leading scholars in the field of United States political parties and elections—Milton Cummings, Everett Carll Ladd, David Mayhew, and Gerald Pomper. Along with myself, each of the contributors answers this book's central questions from his own scholarly perspective. In other words, the contributors to this volume were given the opportunity to write from their own vantage point, to do what they do best. I think the result is a book that is useful to political scientists, grad-

1

uate students, and upper-division undergraduates, as well as accessible to the general reader.

As the subtitle of this book suggests, the subject matter clusters around process, policy, and political change. In the real world of presidential elections, these three are inextricably tied together, thus every chapter touches upon each of them in one way or another. For example, policy is not only a possible aftereffect of an election, but it is also a concern of voters, a strategic tool for parties and candidates, a checklist by which to gauge party effectiveness, and a reflection of societal need.

This said, however, there are decided emphases among the chapters. The presidential selection process is described in basic detail in chapter 1 by Harvey Schantz, and much of chapter 2 by Milton Cummings is devoted to the unfolding and outcome of this process in 1992. The substance of major waves of congressional policy making is highlighted in chapter 5 by David Mayhew, who also attempts to account for their causes.

Political change is perhaps the most touched-upon cluster of topics in this book. In 1960, E. E. Schattschneider asked in a chapter title, "What Does Change Look Like?"[2] His answer was that change had largely to do with new policy agendas, new lines of partisan conflict, and new electoral patterns. These are, in different ways, the concerns of chapter 3 by Harvey Schantz and chapter 6 by Everett Carll Ladd. Gerald Pomper devotes much attention to changing electoral patterns, but is mostly concerned with changes in the organizational effectiveness of the political parties.

The chapters in this book are loosely ordered from those focused on the election process and election outcomes, to those mostly concerned with the relationship among presidential elections, the political system, and society. Furthermore, the first two chapters provide much of the basic material necessary for a complete understanding of the chapters that follow. Let us now discuss each chapter in turn.

SCHANTZ ON THE PRESIDENTIAL SELECTION PROCESS

The first chapter of this book is a primer on the contemporary presidential selection process, including discussion of how it has evolved through the years. The first four parts of this chapter follow the quadrennial sequence of events: the pool of candidates; the nomination process; the general election campaign; and voting. The fifth part of this chapter attempts to place electoral outcomes in historical perspective by examining partisan and electoral trends since 1789. Chapter 1 details for the student and general reader how presidents are selected.

CUMMINGS ON POLITICAL CHANGE
SINCE THE NEW DEAL

The election of Franklin D. Roosevelt in the 1932 presidential election inaugurated the New Deal political era. For the next twenty years the Democrats controlled the White House and almost always elected majorities to the U. S. House and Senate. This Democratic success was reflected in public opinion surveys of party identification. A key component of Democratic strength was solid support from the southern states. The Democratic coalition of support also included solid electoral majorities from Catholics, Blacks, Jews, labor union households, and those with lower incomes.

In his chapter, Milton Cummings examines political change since the New Deal era. He details presidential and U. S. House election results in order to document the movement of the South from the Democrats to the Republicans. Cummings traces trends in party identification for the last one-half century. He also comments upon changes in the Democratic voting coalition evident in the 1992 presidential results.

Cummings also provides singular coverage of our last presidential election. According to Cummings, the 1992 election was one of those relatively infrequent election years when a new leadership team and party was returned to power—the ninth time this has happened in the twentieth century. In his chapter, Cummings describes the dynamics of the campaign and the pattern of the vote. He contrasts the 1992 outcome with the election results in 1984 and 1988. Cummings finds that in 1992 many short-term situational and strategic factors favored the Democrats. A long-time observer of national elections, Cummings classifies the 1992 election as, fundamentally, a vote of lack of confidence in the incumbent party.[3]

SCHANTZ ON SECTIONALISM

The actual votes cast in an election are extremely useful data for analyzing a single election and comparing a set of elections. Election results allow us to analyze presidential elections for the totality of U.S. history, whereas voter surveys extend back only as far as the 1930s. Election returns, which are often termed "aggregate data" by analysts since they add up the votes of many people, do not allow us, however, to study the motivations of individual voters.

In any one presidential election the partisan percentage of the vote is not uniform throughout the United States. It varies from county to county, state to state, and section to section. One might usefully study the pattern of the vote—the degree of uniformity or variance in the partisan percentage—in a single election. Such a study is termed a cross-sectional analysis. In presidential election studies, the unit of analysis is usually the county, state, or section. An election in which there are great differences in the partisan percentages across the regions is said to be sectional. A vote pattern in which partisan percentages are fairly uniform across the country is called a national vote pattern.

Another type of study compares sequential or select presidential elections. Such over time examinations are termed longitudinal studies. These studies look at vote totals over time for a political unit, be it section, state, or county. These examinations seek stability or change in vote totals.

Research designs frequently combine the features of cross-sectional and longitudinal studies. That is to say, they seek stability or change in the cross-sectional pattern of the vote in two or more presidential elections. In this book, the electoral analyses by Harvey Schantz and Gerald Pomper are examples of such studies.

Harvey Schantz examines sectional electoral patterns in presidential elections from 1824 to 1992, building on his earlier work.[4] He chronicles sectional diversity in the presidential vote and vote swing throughout American history, documenting an important perspective on U.S. political parties and elections. Schantz records periods of high sectionalism, such as before the Civil War and at the turn of the twentieth century, along with periods of national vote patterns, especially in contests between the Whigs and Democrats from 1840 to 1852 and between the Republicans and Democrats since the New Deal era of the 1930s.

POMPER ON THE STATE OF THE PARTIES

In his chapter, Gerald Pomper combines two of his long-standing research concerns, analysis of state-level presidential election results and evaluations of the effectiveness of U.S. political parties in the democratic process.[5] Pomper examines election returns since 1956 through a variety of now standard statistical techniques that he helped to popularize for these purposes in 1967. In particular, these include the correlation of successive and nonsuccessive elections to measure electoral coalition continuity and to identify clusters of elections with similar vote patterns. His findings lead Pomper to conclude that there has indeed been a realignment of electoral patterns since 1968 and that voters have now settled into a new stable alignment.

Throughout the 1970s and 1980s numerous commentators portrayed U.S. political parties as being in a state of organizational and functional decline. In the past, Pomper has subscribed to these arguments and findings, and has long been an advocate of a more effective party system. In this book, though, he argues that the premise of the decline of party thesis is, in part, based on a mistaken view of political parties that sees them as "collections of voters," rather than competing organizations. He also concludes that the parties are now more vital organizationally and functionally than they were at their nadir in the late 1960s and early 1970s, gaining power over the presidential nomination and finance processes, as well as cohering ideologically.

MAYHEW ON POLICY CHANGE

One of the major premises held by many political scientists, politicians, and members of the general public is that there is a strong causal link between presidential elections and public policy initiatives. Major policy change, as opposed to incremental movement, is believed to depend upon realigning elections or elections that confer a mandate upon government leaders. Policy change is facilitated by the processes of leadership turnover and the conversion of incumbent leaders who interpret the election returns.

In his chapter, David Mayhew sets out to test the link between elections and major policy change, extending and borrowing from his path-breaking and controversial study about the impact of divided government on politics and policy making in Washington, D.C.[6] To accomplish his goals, Mayhew isolates four preeminent legislative surges in U.S. history. These occurred during the Civil War and Reconstruction, the Progressive Era, the time of the New Deal, and the 1960s–1970s. He then investigates the extent to which this activity may be explained by elections, political parties, the economy, and public moods and movements.

Mayhew finds moods and movements to be a particularly powerful explanation. "As for presidential elections—the chief concern of this essay—they play a role but not as consequentially or frequently as we imagine," writes Mayhew.

LADD ON POSTINDUSTRIALISM

In his writings, Everett Carll Ladd has frequently been interested in the relationship between society and the political system, which primarily involves accommodations of the parties and elections system to major changes in the wider society.[7]

Over the "sweep" of U.S. history the parties have been nested in four different socioeconomic eras: the rural Republic, stretching roughly from independence to the Civil War; the industrializing nation, dating from the Civil War to the Great Depression; the industrial state, from 1929 to approximately 1970; and postindustrial society, our current era.

A postindustrial society is one in which there is general affluence, widespread access to higher education, and instantaneous means of national communication. In a postindustrial society a shrinking percentage of the workforce is devoted to manufacturing and agriculture. High technology fuels economic development, and the growing middle class is largely involved in "technical and professional" occupations. The nature of service industries changes, with growth in human services, research, and data analysis. There are growing employment opportunities for women.[8]

In his chapter, Ladd offers a current summary statement and extension of his analyses concerning the impact of postindustrial society on the parties and elections system. While Ladd takes into account the latest developments, such as "Ross Perot and 'Perotism'," he is primarily concerned with underlying trends. These include the communications revolution and increased education levels that have combined to weaken the role of the parties in elections and to instigate independent voting habits among the electorate. Affluence, Ladd argues, has undermined a class-based politics and has accentuated cultural differences. Increased female participation in the workforce is an antecedent of the well-known gender gap in elections, whereby women are more prone than men to vote Democratic. In all, Ladd portrays a political system that is markedly different than it was before 1970, the approximate advent of the postindustrial era.

NOTES

1. V. O. Key, Jr., "The Politically Relevant in Surveys," *Public Opinion Quarterly* 24 (Spring 1960): 54–61, quotation, p. 55.
2. E. E. Schattschneider, *The Semisovereign People: A Realist's View of Democracy in America* (Hinsdale, Ill.: Dryden Press, 1960), p. 114.
3. See, for example, Milton C. Cummings, Jr., *Congressmen and the Electorate: Elections for the U.S. House and the President, 1920–1964* (New York: The Free Press, 1966); and Cummings, ed., *The National Election of 1964* (Washington, D.C.: Brookings, 1966).
4. Harvey L. Schantz, "The Erosion of Sectionalism in Presidential Elections," *Polity* 24 (Spring 1992): 355–377. This article, which is included in chapter 3, is reprinted with permission of *Polity*.
5. Gerald M. Pomper, "Classification of Presidential Elections," *Journal of Politics* 29 (August 1967): 535–566; "The Decline of Partisan Politics," in *The Impact of the Electoral Process*, ed., Louis Maisel and

Joseph Cooper (Beverly Hills, Calif.: Sage, 1977), pp. 13–38; and Pomper, ed., *Party Renewal in America: Theory and Practice* (New York: Praeger, 1980).

6. David R. Mayhew, *Divided We Govern: Party Control, Lawmaking, and Investigations, 1946–1990* (New Haven: Yale University Press, 1991).

7. Ladd's writings on this topic have appeared in numerous forums, but he has most fully developed his thoughts in two major books, Everett Carll Ladd, *American Political Parties: Social Change and Political Response* (New York: Norton, 1970); and, with Charles D. Hadley, *Transformations of the American Party System: Political Coalitions from the New Deal to the 1970s,* 2nd ed. (New York: Norton, 1978).

8. This paragraph is partly based on Daniel Bell, *The Coming of Post-Industrial Society: A Venture in Social Forecasting* (New York: Basic Books, 1976; originally published 1973), esp. pp. xvi–xix.

CHAPTER 1

The Presidential Selection Process

HARVEY L. SCHANTZ

Presidential elections are at the core of representative democracy in the United States. In these contests, voters, through the electoral vote system, choose our nation's chief executive for the subsequent four years. The election results also signal victory for a particular political party and leadership team, the ascendancy of a voting coalition and, most likely, a shift of public policy in one direction or another.[1]

Presidential elections have a number of indirect effects: they facilitate a legitimate and stable government, offer protection for individuals from their leaders, and provide an opportunity for citizen growth and education.[2] Elections are a central mechanism by which our society resolves conflicts. More cynically, presidential elections are a process of regime renewal, as voters once again grant legitimate authority to their leaders in this most central of state-sponsored democratic rituals.[3]

Presidents of the United States are selected in a two-step process: a major political party nomination and a general election. Although only the general election is called for in the Constitution, all presidents, aside from George Washington, have won the presidential general election as the nominee of a major political party. The Constitution, which specifies eligibility for the presidency, combines with extra-constitutional norms to set the amorphous boundaries of the pool of candidates. The purpose of this chapter is to describe and explain the basics of the presidential selection process. Our discussion follows the quadrennial sequence of events: political prominence; the nomination process; the general election campaign; and voting.

"POLITICAL PROMINENCE": THE POOL OF CANDIDATES

"Political prominence" defines the set of individuals considered seriously for the presidency.[4] "A prominent individual, in these terms," according to Gerald Pomper, "is one who has caught the attention of voters and political leaders by his traits of personality, his performance in some task of public significance, or his identification with important issues and interests." The criterion of prominence superseded presidential availability, which emphasizes conformity, during the middle of the twentieth century. Political prominence combines at least four elements: constitutional eligibility; career positions; personal and social characteristics; and "winnowing."

Constitutional Eligibility

From our nation's beginning there have been few constitutional limitations on citizen eligibility for the presidency.[5] Article II, Section 1 says that a president must be a natural born citizen of the United States, be thirty-five years of age, and have resided in the United States for fourteen years. The Twelfth Amendment to the Constitution, ratified in 1804, separates the electoral vote balloting for president and vice president and applies the rules of presidential eligibility to the vice president.

Members of the legislative branch may not serve as president according to Article I, Section 6. Presumably, this prohibition also applies to judicial branch members. These officials may run for the presidency, though they must resign their positions prior to taking office. A Texas state law, in fact, allowed Lyndon Johnson in 1960 and Lloyd Bentsen in 1988, to simultaneously run for the U.S. Senate and the vice presidency.

The Twenty-second Amendment, ratified in 1951, limits presidents to two full terms or a maximum of ten years in office over a lifetime.[6] It was added to the Constitution partly as a reaction to Franklin Roosevelt, who was elected president four times, in 1932, 1936, 1940, and 1944—the only person to be elected more than twice. The only two presidents restrained from running for a third term so far have been Dwight Eisenhower and Ronald Reagan.

Career Positions

Prominent positions in the government or military have been a staple of the careers of presidents and presidential candidates throughout our nation's history. The last public office held prior to election to the presidency has most often been a state governorship (nine presidents), the vice presidency (five), a U.S. Senate seat (five), a cabinet position (five), or a military generalship (four).[7] An additional nine vice presidents succeeded to the presidency during a term of office. Early in U.S. history, the position of secretary of state was a crucial pathway to the presidency. Since 1932, governors and former governors have most often been elected president.

These numbers do not reflect the large numbers of U.S. senators that bid for the presidency. Between 1868 and 1972, presidential contenders were most often senators.[8] But only five senators won party nominations, as compared to fourteen governors. Fifteen senators did, however, win vice presidential nominations in these years.

In short, to be considered presidential material today, a person has to be or have been a vice president, a governor, or a U.S. senator. Cabinet secretaries do not have the popular appeal of yesteryear. Colin Powell, in 1995, was the first general since Dwight Eisenhower to be considered presidential material.

Personal and Social Characteristics

There are, in addition to the constitutional requirements and expected career positions, informal widely-held expectations concerning the personal and social characteristics of presidential nominees. These evolving standards include a potential nominee's gender, race, religion, family life, and aspects of personal behavior.

In his classic treatment of the subject, Clinton Rossiter wrote that a person who aspires to the presidency "must be, according to unwritten law: a man, white, a Christian. . . . He cannot be, according to unwritten law: a Negro, a Jew, an Oriental, a woman, an atheist. . . ."[9] Nothing that has happened since Rossiter wrote about the subject nearly forty years ago has completely contradicted these unwritten laws. All major party nominees for president have been male, White, and Christian. Among Christians, John F. Kennedy, elected in 1960, is the only Roman Catholic ever to be president. Governor Al Smith of New York, a Roman Catholic, had been nominated by the Democrats in 1928, but lost the general election.

Voter acceptance of presidential candidates of diverse backgrounds, as expressed in opinion polls, has, however, increased greatly since the late 1950s. Today, overwhelming majorities of voters say they would vote for a qualified Jewish (89 percent), woman (82 percent), or African American (79 percent) candidate.[10] Furthermore, opinion polls throughout 1995 found General Colin Powell, an African American, quite popular among adult Americans.[11] Powell had risen to national prominence during the 1991 war with Iraq, which he helped direct in his position as chairman of the Joint Chiefs of Staff.

Rossiter also included less severe rules for presidential hopefuls. They "ought not to be: . . . divorced, a bachelor. . . ." They "ought to be: . . . a veteran."[12] Two of these requirements have been broken by recent presidents. Ronald Reagan was divorced and remarried. Bill Clinton was not a veteran of U.S. involvement in Vietnam. Marital infidelity marked the denouement for candidate Gary Hart in his quest for the 1988 Democratic nomination. But Clinton's similar activity, along with his possible drug use, was overlooked by voters in the 1992 nominating contests and general election.

"Winnowing"

Constitutional eligibility, career positions, and personal and social characteristics delimit the pool of viable presidential candidates. "Pre-election-year winnowing" according to Erwin Hargrove and Michael Nelson, "sifts out from this pool a relatively small number of ambitious and 'serious' candidates."[13] Thomas Cronin reckons that at any given time the potential candidate pool is made up of about fifty individuals, but that there are only a "score or so of activist politicians who inevitably become the serious candidates."[14] In election year polls from 1936 to 1980, on average, about twenty-three candidates received 1 percent or more support in Gallup polls and about half that number achieved at least a 5 percent rating.[15]

A number of factors limit the size of the candidate pool. One of these is the press. In order to be considered a "presidential possibility" by the public, a candidate must be portrayed in that role by the press. The elite news organizations decide which of the candidates deserve such coverage, thereby heightening the chances of the so anointed.[16] The role of the press is greatest in this early stage of the selection process, when the candidates are less well-known.

The ability to attract large amounts of campaign money has traditionally been a sign of a candidate's seriousness.[17] In early 1995, Senator Phil Gramm proudly emphasized his fund-raising ability. And many pundits speculated that former Vice President Dan Quayle declined to run because of funding difficulties.

But for the most part, since the beginning of government finance in 1976, a crucial rite of passage has been a candidate's ability to raise enough money ($100,000 in contributions of $250 or less, with no more than $5,000 from any state) to qualify for matching government funds. The ability to so qualify is interpreted to mean widespread support among voters and also enhances the finances of the candidate.[18]

The winnowing process is crucially furthered by candidates' presidential ambition and risk-taking propensity. According to Stephen Hess, the characteristic that sets "the contours" of the candidate pool is presidential ambition, a deep desire to be president.[19] "The only common denominator," wrote Hess, "for those who would be president is the depth of their ambition . . . the serious candidates are a self-anointed breed. . . ."

John Aldrich, in contrast to Hess, feels that presidential ambition, or progressive ambition, is a given for all vice presidents, senators, and governors.[20] "The calculus of candidacy," however, "includes the costs of running for office, the probability of winning it, and the risks associated with the race." Given the same cost-benefit analysis, not all politicians are equally likely to enter the presidential race. According to Aldrich, "a demonstrated willingness to enter high-risk situations further differentiates presidential candidates from those who start with similar opportunities."

In conclusion, the group of individuals that is "politically prominent" at any one election is very small, limited by constitutional, professional, social, and psychological barriers. To those who do "throw their hat into the ring" and seek the presidency, the first hurdle is winning the nomination of their party.

NOMINATION PROCESS

In a number of important ways the nomination process is the most crucial step in the presidential selection process.[21] Once the nominations have been made only the two major party candidates have a realistic opportunity of winning the presidency. More potential presidents are eliminated at the nomination stage than in November. Nominations also determine the quality of the November choice and greatly affect the November outcome.

In order to formally gain their presidential nomination, both major political parties require a candidate to win a majority of the delegate support at the party's national convention. The delegates to the convention are mostly selected in a local caucus-state convention process or by presidential primaries in each of the states, the District of Columbia, and those territories allocated delegates by the national party committees.

Delegate Selection

In 1996, there will be 4,295 delegate positions for the Democratic National Convention and 1,984 delegate slots for the Republican National Convention.[22] The delegates selected to participate in a national party convention formally choose the presidential candidate of their party. They also collectively decide the vice presidential nominee, the party platform, and the party rules. The methods used to select delegates affect which delegates are chosen and therefore have an impact on a party's presidential ticket and its policy direction.

Historical Development. Political parties have held presidential nominating conventions since the 1830s. From 1832 to 1908, according to Leon Epstein, "virtually all delegates were chosen within each state by party caucus, district convention, state convention, executive committee, leadership, or some combination of such organizational agencies."[23] Between the years 1912 and 1968, with the exception of 1912 and 1916, when primaries temporarily peaked in use, the state caucus and conventions dominated delegate selection but a substantial minority of states selected delegates by a presidential primary. Since 1972, the presidential primary has been the method by which most convention delegates have been chosen.

National party conventions prior to 1972 were generally under the control of state party leaders. But the caucus-convention delegate selection process did afford an opportunity for "popular participation" and held out the possibility of "takeovers by new groups outside the established party leadership."[24] An example of this is the conservative movement and the nomination of Barry Goldwater by the Republicans in 1964.[25] This caveat notwithstanding, political party textbooks tell us that power and control over delegates were historically held by state party leaders.[26] In 1968, when Hubert Humphrey won the Democratic party nomination for president, his major strategy was the courtship of party leaders. He did not even enter a single primary.[27]

The increase in primaries in 1972 and in subsequent election cycles grew out of discontent over the process that nominated Humphrey.[28] In response to the divisive Chicago national party convention the Democratic National Committee adopted changes, suggested by the McGovern-Fraser Commission, designed to make state presidential caucuses more accessible to the party rank-and-file. In so doing, the party hoped to open up the nominating system while avoiding the demands for more presidential primaries. But rather than conduct party business under the new, more stringent rules prescribed by the national party, Democratic state parties opted for holding presidential primaries. In addition, newly adopted campaign finance legislation, the growing influence of television, and the atrophy of state and local party organizations contributed to the growth of primaries. In some instances, Republicans were pulled along by newly adopted state statutes.

Since 1972, all presidential nominations have been won by those candidates able to successfully negotiate the primary election gauntlet. Presidential nominations are decided by voters and candidates. Party leaders have relatively little influence. The new process has also increased the influence of the mass media, especially television, in nomination politics. In today's presidential nominating campaigns, candidates have to endure a year or more of intensive campaigning throughout the nation.

In 1992, Governor Bill Clinton and President George Bush had to succeed in an obstacle course of state presidential primaries to win their party nominations. Bill Clinton did very well. He won thirty-two of thirty-nine Democratic primaries, garnering 10,471,965 total votes, or 51.9 percent of the ballots cast. This percentage of the total primary vote made Clinton "the strongest vote-getter the Democrats have had since the primary-oriented nominating system came into being two decades ago."[29]

In 1992, George Bush swept all thirty-nine Republican primaries, receiving 9,512,142 total votes, or 73.0 percent of all the ballots cast. Although Bush ran strongly, his showing was not up to the standards attained by Richard M. Nixon or Ronald Reagan. Gerald R. Ford obtained a bare majority of the primary vote, but lost in November 1976. In essence, then, Bush's showing in the 1992 presidential primaries was a harbinger of the results of the November election, a point that pundits made as soon as the New Hampshire results were counted in February.[30]

The Mechanics. Today, the delegate selection process is, as it has always been, a state-based procedure that operates within the context of a national party. National parties allocate delegate positions to each of the states, the District of Columbia, and territories. Each state then determines how its delegates will be selected. Since 1972, the national parties, especially the Democrats, have placed some guidelines on states' nominating options.[31]

The Democratic National Committee (DNC) and the Republican National Committee (RNC) allocate delegate slots to the states based on a state's population and its partisan support.[32] In the Democratic party, the size of a state's electoral vote and its average Democratic percentage in the three preceding presidential elections are weighted equally. Republican delegations reflect statehood, House districts, and state success in electing Republican officials. In both parties, there is some controversy over the allocation formula.

Each state, through its legislative process, chooses a method and date for delegate selection.[33] In some states the parties have an option regarding their nominating method. Basically, the states and state parties choose one of two methods: either a local caucus-state convention process or a presidential primary. In practice, however, this basic distinction covers a wide variety of state nominating methods. In addition to conventions and primaries, Democrats send selected party and elected officials as delegates to their convention.

Primaries.   Presidential primaries vary along a number of dimensions. Chief among these are the rules governing who may participate; the translation of popular votes into delegates; and the area covered by a primary. Voter eligibility is determined by state law. For the Democrats, voter access requirements must also be consistent with national party guidelines. In an open primary system, registered voters may participate in the party primary of their choice. In states with a closed primary, voters may only participate in the primary of their own registration. In practice, the distinction between the states is not as simple as open or closed. There is variation as to how long before primary day a voter must be registered with a political party in order to be eligible for a primary. In some closed primary states, a voter may switch registration on primary day.

The Democratic national party prohibits use of an open primary for delegate selection.[34] In a challenge to the national party, Wisconsin Democrats insisted on selecting delegates in an open primary in 1980. The United States Supreme Court, in a 1981 case, *Democratic Party of the United States v. Wisconsin ex rel La Follette*, held that national party rules are superior to state laws. In 1984, Wisconsin used a caucus nomination system, as the state legislature refused to alter the traditionally open Wisconsin primary. In 1988, the national party granted an exception to Wisconsin and Montana.

The translation of popular votes into delegates takes two basic forms. In a winner-take-all system, the candidate with a plurality of the popular vote receives all the delegates at stake. In a proportional system, candidates receive delegates in rough proportion to their popular vote percentage. National Democratic party rules, which were newly strengthened for 1992, require that delegates be divided up proportionally among all candidates receiving at least 15 percent of the vote.

Republican party rules allow states to adopt either a winner-take-all or a proportional system. State Republican parties also have discretion to determine the threshold, or the percentage of the vote necessary, for a candidate to qualify for delegates.

A third basic facet of the primary election system is whether the primary is a statewide contest or is broken down by congressional districts. Democratic party rules require that 75 percent of a state's delegates be chosen at the congressional district level or lower and that 25 percent of the delegates be elected at-large. Republicans allow this decision to be made by the states.[35]

Caucus-State Convention System. In many of the smaller states presidential convention delegates are selected in a series of party meetings. This multitiered process begins with precinct caucuses, includes county and congressional district level caucuses, and culminates in a state convention. The delegates chosen at the state party convention and, in some instances, at other levels, attend the national party convention. The state meetings are held approximately six weeks apart, stretching over a few months between February and June. Like the primaries, precinct-level caucuses may be open or closed, although they are almost always closed.

In a party precinct caucus, local voters meet and discuss issues of public policy and candidate preference. Those attending the meeting split up into groups according to their candidate preference. Delegates to the county conventions from each precinct are allocated to the candidate support groups in approximate proportion to that group's percentage of attendees at the precinct caucus. This process of discussion, allocation, and selection of delegates continues at the county, congressional district, and state levels.

One of the impacts frequently attributed to the rise of presidential primaries is the weakening of the role played by state party leaders in the presidential nomination process. But the local caucus-state convention system has by no means remained a tool of the party establishment, either. Presidential candidates capable of mobilizing large numbers of activists are able to dominate precinct caucuses. George McGovern in 1972 demonstrated the permeability of party caucuses to candidate activists. The Iowa caucuses were the cornerstone of Jimmy Carter's 1976 campaign. The successes of Jesse Jackson and Pat Robertson in 1988 showed that these low turnout affairs are particularly amenable to ideological candidates.[36] In truth, as Everett Carll Ladd has said, "Party caucuses in the modern sense are nothing more than restrictive primaries."[37]

The Calendar. Each of the states must also determine the date for delegate selection. Primaries and caucuses-state conventions run from

February until June. Democratic party rules allow these events to be held from the first Tuesday in March to the second Tuesday in June. A few states are granted exceptions to this rule, most notably Iowa and New Hampshire. The RNC does not prescribe the delegate selection calendar, leaving the scheduling of primaries and caucuses to the states and state parties.

Traditionally, nomination struggles begin in the snows of New Hampshire in February and finish in June as candidates campaign in California and New Jersey. Since 1976, the Iowa caucus has joined the New Hampshire primary as an early focus of attention. These early states, because of the momentum picked up by the winning candidates, have a disproportionate level of influence in the nominating process. Only if the nomination is undecided will the June California primary have any significance.

After the nomination of Walter Mondale in 1984, many southern Democratic party leaders felt that the nominating process was weighted in favor of northern liberal states. To counter this, many southern and border states brought their nominating event forward, a process called frontloading, to an early Tuesday in March. This Tuesday, commonly called Super Tuesday, was instrumental in the 1992 Clinton nomination, validating the strategy of southern Democratic leaders.

Frontloading continues for 1996. The New York primary will be held on March 7, the California primary on March 26. Super Tuesday is set for March 12. Most of the delegates will be selected by the end of March. This means the crucial primary election season has been compressed into February and March.[38]

The Media.   The role of the media, particularly television, is greater in the nomination process than during the general election campaign.[39] The nomination process is more complex, and generally, there is less information available. Also, the nomination process is an intraparty struggle, so voters are unable to rely on partisan cues.

According to Nelson Polsby and Aaron Wildavsky, "Television news coverage plays a significant role in determining who wins the nomination. . . ." As we noted in our discussion of "winnowing," the media decide which candidates are worthy of attention. They also emphasize one nomination contest or another. The media also set the public's expectations for the various candidates and interpret victory or defeat. A losing candidate is deemed a winner if he or she exceeds the media's expectations. Likewise, a winner is tarred with defeat if he or she does not meet the standards set by the media.

Presidential candidates, of course, try to influence media coverage.[40] A favorite tactic is to downplay one's prospects, so that expectations are not heightened. This increases the likelihood of meeting expectations. Candidates choose to emphasize one nomination contest or another.

Professional Delegates.   To increase the influence of elected officials at their convention, the Democrats require that each state party add delegate slots, equal to 15 percent of their basic allocation, for party and elected officials.[41] Additional delegate positions, called superdelegates, are allotted by formula to holders of high office, such as senators and representatives. The Republican party has no equivalent to these. However, "a rule change in 1988 allowed all GOP governors and members of Congress access to the floor and permission to be seated with their state delegations—even if they are not delegates."

National Party Conventions

In the summer of a presidential election year each of the major political parties holds a convention to formally choose the party's presidential and vice presidential nominee and to amend and approve the party rules and platform. Presidential nominating conventions originated in the 1830s, and 1840 was the first year that they were held by both major parties (which were then the Democrats and the Whigs).

Before Conventions.   Prior to the national convention there was a variety of short-lived presidential nominating methods. Chief among these was the congressional caucus, a meeting of a party's legislative contingent. This method was used for nominating Democratic-Republican candidates from 1800 to 1824, and the Federalists used it from 1800 to 1808. In 1796, congressional party leaders had nominated presidential candidates. The last two Federalist nominations, in 1812 and 1816, were made in closed meetings of leading party officials. The 1824 Democratic-Republican congressional caucus was not effective, as party factions ignored the caucus decision and a total of four party candidates entered the November race. In 1828, there were no congressional caucuses, and presidential candidates were nominated by state legislatures.[42]

Date and Site Selection.   During the presidential election year the party that is not in the White House holds its convention in July and the party of the president assembles in August.[43] This tradition is an attempt to afford each party an exclusive month of public and media attention. The party professionals believe the president's party will generally be more unified than the "out" party. The challenging party, therefore, holds its convention earlier and the president's party later in the summer. This gives the challenging party increased opportunity to unify after a possibly bruising nominating contest. This calendar may sometimes have disastrous results for the incumbent party. In 1968, for example, Democratic presidential candidate Hubert H. Humphrey was nominated at a divided and rancorous convention and was unable to unify the party and get his campaign strongly underway until late September. In 1992, George Bush delayed his campaign when he went fishing during the Democratic National Convention; he waited until his own formal nomination to begin campaigning in earnest.

The location of the national convention is determined by the site selection committee of each party's national committee. Potential cities must have a large modern arena, many first-class hotel rooms, a secure environment, and adequate transportation and dining facilities. Potential city governments, along with local corporate sponsors, compete for the conventions by offering financial packages that include setting up the convention hall, hosting parties, and providing security. Since 1976, national conventions have been financed by the national government, as provided in the Federal Election Campaign Act of 1974, so that the symbolic significance of a city has become more important than its financial package. Thus, between 1968 and 1992, five of seven Republican conventions were held in the South, though previously none had ever been held there. Recently, the Democrats have frequently found themselves in New York City, in 1976, 1980, and 1992.

In 1996, the conventions will be held later than usual—after the completion of the summer Olympic Games in Atlanta. The Republicans will meet in San Diego, on August 12–16, with an eye toward California's fifty-four electoral votes. The Democrats will assemble two weeks later in Chicago, the first party convention in the "windy city" since the highly divisive Democratic gathering in 1968.[44]

Schedule of Events.   Party conventions are four-day affairs, stretching from Monday until Thursday.[45] Most of the highlights are staged during prime-time hours for maximum television coverage. The three major networks no longer provide gavel to gavel coverage, leaving this task to CNN (Cable News Network) and C-SPAN (Cable Satellite Public Affairs Network).

The highlight of the first night is the keynote address, which is designed to get the convention off to a rousing start. In 1992, the Democrats had three keynoters, "each with a different constituency."[46] In

1992, the Republican keynote speaker, Phil Gramm, spoke on Tuesday. Monday night, however, featured more memorable speeches by Patrick Buchanan and former President Ronald Reagan.

On Tuesday, conventions decide three matters: the credentials of the delegates who wish to be seated; the party rules governing the convention and nomination process; and the party platform, which is a statement of the principles and policy positions of the party. Most often, convention floor challenges to the credentials of delegates or to the convention rules are tied to rivalry between candidate camps. Although there have been no large-scale battles over credentials in recent years, rules fights were closely tied to rivalry between Reagan and Ford in the 1976 Republican Convention and between Edward Kennedy and Carter in the 1980 Democratic National Convention.

The party platform is written in the weeks before the convention in a complicated process that reflects the relative delegate strengths of the competing candidates.[47] Thus, in 1992, the campaign staffs of Clinton and Bush (although press reports were to the contrary) were able to dictate the contents of their party platforms. At the conventions, delegates occasionally have the opportunity to vote on "minority planks." In 1992, however, the platforms were approved by voice vote without amendment.

Very often it is alleged by the popular press that party platforms serve no purpose and that they are forgotten once the election is over. But careful research by Gerald Pomper demonstrates that party platforms help voters reach informed electoral decisions and aid the party election effort. Furthermore, after the election, party platform pledges are overwhelmingly fulfilled by the winning party and even by the losing one.[48]

On the third night of the convention the presidential nominee is formally chosen. There are nominating speeches and seconding speeches. These are followed by a roll call of the states, in which each delegation, in response to the convention chair's inquiry, touts the virtues of its state and announces how the state's delegates will be divided between the presidential hopefuls.

A candidate is formally nominated when an aspirant receives a majority of the delegate support. In previous years, it was frequently necessary to hold more than one ballot. The record number of roll calls totaled 103 at the Democratic Convention in 1924, which then required two-thirds of the delegate support to formally nominate.

Since 1956, all major party conventions have nominated on the first ballot. This is due to the fact that delegates are now largely chosen based on their candidate preference and, since 1956, a candidate has always amassed a majority of delegates prior to the national convention. Candidates screen those people who want to run as delegates on their ticket. But delegates are not legally bound to vote for the candidate for whom they have been selected. Rule 11H of the Democratic party delegate selection rules for 1992 states, however, that "delegates elected to the national convention pledged to a presidential candidate shall in all good conscience reflect the sentiments of those who elected them." There is a strong expectation, in both parties, that delegates will vote for the candidate they supported in the primaries or caucuses, but they are legally able to change their minds.[49]

Earlier in American history, nominees were chosen by presidential nominating conventions. But today, as we have seen, conventions put their stamp of approval on the candidate who has emerged in the state primaries and caucuses. In this sense, political party conventions do not decide presidential nominations, but rather confirm or ratify the decisions arrived at in the delegate selection process.

On the fourth night of the convention the vice presidential nominee, nominated by the presidential nominee, is approved by the convention. According to Nelson Polsby and Aaron Wildavsky "vice presidential nominees are chosen to help the party achieve the presidency . . . they must possess those desirable qualities the presidential nominee lacks, and they must be acceptable to the presidential nominee."[50] Often, this means balancing the ticket by geography, ideology, age, or experience; sometimes, it means excluding incompatible personalities.

After the selection of the vice presidential nominee, the convention continues with that nominee's acceptance speech. The presidential nominee acceptance speech is then delivered. The convention concludes with an attempt at a show of party unity.

If the convention now plays a less independent role in the selection of the party nominee, its role in the general election campaign has increased in the television age. Much of the convention is turned over to attacking the opposing party. Candidates look forward to a post-convention bounce in the polls. In many ways, the national party conventions are the beginning of the general election campaign.

THE GENERAL ELECTION CAMPAIGN

Once the parties have decided on their nominees, the general election phase of the presidential selection process begins. Ordinarily, this means the race for the presidency is between two candidates, although in recent years, in 1968, 1980, and 1992, there have been substantial third-party challengers. Our discussion of the general election will cover the electoral vote system and the candidate campaign.

Electoral Vote System

The Mechanics.   To be elected president a candidate must receive a majority of electoral votes. Presidential elections are indirect: voters at the polls do not vote directly for their preferred candidate but, rather, pull the lever for a party's slate of electors. These electors are pledged— but not legally bound—to support the candidate preferred by the voters in their state.

In December, the winning electors head to their state capitol where they cast their presidential and vice presidential ballots. In January, at a joint session of Congress, the electoral votes for president and vice president are added and announced. Typically, electors follow the will of their state's voters, but occasionally an elector strays from the popular verdict.

If no candidate receives a majority of the electoral votes, the selection of president falls to the House of Representatives. In the House, each state delegation has one vote, in a choice limited to the top three electoral vote candidates. Twice, following the elections of 1800 and 1824, the U.S. House chose the president. If no vice presidential candidate receives a majority of the electoral vote, the choice is made in the Senate between the top two candidates. It has been necessary to use this procedure only once, after the election of 1836.

In 1996, there will be a total of 538 electoral votes, and a candidate needs 270 to win. These numbers have held steady since 1964, when the District of Columbia was granted three electoral votes by constitutional amendment and the U.S. House was readjusted from 437 to 435 seats.

Every state is allocated electoral votes equal to its representation in Congress (the House and Senate). There is a great range in the number of electors allocated to the various states. For the elections of 1992, 1996, and 2000, California has the most electors, 54 or one-fifth of those needed to win the presidency. New York, with 33, and Texas, with 32, are next highest. Although it is an unlikely combination, the largest eleven states have 270 electoral votes, all those necessary for victory. By contrast, seven states and the District of Columbia have three electoral votes each.

The number of electoral votes a state has is subject to change as U.S. House seats are reapportioned subsequent to every decennial census.

The next change in electoral votes will come about for the election of 2004. The ups and downs of a state's electoral votes reflect its share of the country's population. In the 1960 election, when John Kennedy was elected, New York cast 45 electoral votes, Massachusetts 16, Texas 24, and California 32. By 1992, New York was down to 33, and Massachusetts to 12. But Texas had 32 and California had 54. There has been a shift of electoral votes from the Northeast and Midwest to the South and West, from the frost belt to the Sun Belt. But most states have maintained a relatively stable number of electors.

Strategies and Impacts.   To maximize their clout, states allocate their electoral votes on a winner-take-all basis. That is to say, in a state, the winner of a plurality of popular votes, even if it is only one, receives all the electors of that state. Only two small states, Maine and Nebraska, do not allocate their delegates on a winner-take-all basis.

The winner-take-all basis encourages candidates to spend more resources and time in the large states than they would if such resources were allocated simply by electoral vote ratios.[51] Thus, Michigan, with 18 electoral votes, will receive more than six times the attention that a state with three electors, like South Dakota would. Candidates are fearful of losing a large state by a small popular vote margin.

In recent decades there has been a strong tendency for the electoral vote outcome to magnify the size of the popular vote margin. In 1984, to cite an extreme example, Reagan received 59 percent of the national presidential vote, however he received 525 out of 538, or 98 percent, of the electoral votes. In 1992, Clinton's 43 percent of the total vote translated into 370, or 69 percent, of the electoral votes.

There are a number of difficulties with the electoral vote system.[52] Perhaps foremost is the possibility of electing a president who does not come in first in the popular vote. This could easily happen if one candidate gained many electoral votes with small pluralities, while the other candidate was running up large popular pluralities in the other states. Twice in U.S. history, in 1876 and 1888, the popular vote winner lost the electoral college.

The Candidate Campaign

The general election campaign has traditionally stretched from Labor Day to Election Day. But in 1992, the Democrats began their campaign immediately after their July convention with a Bill Clinton-Al Gore bus tour from New Jersey to Missouri. In a campaign, each party seeks to maintain its base of support and to add enough additional electoral votes to win.

Essential considerations for each candidate's campaign deal with organization, finance, the search for votes, their message, and their desired image.[53] Today, candidates must participate in nationally televised debates. To a substantial degree, these considerations are affected by the incumbency status and party of the candidates.

Organization. Each presidential candidate, as required by the Federal Election Campaign Act of 1971, assembles a campaign organization distinct from the national party committee staff.[54] The campaign organization includes an inner circle of advisers, a staff that travels with the president, and professional and support staff at national headquarters. The candidate's campaign organization conducts an independent effort, as well as coordinates the efforts of the national, state, and local party organizations.

The inner circle of advisers includes a campaign director or chairman, a campaign manager, a chief pollster, and a communications director or press secretary. These advisers work with the presidential candidate to set the strategy and to coordinate the campaign. Frequently, the inner circle of advisers is drawn from the candidate's home state, where they have previously served the candidate in comparable positions. But presidential candidates may also draw on individuals with national party affiliations and reputations, especially when it comes to selecting pollsters. Attached to the inner circle are policy advisers, usually unpaid, who are drawn from the ranks of academia.

Modern day presidential candidates are accompanied by key staff as they crisscross the country in search of votes. These key advisers include press aides and speech writers. The presidential contingent is greeted by advance people who have set up shop prior to the candidate's appearance, in hopes of assuring a large and friendly crowd and a large local media contingent. If their candidate wins, the top personnel employed by the candidates look forward to a choice job in the new administration.

Finance. For most of U.S. political history, presidential candidates used private donations to fund their campaigns; as the costs of campaigns rose, so did the size of the donations.[55] However, in response to rising costs and perceived corruption, the Congress and president passed legislation in the 1970s, primarily the Federal Election Campaign Act (FECA) and Amendments, which, among other things, provide government financing of general election campaigns.

The amount of the subsidy for each major party's nominee was set in 1974 dollars at $10 million. Increased for inflation, the subsidy for 1992

was $55.2 million. Candidates accepting this money, an option pro-
vided by the Supreme Court in *Buckley v. Valeo* (1976), agree not to
spend any additional funds. Third parties and independent candidates
who did not garner at least 5 percent of the previous presidential vote,
are eligible for funds, on a sliding scale according to their vote percentage, after the election.

Since the subsidies began in 1976 all major party candidates have
accepted the government money, thereby agreeing to a spending cap.
Not to do so is to be open to charges of buying the election. Also, it is
very difficult to raise large sums with the $1,000 contribution limit also
contained in FECA. John Anderson received money after the 1980 election, using it to pay off his campaign debt. In 1992, Ross Perot did not
seek federal money, a point he drove home to audiences, so he was able
to exceed the expenditure limits.[56]

Although major party candidates do not have to spend as much time
as they used to raising money for their campaign, the disclosure
requirements of FECA require candidates to employ a battery of
accounting and legal staff. The campaign subsidies, furthermore, have
by no means solved all the problems of campaign funds. Two loopholes
in the law are independent expenditures made by others on behalf of
candidates, and "soft money," contributed by large donors to the parties. In 1992, "soft money" spending on behalf of each major candidate
dwarfed the subsidies and Perot's total spending.[57]

Presidential candidates spend more than half their money on television advertising. Although production and airtime are expensive, television is the most efficient way for candidates to reach voters. Large
expenditures are also typically made for travel, staff salaries, polling,
and political consultants.[58]

Geographic Appeals.   The search for votes must extend to enough
states for the candidate to win at least 270 electoral votes. Candidates
must calculate the odds of winning each state and devote a disproportionate share of their resources to large states—with doubtful outcomes.
These calculations should be made before Labor Day, but they must
remain flexible enough to change as the campaign unfolds.[59]

Many commentators tell us that each party begins with an electoral
vote base. Before the 1992 election, the Republicans were said to have
had a huge base in the South and West; the Democrats, a small one in
New England. However, the Democrats won the 1992 presidential election with 370 electoral votes. The reality of present-day politics is that
all states (except for the District of Columbia) are potentially within the
grasp of either party. As Polsby and Wildavsky wrote in 1991, "There is

scant basis for the belief that Republicans have solid turf they can count on no matter what may happen any more than the Democrats do. Both will have to work for their electoral votes."[60]

Group Appeals. Although the search for votes is conducted with the electoral college in mind, candidate appeals are directed at groups of voters.[61] The first task of both candidates is to encourage a high turnout and loyal voting among their party's usual voting coalition. The Democratic coalition includes lower income groups, African Americans, Jews, teachers, and women. Republicans rely on heavy support from upper income groups, Whites, Protestants, business people, and men. Groups highly concentrated in large electoral vote states, such as the Jewish community in New York and California, receive attention greater than their numbers. Both parties encourage their partisan identifiers to go to the polls and loyally support their party's ticket.

The search for votes extends to voters who are not secure in either camp. In recent years, these have included Catholic, middle class, and blue collar voters. The large number of independent identifiers is a crucial source of votes for both parties.

A daring strategy seeks to extend the search for votes to groups ordinarily extremely loyal to the opposition. In 1968 Nixon's southern strategy was a highly successful appeal to Whites in that region. In 1896, on the other hand, William Jennings Bryan's appeal to eastern urban factory workers was unsuccessful. Such gambits often lead to permanent changes in the voting coalitions for president, with both positive and disastrous results for party electoral success.

The Message. The candidate's message is crucial in the appeal for votes. To a large degree, though, the message is molded by the party and incumbency status of the candidates.[62] The Democrats must present an economic message geared to the lower to middle income groups, while the GOP must appeal to upper income groups and business people. The Democrats' message must further the cause of minorities, feminists, and organized labor. The Republicans must champion the causes of small and big business. Both parties must appeal to the middle classes and suburbanites.

The incumbency status of the candidates has an even larger effect on their messages. Incumbents must emphasize the accomplishments of the last four years and promise continuity. Challengers must call into question the accomplishments of the immediate past and promise a brighter future. A favorite challenger refrain is to offer change. An incumbent who offers change, as Bush did in 1992, appears foolish.

Incumbents stress their experience, while challengers stress their Washington outsider status.

In an election without an incumbent there is more latitude for candidate messages. A vice president of the outgoing administration who is nominated for president, though, is closely associated with the record of the previous administration. Most often this has been a liability for these nominees, as they are held accountable for the shortcomings of the outgoing administration, but are not able to claim credit for most of its accomplishments. George Bush was the first sitting vice president elected president in the 152 years since Martin Van Buren won in 1836.

The Image.   The image and identity of the candidates is another important component of their search for votes. The attributes that Americans look for in a president are exalted, and include qualities of "leadership," "competence," "integrity," and "empathy."[63]

Incumbents have both advantages and disadvantages in projecting a winning image. A president has ample opportunity to demonstrate his or her positive attributes. On the other hand, however, presidents are well-known and therefore have little leeway for sprucing up their image.

The goal for would-be presidents is to appear presidential. Nonincumbents must demonstrate the personality and cognitive skills necessary for the job. Nominees emphasize the value of their previous experiences. A presidential challenger is often portrayed as less than presidential timber by the incumbent. Televised presidential debates are an excellent opportunity for challengers to project a winning image to a huge audience.

Presidential Debates.   The central events of contemporary presidential campaigns are the presidential and vice presidential debates. These debates have consistently attracted huge television audiences of over 60 million people.[64] The first nationally televised debates were held in 1960 between John Kennedy and Richard Nixon. Since 1976, these debates have been held during each election campaign. Presidential candidates no longer have the strategic option of declining to debate, for these events have "become a recognized institution. . . ."[65] Vice presidential candidates have also entered debates in 1976, 1984, 1988, and 1992.

Although there is not complete consensus on the impacts of the presidential debates, a few propositions are widely believed. The first is that a challenger has much more to gain from a debate than a sitting president does. Challengers appearing on the same stage with a president, suddenly become "presidential" themselves. Challengers are also able to present themselves to a national audience, an opportunity to dispel negative portrayals. For example, in 1980, challenger "Reagan gained ground by displaying an affable, apparently relaxed manner, thereby offsetting Carter's previous warnings that the Republican nominee was an aggressive hawk who might lead the country into a military adventure."[66]

A second widely-held proposition is that "debates are more about accidents and mistakes than about enlightenment on the capacities of candidates to govern."[67] Front-runners must avoid mistakes to maintain their lead, and those trailing in the polls cannot afford an error. Mistakes include poor image control, such as Nixon's makeup in 1960 or Michael Dukakis's coolness in 1988; misstatements, notably Ford's 1976 remark about Eastern Europe; and poor preparation, such as Reagan in the first debate of 1984. In the second presidential debate of 1992 Bush stumbled when he was not able to quickly reply to an audience member who asked him how the poor economy affected him personally.

Other widely-held beliefs, which may be more election specific, are that debates reinforce preexisting voter attitudes; that voters are more interested in the style than the substance of the debate; and that the public's evaluation of the debate is greatly influenced by media interpretation. Nevertheless, presidential debates are a wonderful opportunity for the public to gain information about the presidential candidates in preparation for voting.

VOTING

On Election Day the voters choose the electors who in turn select the next president. Aggregate patterns in voter turnout and choice are usually related to salient socioeconomic status characteristics and group memberships, including income, religion, race, and residency.[68] Voting, however, is not a socially determined activity.[69] Whether or not a person votes, and how he or she does vote, are matters of individual choice that are dependent upon individual beliefs and attitudes.[70]

Voter Turnout

The Numbers. In recent presidential elections only about one-half of the voting age population has participated.[71] Since 1972, turnout has varied between a high of 55.2 percent in 1972 and 1992 and a low of 50.1 percent in 1988 (Table 1.1). Turnout levels were rather uniform and on a slightly higher plateau in the 1950s and 1960s, varying between 59.3 percent of the voting age population in 1956 and peaking in 1960 at 62.8 percent.

Table 1.1.   *Voter Turnout in Presidential Elections, 1920–1992*

Year	Turnout (%)[a]	Year	Turnout (%)[a]
1920	44.2	1960	62.8
1924	44.3	1964	61.9
1928	52.3	1968	60.9
1932	52.5	1972	55.2
1936	56.9	1976	53.5
1940	58.9	1980	52.6
1944	56.0	1984	53.1
1948	51.1	1988	50.1
1952	61.6	1992	55.2
1956	59.3		

Sources: 1920–1928, U.S. Bureau of the Census, Statistical Abstract of the United States: 1962 (83d ed.) (Washington, D.C., 1962), p. 373, Table No. 497; and 1932–1992, U.S. Bureau of the Census, Statistical Abstract of the United States: 1993 (113th ed.) (Washington, D.C., 1993), p. 284, Table No. 455.

From 1928 to 1948 turnout levels varied from 51.1 percent to 58.9 percent. In the 1920 and 1924 elections turnout was much lower, about 44 percent.

The Decline Since 1960.   The 1960 turnout figure is the highest percentage of the voting age population ever to vote in a presidential election.[72] It is also the highest turnout among eligible voters since 1908. The closeness of the Kennedy-Nixon contest combined with social trends—rising education, decreased immigration, and a female population accustomed to voting—to promote this peak in turnout.

Since 1960, turnout has declined in every presidential election, except in 1984 and 1992. In 1988, turnout was only 50.2 percent of the voting age population, the lowest level of participation since 1924. This decline occurred despite increased education levels and the easing of suffrage restrictions for minority populations in the South.

There was a surprisingly substantial increase in voter turnout in 1992, however. In this election, 55.2 percent of the voting age population participated, the highest turnout level in twenty years. News reports attributed much of the 1992 increase to the Ross Perot candidacy and the change orientation of the electorate. One survey found that "about 15 percent of Perot voters would have stayed home if Perot had not been on the ballot."[73]

The most convincing explanation of the decline of voter turnout since 1960 emphasizes psychological changes among voters. Specifically, Paul Abramson and John Aldrich demonstrate that the decline in turnout is associated with a weakening of party loyalties and an erosion of a sense of external political efficacy among voters.[74] According to Abramson, Aldrich, and David Rohde these two factors account for 62 percent of the turnout decline between 1960 and 1988, with most of the drop-off accounted for by the decline in political efficacy. Additional turnout decline is explained by short-term factors, such as the widespread perception that Bush would win easily in 1988.

Implications. In their study of the 1988 election, Abramson, Aldrich, and Rohde found some differences in policy preference between voters and nonvoters. But they concluded that "there is no reasonable scenario under which increased turnout would have altered the outcome of the presidential election." However, these authors are concerned that turnout is low among disadvantaged Americans and that low turnout "may undermine the legitimacy of elected political leaders."[75]

Walter Dean Burnham is particularly distressed by the decline in turnout. He finds that the current situation is a demobilization of the working class. The decline in turnout is concentrated among the poor and working class; professionals and rich are turning out at a 90 percent rate. This greatly advantages the Republican party and hurts the Democrats.[76]

The right to vote is one of the defining features of democracy. Yet millions of eligible voters do not exercise their suffrage. In 1992, almost 85 million Americans of voting age did not vote. These nonvoters outnumbered the combined vote for Clinton and Bush. Perot's 19.7 million votes pale by comparison. And the popular vote difference between Clinton and Bush was less than 6 million. E. E. Schattschneider was onto something when he pointed out long ago that "All that is necessary to produce the most painless revolution in history, the first revolution ever legalized and legitimatized in advance, is to have a sufficient number of people do something not much more difficult than to walk across the street on election day."[77]

Voter Choice

For most of the electorate, voting decisions are heavily influenced by their party identifications, perceptions of the candidates, and issue preferences. The particular mix of these factors changes from election to election and is somewhat dependent on the candidates' campaigns and the nature of the times.[78]

Party Identification.   Party identification is a psychological attachment or feeling of loyalty that a voter has for a political party.[79] For many voters, party identification is a long-term core belief that influences their political thinking and behavior. People view political issues and presidential candidates through the lenses of their party identification, generally favoring the positions and nominees of their party.

The party identification of the electorate is measured by the Center for Political Studies of the University of Michigan from responses to a set of two questions administered to a random sample of U.S. citizens. Those surveyed are asked: "Generally speaking, do you usually think of yourself as a Republican, a Democrat, an Independent, or what?" Those who respond Republican or Democrat are then asked: "Would you call yourself a strong (Republican, Democrat) or a not very strong (Republican, Democrat)?" Those who say that they view themselves as Independent are then asked: "Do you think of yourself as closer to the Republican or the Democratic party?" The questions and responses yield a seven-category distribution of party identification: Strong Democrat, Weak Democrat, Independent that leans to the Democrats, Pure Independent, Independent that leans to the Republicans, Weak Republican, and Strong Republican.

The distribution of party identification since 1952, as measured by the Center for Political Studies, is presented in Table 1.2.[80] These data show that throughout this period more voters have identified with the Democratic party than with the Republican party. This is true whether or not we include Independent leaners as party identifiers. Chief among the trends evident in Table 1.2 is the relative increase in Republican support since 1952. There is also an increase in Independent voters and a decline among strong party identifiers, mainly among the Democrats.

The direction and strength of party loyalties are reflected in the voting booth.[81] Republican identifiers tend to vote Republican and Democratic identifiers generally vote Democratic. In each party, strong identifiers are more loyal to their party than weak identifiers. Overall, Republican identifiers are usually less likely to defect from their party than are Democrats.

Independent Democrats and Independent Republicans both usually vote for the party to which they lean. In fact, they are more loyal to their party than the weak identifiers of each party. Republicans have generally done very well with the pure Independents.

Candidate Evaluation.   A crucial component of voter decision-making in presidential elections is evaluation of candidates. Voters may cast

Table 1.2. Party Identification in the United States, 1952–1992
(*University of Michigan Poll*)

	1952 (%)	1956 (%)	1960 (%)	1964 (%)
Strong Democrat	22	21	20	27
Weak Democrat	25	23	25	25
Independent leaning Democrat	10	6	6	9
Pure Independent	6	9	10	8
Independent leaning Republican	7	8	7	6
Weak Republican	14	14	14	14
Strong Republican	14	15	16	11
Apolitical, don't know	3	4	3	1
Total percent[a]	101	100	101	101
	1968 (%)	1972 (%)	1976 (%)	1980 (%)
Strong Democrat	20	15	15	18
Weak Democrat	25	26	25	23
Independent leaning Democrat	10	11	12	11
Pure Independent	11	13	15	13
Independent leaning Republican	9	11	10	10
Weak Republican	15	13	14	14
Strong Republican	10	10	9	9
Apolitical, don't know	1	1	1	2
Total percent[a]	101	100	101	100
	1984 (%)	1988 (%)	1992 (%)	
Strong Democrat	17	18	18	
Weak Democrat	20	18	18	
Independent leaning Democrat	11	12	14	
Pure Independent	11	11	12	
Independent leaning Republican	12	13	12	
Weak Republican	15	14	14	
Strong Republican	12	14	11	
Apolitical, don't know	2	2	1	
Total percent[a]	100	102	100	

Source: American National Election Studies, Center for Political Studies, University of Michigan.

[a]Does not always add to 100 percent due to rounding.

their ballot on the basis of their positive and negative evaluations of the rivals.

In his study of presidential elections from 1952 to 1988, Herbert Asher found that Republicans have generally nominated more popular candidates than have Democrats. This has helped the GOP win many presidential elections despite their lag in party identification.[82] In 1992, though, the Republican incumbent was seen in a more unfavorable light than his Democratic challenger.[83]

Issue Preferences.   Voters also take into account questions of public policy when casting their ballots. In so doing, the electorate considers promises for the future as well as party performance over the past four years. Political scientists call these two forms of balloting, prospective and retrospective voting, respectively.

There is substantial evidence that the electorate practices prospective voting. For example, voters will overwhelmingly choose the candidate whose position they prefer on the issue they feel is most important. Furthermore, most voters will, if necessary, defect from their party identification to vote consistently with their most important issue preference.[84] Also, on most issues, evaluated individually or as part of an issue composite, voters will most often choose the candidate whose position they perceive to be closer to their own.[85]

More simply, most important issue selections are related to vote choice. In 1992, for example, voters citing as their issue priorities the environment, health care, education, or jobs gave majority support to Clinton. Bush received majority support from those pointing out the importance of foreign policy, family values, taxes, or abortion. Perot received a plurality of the vote among those singling out the deficit as the most important problem.[86]

Retrospective voting is a crucial component of voter decision-making.[87] Individual perceptions of the national economy and of personal standards of living are central to voter evaluations of the past four years and are closely tied to voter choice. Other retrospective judgments tied to voter choice concern presidential job performance, the president's handling of foreign affairs, and the government's handling of a voter's self-selected most important problem. In all of these evaluations, considered both singly and compositely, a positive assessment benefits the incumbent party and a negative assessment benefits the challenging party.

Assessment.   A central aim of research on voting is to sort out the relative importance of party identification, candidate evaluations, and issue preferences in influencing how people vote.[88] Initially, the psychological orientation in voting behavior research, as exemplified by *The American Voter,* published in 1960, emphasized party identification as the dominant influence. Since the mid-1970s, however, this view has been challenged on at least two counts.

The first challenge to the hegemony of party identification points out that there is variability from election to election in the relative influence of the three key psychological variables.[89] Thus, for example, while the predominance of party identification accurately describes voting behavior in the 1950s, in 1964 and 1972 issue preferences were a larger influence on voters.

The second challenge to a party identification explanation of voting behavior emphasizes that the three psychological variables are entangled. That is to say, a person's party identification, candidate evaluations, and issue preferences all influence—and are influenced by—each other. This is a marked contrast to the earlier psychological tradition that viewed party identification as a long-term core belief that was very influential but stable—"the 'unmoved mover',," in the words of Jack Dennis.[90] The complexity of the causal relationships, means, according to Asher, that "analysts should exercise caution in making claims about the unique effects of each of the explanatory variables."[91]

PARTISAN AND ELECTORAL TRENDS

Every presidential election is a unique blend of particular candidates, issues, and circumstances. But as V. O. Key, Jr. noted, "the wars of domestic politics . . . are not events of a moment but extend through the years."[92] To understand the nature of the verdict in a presidential election, then, it is also necessary to appreciate long-term partisan and electoral trends. In this section we will consider three of the most important: winning political party, party turnovers and reelections, and incumbency.

Winning Political Party

All presidents, aside from George Washington, have been elected as party standard-bearers. In our nation's fifty-two presidential elections, though, only five political parties have been victorious—the Federalists, Democratic-Republicans or Jeffersonians, Democrats, Whigs, and Republicans[93] (Table 1.3).

Federalists. The Federalists contested the six presidential elections from 1796 to 1816, but their only victory was the 1796 election of

Table 1.3. Political Party Success in Presidential Elections [a]

Political Party	Elections Contested	First Contest	Last Contest	Elections Won	First Win	Last Win	% of Contests Won
Federalist	6	1796	1816	1	1796	1796	16.7
Democratic-Republican [b]	8	1796	1824	7	1800	1824	87.5
Democratic [c]	42	1828	1992	19	1828	1992	45.2
Whig	6	1836	1856	2	1840	1848	33.3
Republican	35	1856	1992	21	1860	1988	60.0

Source: Based on Appendix.

[a] Does not include two victories by George Washington, in 1789 and 1792, which are classified as No Party Designation.

[b] Sometimes called the Jeffersonians.

[c] The election of Andrew Jackson in 1828 is counted as a Democratic victory.

John Adams. Adams lost his 1800 reelection bid, however, and the Federalists would go on to lose four more presidential elections before disappearing.

The Federalist party developed its "constituency organization" during the Adams administration, but Federalist leaders successfully championed a number of important causes prior to that period, including adoption of the U.S. Constitution, assumption by the national government of the state and national debts, and a national bank.[94] The Federalists were the party of national integration, receiving their greatest electoral support in New England and the northern Atlantic states. The Federalists drew some agricultural support, but in essence "trade and commercial interests, such as they were in the new society, looked to the Federalists to represent their interests." The Federalists lost broad-based popular support because of the passage of the Sedition Act, which tried to outlaw political dissent during the Adams administration, and because they were considered out of step with the evolving American democracy.

Democratic-Republicans or Jeffersonians.   The Democratic-Republican party, or the Jeffersonian Democrats, were the most successful party in presidential elections, winning seven consecutive elections between 1800 and 1824 and losing only in 1796. So successful was the Democratic-Republican party that it formed a virtual coalition of the whole, a monopoly on the presidency, during the Era of Good Feelings of the early Monroe years. The Jeffersonians elected three two-term presidents, Thomas Jefferson (1800, 1804), James Madison (1808, 1812), and James Monroe (1816, 1820), as well as John Quincy Adams (1824).

The Jeffersonians were most popular in the hinterlands and in the South.[95] Their appeal was directed to small farmers and the poorer elements of society. The Democratic-Republicans argued for a limited central government or, more accurately, state autonomy, and approved of suffrage expansion in the various states. The hegemony of the Democratic-Republicans was ended, or redirected, by the ascent of Andrew Jackson.

Democrats.   The Democratic party is the longest surviving political party in the world, originating as the Jacksonian wing of the Democratic-Republican party. Democrats have contested every presidential election since Jackson's 1828 campaign. The Democratic party has won nineteen of the forty-two presidential elections that it has contested, or 45.2 percent. In opposition to the Republican party, the Democratic party has won the presidency with eight different candidates since

1884, with only Franklin Roosevelt (four elections), Grover Cleveland, and Woodrow Wilson winning more than once. Prior to the Civil War, the Democrats won six elections with five candidates, including two victories for Jackson. Democrats have lost twenty-three presidential elections, with three of these defeats absorbed by William Jennings Bryan and two by Adlai E. Stevenson.

During its long history the Democratic party has represented various interests and messages.[96] Most familiar is the role the Democratic party has fulfilled since the New Deal, as the party of organized labor, government welfare programs, and economic assistance for individuals. But during the years of the second party system, from the 1830s to the 1850s, the Democratic party represented small farmers, the hinterland, and laissez-faire economics—although it did also then represent the idea of strong executive authority, which was bound up with the persona of Andrew Jackson. During the era of the industrializing nation, from the 1860s to the 1930s, the Democratic party was largely a party of "agrarian discontent" and southern solidarity, although the Woodrow Wilson interlude was a time of progressive policy making. During the 1920s, the Democratic party began to be dominated by the wing of the party that was "urban, eastern, Catholic and 'wet,'" or against Prohibition, as the foundations of the New Deal era were forming.

Whigs.   The Whig party contested the six presidential elections from 1836 to 1856, and won in 1840 and 1848. Both elected Whig presidents, William Henry Harrison and Zachary Taylor, died in office. The Whigs drew some electoral support from agricultural interests, but their strongest support was found among those favoring economic expansionism, which included federal support for internal improvements such as roads and canals.[97] In its day, the Whig party was competitive throughout the United States.

The Whigs were united in their dislike of Jackson and his political heirs. But they also had an ideology of their own, combining "social conservatism and . . . economic progress." The Whigs—unlike the Federalists—were skillful in campaigning for votes. Ultimately, though, the Whigs were torn apart by the slavery issue.

Republicans.   The Republicans have been quite successful in presidential elections. The Republican party has won the most elections, twenty-one. The GOP has won 60 percent (twenty-one out of thirty-five) of the presidential elections it has contested. Republicans have entered every presidential election since 1856, and their first winning campaign was four years later, in 1860.

The record shows that fifteen men have been elected president on the Republican ticket, including two-time winners Abraham Lincoln, Ulysses S. Grant, William McKinley, Dwight D. Eisenhower, Richard M. Nixon, and Ronald Reagan. Thomas E. Dewey is the only two-time loser in the Republican party's fourteen presidential election losses. The Republicans and Democrats have shared a duopoly on the presidency since the election of 1852; thus, the fourteen Republican losses represent Democratic victories.

The Republican party has represented numerous causes and groups during its history,[98] but chief among these was its opposition to slavery and prosecution of the Civil War and Reconstruction. A second animating cause of Republicanism has been support for industrialization, especially from the 1896 election of William McKinley through the 1920s. In our own time, the Republican party has pushed a traditional position on social issues along with a tough anticommunist foreign policy, and has remained staunchly pro-business.

Party Turnovers and Reelections

A party turnover is the replacement of one party with another in the White House.[99] "In presidential elections," according to Gerald Pomper and Susan Lederman, "the voters' principal role has been to maintain or displace the party in power."[100] Party turnovers may very well represent a popular preference for a break with the immediate past, perhaps an attempt to change the direction of government. On the other hand, a party reelection probably signifies a reaffirmation of popular support for the general direction of government.

In U.S. history there have been forty-nine elections in which there was an opportunity for party change or stability from the previous outcome, from the election of 1800 through the 1992 contest. Our tabulation finds twenty party turnovers and twenty-nine party reelections. (These are listed in Table 1.4.) If the process were random, that is to say decided by the toss of a coin, we would expect to find twenty-four or twenty-five party reelections and a like number of turnovers.[101]

Of the twenty party turnovers in presidential elections (as Table 1.4 shows), four represent the first in an extended series of party victories: 1800 (seven victories); 1860 (six); 1932 (five); and 1896 (four). These elections may be viewed as the beginning of a sustained period of party dominance in the White House.[102]

Three times a party turnover began a trio of party victories, in 1828, 1920, and 1980. Five times a party turnover was the first of a pair of party victories, in 1852, 1912, 1952, 1960, and 1968. Most often, these

Table 1.4. Political Party Turnover in Presidential Elections

Year	Losing Party	Winning Party	Number of Wins in a Row
1800	Federalist	Democratic-Republican	7
1828	Democratic-Republican[a]	Democratic	3
1840	Democratic	Whig	1
1844	Whig	Democratic	1
1848	Democratic	Whig	1
1852	Whig	Democratic	2
1860	Democratic	Republican	6[b]
1884	Republican	Democratic	1
1888	Democratic	Republican	1
1892	Republican	Democratic	1
1896	Democratic	Republican	4
1912	Republican	Democratic	2
1920	Democratic	Republican	3
1932	Republican	Democratic	5
1952	Democratic	Republican	2
1960	Republican	Democratic	2
1968	Democratic	Republican	2
1976	Republican	Democratic	1
1980	Democratic	Republican	3
1992	Republican	Democratic	1 so far

Source: Based on Appendix.

[a]The Democratic-Republicans are more properly identified as an outgoing party because they did not offer a candidate in 1828.

[b]Excludes Andrew Johnson (Democrat), who succeeded Abraham Lincoln.

successes represented a series nested inside a longer period of party dominance. The series beginning in 1912 and 1952, though, were short periods of party success in generally unfriendly eras.[103]

Eight times (including 1992), 40 percent of the time, a party turnover was a lone partisan victory. In these instances party turnovers represented momentary victory in an era of partisan flux.

Incumbency

Advantages and Disadvantages of Incumbency. The most important strategic constraint in a presidential election is the presence or absence of an incumbent.[104] The power of incumbency is an important resource for a candidate. The advantages of incumbency are many: presidents have the aura and experience of the office; they command media coverage; they are able to influence events; and they are able to dispense government grants.

There is one tremendous burden for presidents, however. They are held responsible for the "state of the union"—peace and prosperity—during their years in office—even if they have no control over these conditions. The ups and downs of society have led to a somewhat checkered record of electoral success for presidents.

The Record of Incumbents. In U.S. history, there have been fifty-two presidential elections, yielding fifty-one administration endings. These endings may be summarized as follows:

Scenario	No. of Times
President Reelected	19
President Denied Nomination	5
President Lost Election	10
President Did Not Run	17
1792–1992	51

Most often, nineteen times, a president has been reelected. These nineteen instances include, however, three reelections for Franklin Roosevelt. The latter two-thirds of the nineteenth century had few reelections; only Lincoln (1864) and Grant (1872) followed Jackson (1832) in that century. Four out of the total of nine nonelected presidents were reelected to office.

Only five presidents have been denied renomination—all between 1844 and 1884. Not surprisingly, this fate befell four of the nonelected presidents. The only elected president denied renomination was Franklin Pierce, in 1856.

Ten presidents have lost the general election, including three of the last four—Ford (nonelected), Carter, and Bush. These ten losses represent more than one-third (ten out of twenty-nine) of the incumbents running in November. Combined with the five lost nominations, fifteen out of thirty-four, or 44.1 percent of presidents have been denied another term.

In one-third of the instances, seventeen times, the incumbent president did not seek reelection. Only in the two most recent instances, Eisenhower in 1960 and Reagan in 1988, did the Twenty-second Amendment prohibit the incumbent from seeking reelection. All nine nonelected presidents sought a term of their own.

Seven presidents stepped down after serving two full terms, and Grover Cleveland stepped down after serving two nonconsecutive terms. Four presidents left after serving a partial term plus one full term. Two presidents left after serving only one full term.

Assessment.   Overall, then, the electoral record of presidents is decidedly mixed and trends do not hold out great promise for future presidents seeking a second full term. Although a president has not been denied renomination since 1884, in the twentieth century presidents have occasionally faced difficult opposition for the nomination.[105] Two presidents, Harry Truman in 1952 and Lyndon Johnson in 1968, did not run again, in part, to avoid a nomination challenge.[106] A difficult nomination significantly weakens the incumbent's November chances.[107]

In both the nineteenth and twentieth centuries, five incumbents lost the general election. Three of these defeats, including that of the nonelected Ford, occurred, furthermore, in the five elections between 1976 and 1992. Clearly, incumbency has its negative as well as positive aspects. Moreover, high turnover in office appears to be a significant feature of the contemporary presidency.[108]

CONCLUSION

In this chapter we have presented the major steps of the presidential selection process. In particular we have looked in some detail at the key features of the pool of candidates, the nomination process, the general election, voting, and electoral trends.

The presidential selection process takes place within the context of a constitution that is over 200 years old and of a party system that stretches back almost as far. The process that emerges from this chapter is one that is immutable, but changing; complicated, but understandable; and heavily influenced by the media and money, but ultimately decided by candidates and voters. The presidential election process is often criticized, but it is one that I feel works reasonably well.

NOTES

1. V. O. Key, Jr., *Politics, Parties, and Pressure Groups,* 5th ed. (New York: Crowell, 1964), pp. 5–6, 10.

2. Gerald M. Pomper, with Susan S. Lederman, *Elections in America: Control and Influence in Democratic Politics*, 2nd ed. (New York: Longman, 1980).

3. Benjamin Ginsberg, *The Consequences of Consent: Elections, Citizen Control and Popular Acquiescence* (Reading, Mass.: Addison-Wesley, 1982); and idem, *The Captive Public: How Mass Opinion Promotes State Power* (New York: Basic Books, 1986).

4. Gerald M. Pomper, *Nominating the President: The Politics of Convention Choice* (Evanston, Ill.: Northwestern University Press, 1963), pp. 122–133, quotation, p. 129.

5. Erwin C. Hargrove and Michael Nelson, *Presidents, Politics, and Policy* (Baltimore: Johns Hopkins University Press, 1984), p. 135.

6. Louis W. Koenig, *The Chief Executive*, 5th ed. (New York: Harcourt Brace Jovanovich, 1986), pp. 67–68.

7. Calculated from Norman C. Thomas, Joseph A. Pika, and Richard A. Watson, *The Politics of the Presidency*, 3rd ed. (Washington, D.C.: CQ Press, 1993), pp. 458–460, updated for Clinton.

8. Robert L. Peabody, Norman J. Ornstein, and David W. Rohde, "The United States Senate As a Presidential Incubator: Many Are Called But Few Are Chosen," *Political Science Quarterly* 91 (Summer 1976): 237–258, at 242–243.

9. Clinton Rossiter, *The American Presidency*, rev. ed. (New York: Mentor Books, 1960), pp. 192–196, quotations, pp. 193, 194.

10. Gallup Opinion Poll presented in Milton C. Cummings, Jr., and David Wise, *Democracy Under Pressure: An Introduction to the American Political System*, 7th ed. (Fort Worth: Harcourt Brace Jovanovich College Publishers, 1993), p. 184.

11. For example, John F. Stacks, "The Powell Factor," *Time*, July 10, 1995, pp. 22–29.

12. Rossiter, pp. 194, 193.

13. Hargrove and Nelson, p. 135; emphasis deleted.

14. Thomas E. Cronin, *The State of the Presidency*, 2nd ed. (Boston: Little, Brown, 1980), pp. 28–29.

15. Hargrove and Nelson, p. 136.

16. Donald R. Matthews, "Presidential Nominations: Process and Outcomes," in *Choosing the President*, ed. James David Barber (Englewood Cliffs, N.J.: Prentice-Hall, 1974), pp. 35–70, at 41–43; and Hargrove and Nelson, pp. 154–155.

17. Matthews, p. 43.

18. Herbert B. Asher, *Presidential Elections and American Politics: Voters, Candidates, and Campaigns Since 1952*, 5th ed. (Pacific Grove, Calif.: Brooks/Cole, 1992), p. 218.

19. Stephen Hess, "'Why Great Men Are Not Chosen Presidents': Lord Bryce Revisited," in *Elections American Style*, ed. A. James Reichley (Washington, D.C.: Brookings, 1987), pp. 75–94, esp. pp. 83–89, quotations, pp. 88, 84, 88.

20. John H. Aldrich, *Before the Convention: Strategies and Choices in Presidential Nomination Campaigns* (Chicago: University of Chicago Press, 1980), pp. 22–48, quotations, pp. 29, 41; emphasis deleted.

21. For example, Matthews, pp. 36–37; Austin Ranney, "Changing the Rules of the Nominating Game," in *Choosing the President*, pp. 71–93, at 71; and William R. Keech, "Selecting and Electing Presidents," in *The Presidency Reappraised*, 2nd ed., ed. Thomas E. Cronin and Rexford G. Tugwell (New York: Praeger, 1977), pp. 86–103, at 86–88.

22. Rhodes Cook, "Earlier Voting in 1996 Forecasts Fast and Furious Campaigns," *Congressional Quarterly Weekly Report* 53 (August 19, 1995): 2483–2488, at 2485.

23. Leon D. Epstein, *Political Parties in the American Mold* (Madison: University of Wisconsin Press, 1986), pp. 89–95, quotation, p. 89.

24. Epstein, p. 90.

25. Andrew E. Busch, "In Defense of the 'Mixed' System: The Goldwater Campaign and the Role of Popular Movements in the Pre-Reform Presidential Nomination Process," *Polity* 24 (Summer 1992): 527–549.

26. Epstein, p. 90; Key, *Politics, Parties, and Pressure Groups*, p. 402.

27. Congressional Quarterly Inc., *Politics in America: Edition IV* (Washington, D.C., 1971), pp. 43–48, 95–97; Theodore H. White, *The Making of the President 1968* (New York: Pocket Books, 1969, 1970), pp. 336–337.

28. This paragraph is based on Epstein, pp. 95–99; Austin Ranney, *Curing the Mischiefs of Faction: Party Reform in America* (Berkeley: University of California Press, 1975), pp. 205–206; Richard L. Kolbe, *American Political Parties: An Uncertain Future* (New York: Harper & Row, 1985), pp. 171–175; and Nelson W. Polsby, *Consequences of Party Reform* (New York: Oxford University Press, 1983), pp. 55–59, 62–64.

29. Primary returns are from *Guide to the 1992 Democratic National Convention, Congressional Quarterly Weekly Report* 50 (July 4, 1992, Supplement): 69, 71. Quotation is from Rhodes Cook, "Front-Runners Face Good News, Bad News in Final Phase," *Congressional Quarterly Weekly Report* 50 (May 16, 1992): 1375–1379, at 1375.

30. Primary returns are from *Guide to the 1992 Republican National Convention, Congressional Quarterly Weekly Report* 50 (August 8, 1992, Supplement): 63, 67. Paragraph also based on Cook, "Front-Runners Face Good News, Bad News," and, for example, Ronald D. Elving and Beth Donovan, "Candidates Spread Their Bets in Presidential Gamble," *Congressional Quarterly Weekly Report* 50 (February 22, 1992): 419–422.

31. Stephen J. Wayne, *The Road to the White House 1992: The Politics of Presidential Elections* (New York: St. Martin's Press, 1992), pp. 87–103; and Epstein, pp. 225–235.

32. Wayne, pp. 101–103; Paul Allen Beck and Frank J. Sorauf, *Party Politics in America*, 7th ed. (New York: HarperCollins, 1992), pp. 282–285.

33. A complete "state-by-state" special report of 1996 delegate nominating systems is *Congressional Quarterly Weekly Report* 53 (August 19, 1995).

34. This paragraph is based on Epstein, pp. 229–233; and Wayne, pp. 100–101.

35. Wayne, p. 99.

36. Nelson W. Polsby and Aaron Wildavsky, *Presidential Elections: Contemporary Strategies of American Electoral Politics*, 8th ed. (New York: The Free Press, 1991), p. 128.

37. Ladd, quoted in Epstein, p. 96; emphasis deleted.

38. Rhodes Cook, "Primary Calendar Shaping Up as a Tough Timetable," *Congressional Quarterly Weekly Report* 53 (April 29, 1995): 1195–1197.

39. Asher, pp. 259–275; Polsby and Wildavsky, pp. 71–85, quotation, p. 79.

40. Polsby and Wildavsky, pp. 114–115; Asher, pp. 271–273.

41. Polsby and Wildavsky, pp. 126–127; Wayne, pp. 96–97; and Ronald D. Elving, "Convention: A Traditional Revival," in *Guide to the 1992 Republican National Convention*, pp. 25–28, quotation, p. 27.

42. Wayne, pp. 6–9; Key, pp. 396–398.

43. Polsby and Wildavsky, p. 135.

44. Republican National Committee, Chief Counsel's Office, "Tentative 1996 Presidential Primary/Caucus Dates; 1996 Republican National Convention Preliminary Delegate Allocation," (Washington, D.C., December 1994). This report was provided to me by Charles A. Moynihan, student intern from the State University of New York, Plattsburgh.

45. Wayne, pp. 137–170; Beck and Sorauf, pp. 278–302.

46. Jeffrey L. Katz, "Facing Forward," in *Guide to the 1992 Democratic National Convention*, pp. 17–20, at 18–19, quotation, p. 18.

47. L. Sandy Maisel, "The Platform-Writing Process: Candidate-Centered Platforms in 1992," *Political Science Quarterly* 108 (Winter 1993–94): 671–698.

48. Pomper, with Lederman, *Elections in America*, pp. 128–178.

49. Quotation from William J. Keefe, *Parties, Politics, and Public Policy in America*, 7th ed. (Washington, D.C.: CQ Press, 1994), p. 103; also see Polsby and Wildavsky, p. 142.

50. Polsby and Wildavsky, p. 166.

51. This proposition could probably use more current verification, but see Steven J. Brams and Morton D. Davis, "The 3/2's Rule in Presidential Campaigning," *American Political Science Review* 68 (March 1974): 113–134.

52. For discussion of problems, strengths, and reforms, see, for example, Polsby and Wildavsky, pp. 307–317; and Wayne, pp. 14–21, 290–297.

53. Discussion of candidate campaigns draws on Polsby and Wildavsky, pp. 206–258.

54. L. Sandy Maisel, *Parties and Elections in America: The Electoral Process* (New York: Random House, 1987), pp. 204–216; Wayne, pp. 176–180.

55. Wayne, pp. 29–30.

56. Cummings and Wise, p. 296.

57. F. Christopher Arterton, "Campaign '92: Strategies and Tactics of the Candidates," in *The Election of 1992*, ed. Gerald M. Pomper (Chatham, N.J.: Chatham House, 1993), pp. 74–109, at 82–84; Candice J. Nelson, "Money and Its Role in the Election," in *America's Choice: The Election of 1992*, ed. William Crotty (Guilford, Conn.: Dushkin, 1993), pp. 101–110, at 104–106; and Beth Donovan, "Much Maligned 'Soft Money' is Precious to Both Parties," *Congressional Quarterly Weekly Report* 51 (May 15, 1993): 1195–1200.

58. See, for example, Herbert E. Alexander, with the assistance of Brian A. Haggerty, *Financing the 1980 Election* (Lexington, Mass.: D. C. Heath, 1983), pp. 303–308, 328–333.

59. Maisel, p. 217.

60. Polsby and Wildavsky, p. 199

61. Asher, pp. 309–313.

62. Wayne, pp. 181–191.

63. Thomas, Pika, and Watson, pp. 77, 80.

64. George C. Edwards III and Stephen J. Wayne, *Presidential Leadership: Politics and Policy Making*, 3rd ed. (New York: St. Martin's Press, 1994), p. 74.

65. Wayne, p. 225; also Polsby and Wildavsky, p. 245.

66. Cummings and Wise, p. 281.
67. Polsby and Wildavsky, p. 246.
68. The first major theoretical work in the "sociological" tradition of voting behavior studies is widely considered to be Paul F. Lazarsfeld, Bernard Berelson, and Hazel Gaudet, *The People's Choice*, 3rd ed. (New York: Columbia University Press, 1968). Originally published in 1944 by Duell, Sloan, and Pearce.
69. V. O. Key, Jr. and Frank Munger, "Social Determinism and Electoral Decision: The Case of Indiana," in *American Voting Behavior*, ed. Eugene Burdick and Arthur J. Brodbeck (Glencoe, Ill.: The Free Press, 1959), pp. 281–299; and V. O. Key, Jr., with the assistance of Milton C. Cummings, Jr., *The Responsible Electorate: Rationality in Presidential Voting 1936–1960* (Cambridge, Mass.: Harvard University Press, 1966), pp. 7–8, 70.
70. Angus Campbell, Philip E. Converse, Warren E. Miller, and Donald E. Stokes, *The American Voter* (New York: Wiley, 1960), pp. 12–17.
71. U.S. Bureau of the Census, *Statistical Abstract of the United States: 1993* (113th ed.) (Washington, D.C., 1993), p. 284, Table No. 455; idem, *Statistical Abstract of the United States: 1962* (83rd ed.) (Washington, D.C., 1962), p. 373, Table No. 497.
72. Paul R. Abramson, John H. Aldrich, and David W. Rohde, *Change and Continuity in the 1988 Elections* (Washington, D.C.: CQ Press, 1990), pp. 93–94; and Walter Dean Burnham, "The Turnout Problem," in *Elections American Style,* pp. 97–133, at 113–114.
73. Rhodes Cook, "Clinton Picks the GOP Lock on the Electoral College," *Congressional Quarterly Weekly Report* 50 (November 7, 1992): 3548–3553, quotation at 3553.
74. Paul R. Abramson and John H. Aldrich, "The Decline of Electoral Participation in America," *American Political Science Review* 76 (September 1982): 502–521; Abramson, Aldrich, and Rohde, pp. 102–107, esp. pp. 105–106.
75. Abramson, Aldrich, and Rohde, pp. 108–113, quotations pp. 111, 112.
76. Burnham, "The Turnout Problem," pp. 123–133.
77. E. E. Schattschneider, *The Semisovereign People: A Realist's View of Democracy in America* (Hinsdale, Ill.: Dryden Press, 1960), p. 99.
78. Key, *Responsible Electorate*, pp. 2–3; Mark A. Schulman and Gerald M. Pomper, "Variability in Electoral Behavior: Longitudinal Perspectives from Causal Modeling," *American Journal of Political Science* 19 (February 1975): 1–18; and Asher, pp. 104–108.
79. This section is based on Campbell et al., *The American Voter*, pp. 120–167; Asher, pp. 39–47, 60–90; and Abramson, Aldrich, and Rohde, pp. 201–225.

80. Data from American National Election Studies, conducted by the Center for Political Studies, University of Michigan. The data were provided to me by Thomas M. Ivacko, NES Administrator.
81. Asher, pp. 87–88; Abramson, Aldrich, and Rohde, pp. 210–212.
82. Asher, pp. 122–195; and, for example, Keech, "Selecting and Electing Presidents," p. 98.
83. Kathleen A. Frankovic, "Public Opinion in the 1992 Campaign," in *The Election of 1992*, ed. Pomper, pp. 110–131.
84. Asher, pp. 102–104.
85. Abramson, Aldrich, and Rohde, pp. 166–173.
86. Gerald M. Pomper, "The Presidential Election," in *The Election of 1992*, pp. 132–156, at 146.
87. Abramson, Aldrich, and Rohde, pp. 179–200.
88. Herbert B. Asher, "Voting Behavior Research in the 1980s: An Examination of Some Old and New Problem Areas," in *Political Science: The State of the Discipline*, ed. Ada W. Finifter (Washington, D.C.: American Political Science Association, 1983), pp. 339–388; and Jack Dennis, "The Study of Electoral Behavior," in *Political Science: Looking to the Future, Vol. 3 Political Behavior* (Evanston, Ill.: Northwestern University Press, 1991), pp. 51–89.
89. Schulman and Pomper; and see the research update, Frederick Hartwig, William R. Jenkins, and Earl M. Temchin, "Variability in Electoral Behavior: The 1960, 1968, and 1976 Elections," *American Journal of Political Science* 24 (August 1980): 553–558.
90. Dennis, p. 60.
91. Asher, "Voting Behavior Research," p. 350.
92. Key, *Politics, Parties, and Pressure Groups*, p. 166.
93. For a complete listing of election outcomes, see Appendix.
94. Discussion of the Federalists is based on Everett Carll Ladd, *American Political Parties: Social Change and Political Response* (New York: Norton, 1970), pp. 79–88, quotations, pp. 81, 86; and A. James Reichley, *The Life of the Parties: A History of American Political Parties* (New York: The Free Press, 1992), pp. 38–63.
95. Discussion of the Jeffersonians is based on Ladd, *American Political Parties*, pp. 79–88; and Reichley, pp. 64–84.
96. My reading of history is based on Ladd, *American Political Parties*; Reichley; Arthur N. Holcombe, *The Political Parties of To-Day: A Study in Republican and Democratic Politics*, 2nd ed. (New York: Harper and Brothers, 1925); and James L. Sundquist, *Dynamics of the Party System: Alignment and Realignment of Political Parties in the United States*, rev. ed. (Washington, D.C.: Brookings, 1983); quotations, Ladd, pp. 151, 161.

97. Discussion of the Whig party is based on Ladd, *American Political Parties*, pp. 88–93, 103–108; Reichley, pp. 97–110; and Sundquist, pp. 50–73; quotation, Reichley, p. 100.

98. See, Supra, note 96.

99. In our calculations a partisan change is an election outcome different from that of the previous election. Changes of party in the White House in the middle of a term are not tabulated. The only time a president was succeeded during his term by a vice president of another party was in 1865, when Republican Abraham Lincoln was replaced by Democrat Andrew Johnson.

100. Pomper, with Lederman, *Elections in America*, p. 211.

101. This point is the simplified central thrust of Daniel J. Gans, "Persistence of Party Success in American Presidential Elections," *Journal of Interdisciplinary History* 16 (Winter 1986): 221–237.

102. These elections, along with 1828, and substituting 1788 for 1800, are often viewed as the beginning of successive "party systems." The landmark work here is Walter Dean Burnham, "Party Systems and the Political Process," in *The American Party Systems: Stages of Political Development*, ed. William Nisbet Chambers and Burnham (New York: Oxford University Press, 1967, 1975), pp. 277–307. For alternative and more recent perspectives, see Byron E. Shafer, ed., *The End of Realignment?: Interpreting American Electoral Eras* (Madison: University of Wisconsin Press, 1991).

103. The Wilson (1912, 1916) and Eisenhower (1952, 1956) elections are usually classified as "deviating." See Angus Campbell, "A Classification of the Presidential Elections," in *Elections and the Political Order*, ed. Campbell, Philip E. Converse, Warren E. Miller, and Donald E. Stokes (New York: Wiley, 1966), pp. 63–77, at 69–74; and Gerald M. Pomper, "Classification of Presidential Elections," *Journal of Politics* 29 (August 1967): 535–566, at 566.

104. These two paragraphs are based on Asher, *Presidential Elections*, pp. 299–300; Wayne, pp. 186–189; and Polsby and Wildavsky, pp. 86–89.

105. Rhodes Cook, "Bush's Gulf Triumph Stifles Talk of GOP Primary Challengers," *Congressional Quarterly Weekly Report* 49 (March 9, 1991): 584–587, at 586–587.

106. Richard M. Pious, *The American Presidency* (New York: Basic Books, 1979), p. 91.

107. Allan J. Lichtman and Ken DeCell, *The Thirteen Keys to the Presidency* (Lanham, Md.: Madison Books, 1990), esp. pp. 64–68; and Cook, "Bush's Gulf Triumph."

108. Fred I. Greenstein, "Change and Continuity in the Modern Presi-

dency," in *The New American Political System*, ed. Anthony King (Washington, D.C.: American Enterprise Institute, 1978), pp. 45–85, at 63–65; and Harvey L. Schantz, "The Changed Landscape of United States Politics 1960–1993," in *Re-Naming the Landscape*, ed. Jurgen Kleist and Bruce A. Butterfield (New York: Peter Lang, 1994), pp. 203–225, at 208–211.

CHAPTER 2

Political Change Since the New Deal: The 1992 Presidential Election in Historical Perspective

MILTON C. CUMMINGS, JR.

In an election year that produced a number of startling surprises, the most notable feature of the 1992 results was that voters expelled an incumbent presidential candidate of one party from power and brought a new leadership team and party to control of the White House. Clinton's victory over President George Bush was the fifth time in this century that an incumbent President of the United States had been defeated—three of those defeats have occurred in the last two decades. And Clinton's victory marked the ninth time in this century that there has been a change in party control of the presidency.

THE AMERICAN ELECTORATE OF 1992

The size of the voting electorate who brought about this change jumped sharply between 1988 and 1992. Nearly thirteen million more people went to the polls in 1992 than had voted four years earlier. Moreover, although the percentage turnout has been higher in several other presidential elections since World War II, the 1992 total vote of 104.4 million was in one respect a landmark—it was the first time in American history that more than 100 million people voted for president.

In many respects, however, the men and women who voted in 1992 did not differ greatly from the active electorates in other recent presidential elections. By their own report, as shown in Table 2.1, the voters of 1992 were 87 percent White—compared to 8 percent who were African American and 3 percent who identified themselves as Hispanic. A solid majority (63 percent) had family incomes of $30,000 per year or more; the median family income was about $36,000. And more than half (54 percent) of those who went to the polls were women—a trend that first began to assert itself in the 1960s.

One element of change in the active electorate of 1992 is worth noting, however. Two new candidates in 1992—Bill Clinton and Ross

Table 2.1. Those Who Voted in 1992: A Profile by Groups

Groups	Their Percentage of the Total Vote[a]
Men	46
Women	54
White	87
African American	8
Hispanics	3
Age 18–24	11
25–29	11
30–39	25
40–49	24
50–59	13
60 and up	16
Family Income:	
Less than $15,000	14
$15,000–29,999	24
$30,000–49,999	30
$50,000–74,999	20
$75,000 or more	13
Protestants	56
Catholics	27
Jews	4
Democrats	39
Republicans	34
Independents	28

Source: Voter Research and Surveys exit polls for 1992 in *National Journal*, November 7, 1992, p. 2543.

[a]Does not always add to 100 percent due to rounding.

Perot—seemed to energize younger voters; and the voting turnout in 1992 probably produced the youngest group of voters in many years. Nearly half of those who went to the polls (47 percent) reported that they were younger than forty; and, although a huge bloc of voters—30 million—were age fifty or older, there were also 23 million voters who were under thirty.

HISTORICAL BACKGROUND

In every presidential election campaign there are issues, candidates, and dramatic events that are unique to that particular election year. But every American presidential election is also part of a long-term, and ongoing, party battle, in which distinct groupings of the electorate vote for long periods of time for one party, while other groups consistently support the opposite party. John F. Kennedy once underscored the long historical sweep of this battle between the two major U.S. parties, when he was campaigning for the presidency in 1960 against his Republican opponent, Richard M. Nixon. In a September, 1960 speech in Los Angeles, Kennedy declared:

> I think the record of the two parties, and its promise for the future, can be told pretty well from its record of the past. Mr. Nixon and I, and the Republican and Democratic parties, are not suddenly frozen in ice or collected in amber since the two conventions. We are like two rivers that flow back through history, and you can judge the force, the power, and the direction of the rivers by studying where they rose and where they ran throughout their long course. . . .[1]

For most of the twentieth century, election outcomes in the United States were powerfully affected by the existence of two great electoral eras—or "party systems." From 1896 to 1929, there appeared to be an Era of Republican Hegemony, in which the Republican party was the normal majority party of the United States. Then, with the onslaught of the Great Depression, a new electoral majority was formed, and this Roosevelt New Deal Democratic coalition dominated most elections from 1932 to 1968. Finally, from 1968 until the elections of 1992 and 1994, there appeared to be a "two-tiered" party structure, with Democrats dominating Congress and Republicans the presidency.[2] Not every election conformed to this two-tiered model, however. In 1976, the voters elected a Democratic president; and the Republicans maintained Senate majorities for the first six years of the Reagan presidency. The pattern also diverged from the model in 1992 and 1994. In 1992, the

Democrats won the presidency and both houses of Congress. And in 1994 it was the Republicans who won both the Senate and House. Nevertheless, from 1968 to 1992, the normal pattern was Republican control of the White House along with a Democratic Congress.

Presidential Voting Patterns

During the first fifteen years of the New Deal electoral era, the South was a bastion of Democratic strength—in presidential as well as in all other elections. Even in his fourth, and last, successful race for the presidency, in 1944, the Democrats' Franklin Roosevelt polled nearly 71 percent of all the votes that were cast for president in the South. In his first two presidential races, Roosevelt received more than 80 percent of the southern vote. Moreover, in the four presidential elections, from 1932 to 1944, which were dominated by Roosevelt, his share of the popular vote in the South, as shown in Table 2.2, ranged between nineteen and nearly twenty-six percentage points *higher* than his percentage of the vote in the rest of the country. The South was a solid, and potentially enormously important, part of the Democratic presidential electoral coalition.

For the Democrats of the South, however, the 1944 election was a last hurrah—1944 was the last year in which the Democratic party has even come close to achieving the strength in southern presidential voting that Franklin D. Roosevelt regularly attained. This movement of the South from a region that was consistently far more Democratic in presidential elections than the rest of the country to a section that has usually been less Democratic than the rest of the nation in presidential voting is traced in Table 2.2. This table shows the Democratic percentage of the total vote for the South, as well as for the rest of the country, in every presidential election from 1932 through 1992. The right-hand column of Table 2.2 shows by how much the South was more or less Democratic than the rest of the United States.

In the eight presidential contests from 1932 through 1960, the South was more Democratic than the nonsouthern states in every election year. This comparative Democratic edge in the South was very small in 1948, the year of the States' Rights party ("Dixiecrats") revolt, led by a number of prominent southern Democrats. It was also small in 1960, the year the Democrats chose Senator Lyndon B. Johnson of Texas as Senator John F. Kennedy's vice presidential running mate, in an all-out effort to hold their electoral support in the South. Nevertheless, although the contests in several southern states were extremely close in 1948 and 1960, most of the South's electoral votes ended up in the Democratic

Table 2.2. The Democratic Percentage of the Total Vote for President:
The South and the Rest of the United States Compared, 1932–1992*

Year	Democratic Percentage in the South*	Democratic Percentage in the Rest of the U.S.	Democratic Percentage in the South Compared with the Rest of the U.S.
1932	80.8	55.0	+ 25.8
1936	80.6	58.8	+ 21.8
1940	76.0	53.8	+ 22.2
1944	70.9	51.5	+ 19.4
1948	50.0	49.8	+ 0.2
1952	52.2	44.3	+ 7.9
1956	49.1	41.6	+ 7.5
1960	52.1	49.7	+ 2.4
1964	50.5	61.6	− 11.1
1968	31.8	43.9	− 12.1
1972	29.1	40.8	− 11.7
1976	54.8	49.9	+ 4.9
1980	46.0	40.1	+ 5.9
1984	38.0	43.0	− 5.0
1988	41.3	48.0	− 6.7
1992	41.2	43.7	− 2.5

* In the computations for this table, "the South" is composed of the eleven states of the former Confederacy.
Source: Richard M. Scammon and Alice V. McGillivray, comps. and eds., *America Votes* 20 (Washington, D.C.: Congressional Quarterly, 1993), pp. 11–39.

column; and the South was a crucial component of the Democratic party's winning electoral coalition. Without their electoral votes from the South, both Harry S Truman in 1948 and John F. Kennedy in 1960 would have lost their race for the presidency.

Four years later, in 1964, the voting returns from the South showed that another important change in the region's voting had occurred. The 1964 election was held just four months after passage of the Civil Rights Act of 1964, which outlawed discrimination in public accommodations. President Johnson, the Democratic candidate, had strongly backed the Civil Rights Act. Senator Barry Goldwater, his Republican opponent, had voted against it, on the grounds that the bill was unconstitutional. That November, the Democratic presidential ticket, headed by Lyndon Johnson, was a full eleven percentage points weaker in the

South than in the rest of the country.[3] Moreover, with just two exceptions—1976 and 1980, when the Democrats ran Jimmy Carter of Georgia
for President—the Democratic presidential ticket has been weaker in
the South than in the rest of the nation in every presidential contest
since 1964.

U.S. House Election Comparisons

By 1992, the Democratic party had been facing strong competition from
the Republicans in *presidential* elections in the South for forty years. In
three of those elections—1972, 1984, and 1988—the preference among
southern voters for the GOP's presidential ticket was overwhelming.
Republican strength in *congressional* elections in the South, however,
was much slower to assert itself.[4] But in time the Republican party
began to do decidedly better in House elections in the South, as well.
James L. Sundquist sees this growth of Republican congressional
strength as the second stage of the southern New Deal realignment.[5]
This slower growth of Republican successes in contests for the U.S.
House of Representatives in the South is traced in Table 2.3, where the
number of House races won by each major party in the South is compared with each party's number of House victories in the rest of the
United States.

The data in Table 2.3 cover every general election for the House of
Representatives—those in presidential years and those at midterm—
from 1950 through 1994. In 1950, the House results in the South were
much as they had been for more than half a century prior to 1950.[6] The
Democrats won 103 of the House contests in the South. The GOP in the
South won just two. Aided by President Eisenhower's electoral strength
in the region, the Republicans began to win a few more House seats in
the South in the 1950s. Moreover, during the 1960s, they raised the
number of southern Republican representatives to a high of twenty-six
in 1968. Even so, at the end of the 1960s, the Democrats still controlled
75 percent of all the House seats in the South.

Since 1970, however, the Republicans have made House election
contests in the South more competitive. In the 1980s, the share of all
southern House elections that were won by the Democrats hovered
around 66 percent; that is, the Republicans were the winner one time in
every three. And in 1992, the GOP won nearly four of every ten House
contests in the South; the percentage of southern House seats going
Democratic stood at 61.6 percent. Between 1952 and 1992, the gap
between the way southerners voted for president and their voting in
U. S. House elections narrowed substantially. Moreover, in 1994, for the

first time since Reconstruction, more Republicans than Democrats were elected to the House from the eleven states of the former Confederacy.

The figures for U.S. House seats won and lost presented in Table 2.3 highlight a profound change that has taken place in the South between 1950 and the mid 1990s. The Republican party is now competitive in congressional elections in most parts of the region. But while southern Republican congressional strength was going up in the South, another major change was taking place in the North. In the thirty-nine states outside the South,[7] the Democratic party has been doing much better in elections for the House of Representatives than it did in the early 1950s.

In the first four general elections for Congress in the 1950s, the Democrats won only about four out of ten House seats from states outside the South. In 1952, in fact, the last year the Republican party won a House majority before 1994, Democratic House candidates won just over a third of their nonsouthern elections. But then came the midterm elections of 1958, which produced a congressional landslide for the Democratic party. The Democrats gained nearly fifty seats outside the South and lifted the number of nonsouthern House seats they controlled to 55.6 percent. Moreover, between 1958 and 1992, Democrats never won fewer than 49.5 percent of the nonsouthern House seats.

This Democratic congressional strength in the North was particularly pronounced in the series of House elections that ran from 1982 through 1992. During this period, the percentage of House seats outside the South that was in Democratic hands ranged from a low of 56.4 percent to a high of nearly 60 percent. It was this major shift in the relative strength of the two major parties in congressional elections outside the South—as well as continuing Democratic strength in the South—that kept the House of Representatives firmly under Democratic control throughout the 1960s, 1970s, and 1980s.

Party Identification Trends

Nevertheless, at the presidential level, the South has clearly been tilting Republican in most presidential elections since 1972—a change that has deprived the Democratic party of a key component of its old Roosevelt New Deal coalition. Even so, throughout the 1970s and into the early 1980s, the Democratic party continued to hold a large advantage over the Republicans in terms of party identification—the number of Americans who considered themselves to be Democrats compared to the number who were Republicans. This trend line in party identification is detailed in Table 2.4.

Table 2.3. Democrats and Republicans Elected to the U.S. House of Representatives: The South and the Rest of the United States Compared, 1950–1994*

Year	Number of U.S. House Members in the South		Percentage of House Seats Democratic in South	Number of U.S. House Members, Rest of U.S.*		Percentage of House Seats Democratic, Rest of U.S.	Democratic Percentage in South Compared with the Rest of U.S.
	Democrat	Republican		Democrat	Republican		
1950	103	2	98.1	131	197	39.9	+58.2
1952	100	6	94.3	113	215	34.5	+59.8
1954	99	7	93.4	133	196	40.4	+53.0
1956	99	7	93.4	135	194	41.0	+52.4
1958	99	7	93.4	184	147	55.6	+37.8
1960	99	7	93.4	164	167	49.5	+43.9
1962	95	11	89.6	164	165	49.8	+39.8
1964	89	17	84.0	206	123	62.6	+21.4
1966	83	23	78.3	165	164	50.2	+28.1
1968	80	26	75.5	163	166	49.5	+26.0
1970	79	27	74.5	176	153	53.5	+21.0
1972	74	34	68.5	169	158	51.7	+16.8

1974	81	27	75.0	210	117	64.2	+ 10.8
1976	82	26	75.9	210	117	64.2	+ 11.7
1978	77	31	71.3	200	127	61.2	+ 10.1
1980	69	39	63.9	174	153	53.2	+ 10.7
1982	82	34	70.7	187	132	58.6	+ 12.1
1984	73	43	62.9	180	139	56.4	+ 6.5
1986	77	39	66.4	181	138	56.7	+ 9.7
1988	78	38	67.2	182	137	57.1	+ 10.1
1990	77	39	66.4	190	128	59.7	+ 6.7
1992	77	48	61.6	182	127	58.9	+ 2.7
1994	61	64	48.8	141	168	45.6	+ 3.2

* During most of the years between 1950 and 1992, the House of Representatives had 435 members. In 1960, though, there were 437 seats due to the admission of Alaska and Hawaii.

Source: Adapted from Congressional Quarterly Weekly Report, various years.

Table 2.4. Party Identification Among the American Electorate, 1940–1992 (Gallup Poll)

Year	Percentage of Voters Identifying Themselves as:		
	Democrats	Republicans	Independents
1940	42	38	20
1950	45	33	22
1960	47	30	23
1964	53	25	22
1966	48	27	25
1968	46	27	27
1970	45	29	26
1972	43	28	29
1974	44	23	33
1976	46	22	32
1980	47	23	30
1984	41	29	30
1986	40	30	30
1988	43	29	28
1990	40	32	28
1992	38	29	33

Source: Gallup Opinion Index, Report No. 131, June 1976, p. 11; *Gallup Opinion Index*, Report No. 180, August 1980, p. 31; *Gallup Report*, December 1986, No. 255, pp. 27–28; the Gallup poll, August 7, 1988; the Gallup poll, January 1992; and the Gallup poll, January–June 1992.

As late as 1980, a year in which Republicans won the presidency handily, self-described Democrats outnumbered the Republicans by two to one. Then, in 1984, as Ronald Reagan approached his bid for a second term, this Democratic advantage in the arithmetic of party identification narrowed considerably. In 1984, among all potential voters, the Democratic lead over the Republicans stood at twelve percentage points. In 1992, it dropped to nine points. In addition, Republicans usually have a higher percentage turnout than Democrats. In 1992, which was not a vintage Republican year, among the people who actually got to the polls, Democrats outnumbered Republicans by just five percentage points, as shown earlier in Table 2.1.

By the mid-1980s, then, the old Roosevelt New Deal coalition had been weakened by two fundamental changes that reshaped the topography of American presidential elections. The South had shifted to become one of the GOP's most dependable major regions in voting at the presidential level. And the Democrats had lost much of their longtime edge in party identification. It was in this altered strategic setting that the presidential elections of 1984, 1988, and 1992 were fought.

The 1984 and 1988 Presidential Elections

The 1984 presidential election was a virtual Republican landslide, as Ronald Reagan won 62 percent of the vote in the South, and 57 percent of the vote in the rest of the country. The Democrats' Walter Mondale carried only his home state of Minnesota and the District of Columbia. Reagan swept the electoral vote, 525 to 13.

Four years later, with Ronald Reagan off the ballot, the Democrats initially had hopes of defeating the new Republican presidential nominee, Vice President George Bush. In a move that echoed the Massachusetts-Texas alliance of Kennedy and Johnson that had served the Democrats well in 1960, Governor Michael Dukakis of Massachusetts, the Democratic presidential nominee, selected Senator Lloyd Bentsen of Texas as his vice presidential running mate. But normal presidential voting patterns by 1988 were very different from those of 1960; and Bush won another solid presidential victory for the Republicans, defeating Dukakis by 53.9 percent to 46.1 percent in the popular vote. In the electoral college, Bush won with 426 electoral votes to Dukakis's 111.[8]

These 1988 election returns underscored the importance of the Democrats' loss during the first half of the 1980s of their commanding lead in party identification. In 1976, when Democrats outnumbered Republicans by a lopsided margin of two to one (47 percent to 23 percent), the Democratic presidential nominee, Jimmy Carter, was supported by 82 percent of the Democrats. That was enough, however, to give Carter a narrow victory over his Republican opponent, Gerald R. Ford, even though Carter ran well behind Ford among both independents and Republicans.

Twelve years later, in 1988, the Democrats' lead over the Republicans in party identification was narrower. Democrats now outnumbered Republicans by about four to three—41 percent to 29 percent (Table 2.4). In the November, 1988, election, Dukakis ran slightly better than Carter had run among Democrats (Dukakis received 85 percent of the votes cast by Democrats).[9] This time, however, support from 85 percent of the voters who considered themselves Democrats was not sufficient to produce a Democratic victory.

In the South in 1988, once again there was a sweeping victory for the GOP. Even with Lloyd Bentsen on the Democratic ticket, every southern electoral vote went to the Republican party. What received less attention as the returns came in was that, outside the South, Dukakis actually made the 1988 election close. In the thirty-nine nonsouthern states, Dukakis brought the Democratic share of the two-party vote to 48 percent. In Illinois, Pennsylvania, and California, a shift of less than two percentage points toward the Democrats would have given those states to Dukakis.

The vote for Dukakis stood at 49.5 percent in the East, 47.2 percent in the Midwest, and—following large shifts toward the Democrats, once Ronald Reagan was no longer on the ballot—at 47 percent in the entire West.[10] Once the election was over, it was striking how quickly Michael Dukakis ceased to be an important figure—indeed became almost invisible—among national Democratic leaders. The fact is, however, that Dukakis had come closer to making the Democrats competitive for president than had any nonsouthern Democratic candidate since Hubert Humphrey.[11]

The pattern of the 1988 vote is set forth in Table 2.5. In this table, the fifty states and the District of Columbia are ranked according to their Democratic percentage of the two-party presidential vote, starting with the District of Columbia, the most Democratic jurisdiction, and ending with Utah, the state in which the Dukakis-Bentsen ticket was weakest. In the first grouping are the ten states (plus the District of Columbia) that Dukakis carried. In the next grouping, however, are twelve more states where Dukakis ran about even with, or higher than, his 46.1 percent of the vote in the United States as a whole. These states where Dukakis made a respectable or a near-respectable showing included Illinois, Pennsylvania, and California, as well as Maryland, Missouri, Montana, Michigan, and Colorado.

It would, of course, have taken a net shift in the vote toward the Democrats of four percentage points, evenly distributed, to give all twelve of those states to Dukakis. But if the twelve states had all moved into the Democratic column, Dukakis would also have had a narrow margin of victory in the electoral college. (In 1992, eleven of these twelve states went for the Clinton-Gore ticket; the exception was South Dakota.)

The gains Michael Dukakis made in 1988 by no means made it certain that there would be further Democratic gains in future presidential elections. But if an additional tide developed toward the Democratic party, the pattern of the Dukakis vote showed the electoral base around which a winning Democratic presidential coalition might be built.

THE DYNAMICS OF THE 1992 CAMPAIGN

1991: President Bush Gains, and then Loses, Public Support

When President George Bush and his advisers met in the summer of 1991 to discuss plans for the 1992 campaign, the Republican party's electoral

Table 2.5. Democratic Voting Strength, by States, in 1988: States Ranked from Highest to Lowest Democratic Percentage of the Two-Party Vote for President in 1988

	States Dukakis Won			States where Dukakis Lost but Equaled or Bettered his U.S. Percentage	
State	*1988 (%) Democrat*	*Electoral Vote*	*State*	*1988 (%) Democrat*	*Electoral Vote*
D.C.	85.2	3	Ill.	49.0	24
R.I.	55.9	4	Pa.	48.8	25
Iowa	55.1	8	Md.	48.5	10
Hawaii	54.8	4	Calif.	48.2	47
Mass.	54.0	13	Vt.	48.2	3
Minn.	53.6	10	Mo.	48.0	11
W.Va.	52.4	6	N.Mex.	47.5	5
Ore.	52.4	7	Conn.	47.4	8
N.Y.	52.1	36	Mont.	47.0	4
Wisc.	51.8	11	S.Dak.	46.8	3
Wash.	50.8	10	Mich.	46.0	20
			Colo.	46.0	8

States Where Dukakis Lagged Behind His U.S. Percentage

State	*1988 (%) Democrat*	*Electoral Vote*	*State*	*1988 (%) Democrat*	*Electoral Vote*
La.	44.8	10	Ga.	39.8	12
Ohio	44.5	23	Va.	39.6	12
Maine	44.2	4	Miss.	39.5	7
Ky.	44.1	9	Nebr.	39.4	5
Del.	43.8	3	Ariz.	39.3	7
Tex.	43.7	29	Nev.	39.2	4
N.Dak.	43.4	3	Fla.	38.7	21
Kans.	43.4	7	Wyo.	38.6	3
N.J.	43.1	16	S.C.	37.9	8
Ark.	42.8	6	Alaska	37.8	3
Tenn.	41.8	11	N.H.	36.8	4
N.C.	41.8	13	Idaho	36.7	4
Okla.	41.6	8	Utah	32.6	5
Ala.	40.3	9			
Ind.	39.9	12			

1988 Democratic percentage in the U.S.: 46.1
1988 Democratic percentage outside the South: 48.0

Source: Richard M. Scammon and Alice V. McGillivray, comps. and eds., *America Votes 20* (Washington: Congressional Quarterly, 1993), p. 11.

prospects looked very promising indeed.[12] The President's approval rating in the Gallup poll stood at 71 percent, and had been above 65 percent throughout much of his two and one-half years in office. In January and February of 1991, Bush had led an alliance of twenty-eight nations to a decisive military victory over Iraq and dictator Saddam Hussein in the Persian Gulf War. In the aftermath of the war, the number of Americans who approved of the way George Bush was "handling his job as President" had reached 89 percent—the highest rating ever received by an American president in the history of the Gallup poll (Table 2.6).

But after a series of triumphant victory parades and celebrations across the nation, the memories of the Persian Gulf War began to fade. The ravages of the recession—which had begun in 1990—did not. The economy sank to its lowest point in October 1991. Although inflation was low, unemployment was up (Table 2.7). And during the autumn of 1991, President Bush's job approval ratings began to drop—to 66 percent in October, 56 percent in November, and 50 percent (the danger zone for a president seeking reelection) in December. In the middle of January 1992, just one month before the New Hampshire presidential primary, Bush's approval rating fell to 46 percent. And in October 1992, less than one month before the presidential election, only 34 percent of those polled approved of the way Bush was handling his job (Table 2.6).

Bush Versus Buchanan

Since World War II, other incumbent presidents have suffered a sharp drop in public support during the year before they were eligible to run for reelection. During 1951 President Truman's approval ratings dropped markedly, and in March 1952 Truman announced that he would not seek another term. President Lyndon Johnson also bowed out of the presidential race, in 1968, after watching his public support erode in 1967. Throughout the winter of 1991–1992, however, there were no signals from the White House that President Bush was going to step aside. Like President Jimmy Carter in 1980, George Bush was determined to seek a second term.

As it turned out, however, there was at least one other Republican who also wanted to run in 1992. On December 10, 1991, Patrick J. Buchanan, an articulate, staunchly conservative journalist, announced that he planned to challenge Bush for the Republican nomination in their party's primaries and caucuses. Buchanan had worked in the White House in both the Nixon and the Reagan administrations. His entry into the race confronted Bush with a situation that almost no one

Table 2.6. President Bush's Job Rating, 1989–1992*

Date of Interviews	Approve (%)	Disapprove (%)	No Opinion (%)
Bush Elected with 54% of the Vote, November 1988			
Bush Inaugurated January 1989			
January 24–26, 1989	51	6	43
July 6–9, 1989	66	19	15
Panama Invasion, December 1989			
January 4–7, 1990	80	11	9
April 19–22, 1990	67	17	16
Bush Drops "No New Taxes" Pledge, June 1990			
October 18–21, 1990	53	37	10
Persian Gulf War Begins, January 1991			
January 17–20, 1991	82	12	6
Gulf War Victory, February 1991			
February 28–March 3, 1991	89**	8	3
July 25–28, 1991	71	21	8
Soviet Coup Fails, August 1991			
September 5–8, 1991	70	21	9
Recession's Low Point, October 1991			
October 17–20, 1991	66	26	8
November 14–17, 1991	56	36	8
December 12–15, 1991	50	41	9
January 16–19, 1992	46	48	6
April 20–22, 1992	42	48	10
Economic Recovery Stalls, Spring 1992			
June 26–30, 1992	38	55	7
July 31–August 2, 1992	29	60	11
August 31–September 2, 1992	39	54	7
September 17–20, 1992	36	54	10
October 12–14, 1992	34	56	10

* Responses to the question: "Do you approve or disapprove of the way George Bush is handling his job as president?"
** Highest rating in Gallup Poll annals.
Source: Gallup Poll surveys.

Table 2.7. Annual Rates of Inflation and Unemployment in the United States, 1980–1992

Year	Inflation (%)	Unemployment (%)
1980	13.5	7.1
1981	10.4	7.6
1982	6.1	9.7
1983	3.2	9.6
1984	4.3	7.4
1985	3.6	7.1
1986	1.9	6.9
1987	3.6	6.1
1988	4.4	5.5
1989	4.6	5.3
1990	6.1	5.5
1991	3.1	6.7
1992*	3.2	7.4

*1992 figures are the annualized rate for the first ten months of the year.
Source: U.S. Bureau of Labor Statistics.

had expected during the previous summer—Bush had to face a Republican opponent to win renomination.

The New Hampshire primary, as usual the nation's first, was held on February 18, 1992. The state had been particularly hard-hit by the recession. As a result, the voters were receptive to Buchanan's increasingly sharp attacks on the president for not doing enough about the nation's ailing economy.

On primary day, Bush got 53 percent of the vote to Buchanan's 37 percent. (Thousands of other Republicans wrote in the name of Paul Tsongas, a Democrat, rather than vote for either Buchanan or Bush.) Bush won the New Hampshire primary, but because of Buchanan's strong showing, the results were reported in the press as a major embarrassment for the president.

Buchanan never again reached 37 percent in his Republican primary contests with George Bush. And after Buchanan lost eight primaries to Bush in one day on Super Tuesday, March 10, he was never a serious threat to Bush's renomination. Nevertheless, Buchanan continued to run in Republican primaries, all the way to the end in California in June. Moreover, the 15 to 25 percent of the vote that he polled in many of those primaries was a reminder that a substantial number of Republicans were dissatisfied with President Bush's leadership.

Ross Perot

As the Buchanan challenge receded, a new, and potentially more dangerous, threat to Bush's reelection began to appear—a possible independent presidential candidacy by the Texas billionaire, Ross Perot. During the spring of 1992, Perot's thinking seemed to be "driven in part by his disdain for the leadership style of George Bush; he spoke of him privately as a hand-wringer and a whiner. . . ."[13] And he argued that neither of the two major-party candidates would offer the strong medicine that he said was required to fix a four trillion dollar debt.

On February 20, 1992, on the *Larry King Live* television show, Perot implied that he would indeed run for president if there were enough viewers who wanted him to run, and if they put him on the ballot in all fifty states. Eventually, Perot's supporters, many of them paid volunteers, got his name on the ballot in all fifty states and the District of Columbia.

During the spring, Perot's public support began to rise rapidly. By early June he was running first in the polls—ahead of George Bush, and ahead of Bill Clinton, who was by then the certain Democratic nominee (Table 2.8). By this time, however, Perot, like other candidates, began to encounter negative stories and scrutiny in the press. Perot's July appearance in Nashville, before the national convention of the NAACP, was a disaster. In his speech he offended many voters by referring to African Americans as "you" and "your people."[14] And his standing in the polls began to fall. On July 16, the day Bill Clinton accepted the Democratic nomination for the presidency, Ross Perot announced that he was withdrawing from the race.

Democrats

During much of 1991, while President Bush's poll ratings stood at record or near-record highs, it seemed as though most leading Democrats were making news by announcing that they were *not* going to run for president. Among the potential presidential candidates who might have run but did not were Representative Richard Gephardt of Missouri, Senator Jay Rockefeller of West Virginia, Senator Bill Bradley of New Jersey, and Senator Albert Gore of Tennessee. Both Gephardt and Gore had pursued the Democratic presidential nomination in 1988.

Then, late in 1991, two other leading Democrats announced that they would not run. On November 2, the Reverend Jesse Jackson, who had sought the presidency both in 1984 and 1988, declared that he would not be a candidate. And on December 20, New York's Governor Mario Cuomo, probably the Democratic party's best orator, announced that he, too, would not enter the race for president in 1992.

Table 2.8. Voter Support for Clinton, Bush, and Perot: The Gallup Poll's Three-Way Trial Heats Between March and Election Eve, 1992

Date of Interviews	For Clinton %	For Bush %	For Perot %	For Others, No Opinion %
March 31–April 1	25	44	24	7
May 7–10	29	35	30	6
June 4–9	25	31	39	5
July 6–8	28	35	30	7
July 6–8*	40	48		12
Democratic Convention Meets, Perot Leaves Race, July 13–16, 1992				
July 17–18	56	34		10
August 8–10	56	37		7
Republican Convention Meets, August 17–20, 1992				
August 21–22	52	42		6
August 31–September 2	54	39		7
September 17–18	51	42		7
Perot Reenters Race, October 1, 1992				
October 7–8**	50	34	9	7
Televised Debates, October 11–19, 1992				
October 21–22***	43	34	16	7
October 26–27***	40	38	16	6
October 29–30***	42	39	14	5
November 1–2***	44	37	14	5
Election Results	43	38	19	—

* Perot voters assigned to candidate named as their second choice.
** Based on likely voters, responses to question: "If the presidential election were being held today, would you vote for the Republican candidates, George Bush and Dan Quayle, for the Democratic candidates, Bill Clinton and Al Gore, or for the independent candidates, Ross Perot and James Stockdale?"
*** One reason these results may have differed from other polls at the time is that for these surveys, Gallup sampled only "likely voters."
Source: Gallup Poll surveys.

The Democrats who did come forward to seek their party's nomination were less well-known nationally than several of the leading noncandidates. (Some political commentators unkindly characterized the candidates who entered the race as the "B List" of potential Democratic contenders.) The first to announce was Paul Tsongas, a former senator from Massachusetts. In time, five other candidates sought the nomination: Governor Douglas Wilder of Virginia, the first African American to be elected governor of a southern state in the twentieth century; Senator Tom Harkin of Iowa; Senator Bob Kerrey of Nebraska; Jerry Brown, the former governor of California; and Governor Bill Clinton of Arkansas. But Governor Wilder, criticized in his home state for spending too much time running for president, dropped out of the race very early, on January 9. As a result, for the first time in twelve years, there was no major Black candidate seeking the Democratic nomination for president. As it turned out, Wilder's decision helped Clinton, for Clinton was to receive sizable majorities of the votes cast by African Americans in most of the state primaries.

The first Democratic primary took place on February 18, 1992, in New Hampshire. As the campaign got under way, Clinton quickly emerged as the front-runner in the polls.

Then came two startling developments that threatened to destroy the Clinton campaign almost before it began. First, the tabloid *Star* published a story in which Gennifer Flowers, a lounge singer, asserted that she had engaged in a twelve-year affair with Bill Clinton. Clinton, with his wife Hillary, appeared on the CBS television program *60 Minutes* and denied Flowers' allegations.

Next, the *Wall Street Journal* raised a new issue: Clinton's draft record. "A man who had been head of the ROTC program at the University of Arkansas said Clinton had promised to join the program in 1969 as a way of avoiding the draft when he was most vulnerable to being called—and then had reneged on his pledge," the reporter asserted.[15] After bypassing the ROTC program, Clinton drew a high number in the draft lottery and was not called. Questions about the draft, and about his varying explanations of what had occurred, were to plague Clinton throughout the 1992 campaign.

Within a few days, Clinton had fallen behind Paul Tsongas in the New Hampshire polls and was in danger of losing so badly that his campaign would be finished before it really started. The night before the election, when Clinton heard the final New Hampshire tracking poll numbers, he thought that his campaign might well be over. But Clinton ran much better in New Hampshire than he expected. Paul Tsongas was first, but the Arkansas governor was a strong second. The final tally was Tsongas, 33 percent; Clinton, 25; Kerrey, 11; Harkin, 10; and Brown, 8.[16] Most of the primaries immediately ahead lay in the South, a region where Clinton hoped to run strongly among his fellow Democrats.

The South did indeed give a powerful lift to the Clinton candidacy. First there was a crucial primary in Georgia. Clinton won that with 57 percent of the vote to Tsongas's 24 percent. On Super Tuesday, March 10, Clinton swept most of the rest of the South and the Border states.

The governor from Arkansas now had 800 delegates, more than one-third of the number needed to win the Democratic nomination.[17]

By now, Harkin and Kerrey had joined Wilder in dropping out of the race, and a series of primaries in major northern states lay ahead. After Clinton won a decisive victory in Illinois, Tsongas also withdrew. Now Clinton's only announced Democratic opponent was Jerry Brown.

A Brown victory over Clinton in Connecticut—by one percentage point—gave special importance to the upcoming primary in New York State on April 7. Brown sought to strengthen his position among African American voters by promising that, if he won the nomination, he would select Jesse Jackson as his vice presidential running mate. But Clinton still maintained considerable support among New York's Black voters, and he won the New York primary with 40.9 percent of the vote. Tsongas pulled in 28.6 percent of the vote to finish second in New York, where his name remained on the ballot, followed by Brown with 26.2 percent. A Clinton nomination now seemed certain.

Nevertheless, during May and June, Clinton was running third—behind both Bush and Perot—in most of the national polls. Then, during the second and third weeks of July, the strategic outlook for the fall campaign changed dramatically. On July 9, Clinton announced that he had selected Senator Al Gore of Tennessee to be his vice presidential running mate. The two Democrats were presented as a "New Generation" ticket. For the first time, both candidates of a major party had been born after the Second World War—Clinton in 1946, Gore in 1948. And it was also the first all-southern presidential and vice presidential ticket to be offered by a major political party since Andrew Jackson had run with John C. Calhoun in 1828.

The next week, the Democrats dominated political coverage on radio, television, and in the newspapers for four days, in what was generally perceived as a highly successful convention in New York City. And Ross Perot dropped out of the race. The first Gallup poll taken after the Democratic convention brought startling news—Clinton was now ahead of George Bush by twenty-two points, 56 percent to 34 percent (Table 2.8).

It had been a very good two weeks for the Democrats. During a thirteen-day period, in early and mid-July, Clinton had moved from last place in a three-way race to a commanding lead over the president.

The General Election Campaign

Part of the new Clinton lead was undoubtedly a temporary increase in support for a candidate whose party had held a successful convention—the so-called "convention bounce" in the polls. But three weeks later, shortly before the Republican Convention, Clinton still led Bush by nineteen percentage points.

The Republicans now launched their counterattack at their national convention, held in Houston, August 17–20. Many convention speakers emphasized the theme of "family values," and Bush delivered a vigorous statement of the case against the Democrats in his acceptance speech. But a fiery convention address by Pat Buchanan, who charged that the Democratic party was endangering fundamental cultural values, may have been more pleasing to the Republican party's right wing than it was to moderate and independent voters.

When the Republican Convention was over, support for President Bush and his vice presidential running mate Dan Quayle had risen by several percentage points; and the support for the Clinton-Gore ticket had dropped about four points. But the Democrats still led in the Gallup poll by ten percentage points—a lead they would hold through most of the remaining weeks of the campaign (Table 2.8).

A major new development in the campaign season occurred on October 1st. Ross Perot reentered the presidential race, greatly altering the dynamics of the campaign for the final five weeks. The initial impact of Perot's reentry did not seem to benefit Bush, however. The first Gallup poll taken after Perot was again in the race found that Clinton was down by one percentage point, compared with his showing in a Gallup poll taken before Perot was a candidate. But the same two polls suggested that after Perot reentered the campaign, President Bush's support dropped by eight percentage points (Table 2.8).

During the middle of October, from October 11 to October 19, there were four televised debates—three debates among the three leading presidential nominees and one for the candidates for vice president. Enormous audiences—some evenings as high as 93 million people—watched the debates. Once the debates were over, only two weeks of the campaign remained.

Perot had obviously made a favorable impression on many voters, and his standing in the polls began to rise rapidly. He held few campaign rallies; from his headquarters in Dallas he now launched a barrage of television ads and much lengthier "infomercials." Millions of Americans watched the Perot ads.

During the final days of the campaign, there were several dramatic developments. On October 25, Ross Perot claimed he had pulled out of the race in July because he feared that if he stayed in, his daughter would be the victim of Republican "dirty tricks." Perot was unable to substantiate his charge, however, and the uproar that followed seemed for a time to blunt Perot's progress in the polls.

Meanwhile, President Bush began to draw huge, enthusiastic crowds. He was obviously buoyed by their response; he also seemed to feel that he was closing the gap on Clinton, and some of the polls indicated he might be doing so. One Gallup poll, taken October 26–27, reported that Clinton was now only two points ahead of the president among those Americans who were likely to vote (Table 2.8).

As the campaign neared its end, Bush's attacks on his Democratic opponents became harsher. "My dog Millie knows more about foreign policy than these two bozos," Bush said, and he called Gore "Ozone Man," or just "Ozone."[18]

Then, on Friday, October 30, Lawrence E. Walsh, the independent counsel investigating the Iran-contra affair, filed new evidence in court. The key document was a handwritten note by then Defense Secretary Caspar W. Weinberger which seemed to suggest that Bush, while vice president, had attended a high-level White House meeting and had not only known about, but had favored, exchanging arms with Iran for American hostages.[19] Over the final weekend, the president and other Republicans were again on the defensive, denying that the president had been "in the loop."

As election day neared, attention began to focus on a new question: How many of the potential voters would actually turn out to vote? Both Clinton supporters and Perot supporters contended that a large voter turnout would be a "pro-change" vote that could benefit their candidate. On Election Day, bright sunshine and balmy weather prevailed in most of the South and Southeast, and as far north as Philadelphia. (Many politicians believe that good weather usually means more voters will go to the polling places.) But in New York City and New England, and in Chicago and other great cities of the Midwest, there was rain much of the day. And in the iron range of Minnesota, in Colorado, and elsewhere, snow had fallen. Everywhere, however, the people voted—the first day in the history of the nation when more than 100 million Americans went to the polls.

Despite the intense efforts of Bush and Perot to close the gap during the week before the election, Clinton remained in the lead, as he had since the middle of July. Although he received only 43.0 percent of the total vote, Clinton won by a margin of 5.6 percentage points over Bush and by more than 5,800,000 popular votes.

NOVEMBER 3, 1992—THE PATTERN OF THE VOTE

On Election Day, 44.9 million persons cast their ballots for Clinton and about 39.1 million voted for Bush. Perot polled over 19.7 million votes, an unusually strong showing for an independent candidate. In the electoral college, because Perot did not win the popular vote in any state, all of the electoral votes went to Clinton and Bush. The Democratic nominee received 370 electoral votes, reflecting his popular vote pluralities in thirty-one states and his majority victories in the District of Columbia and Arkansas. Bush received 168 electoral votes as a result of popular vote pluralities in eighteen states. Aside from this overall verdict, there were many noteworthy features in the November 3, 1992 vote.

The National Vote

1. About 104.4 million voters went to the polls. The number of people who voted for president was up by almost 13 million from 1988, and the percentage turnout—55.2 percent—was the nation's highest since 1972.[20]

2. The impact of the recession—and of economic concerns—was strongly reflected in the returns. One-third of the voters (34 percent) reported that their family's financial situation was worse in 1992 than it had been in 1988. Among that large group of voters, Clinton ran ahead of Bush by 62 percent to 13 percent (Table 2.9).

3. Clinton's percentage of the *total vote* (43.0 percent) was the lowest percentage received by a winning presidential candidate since Woodrow Wilson won the election of 1912 with 41.8 percent of the vote. Clinton was also only the fifth president in this century (counting Wilson twice) to be elected with less than half of the total vote. The other "minority presidents" were Woodrow Wilson, 1916 (49.4 percent in 1916), Harry S Truman (49.6 percent in 1948), and Richard M. Nixon (43.4 percent in 1968). Nevertheless, despite Clinton's low winning percentage, in the *total vote* for president Clinton ran 5.6 percentage points ahead of Bush.

4. In the voting dynamics that determined the crucial outcome in the electoral college, the popular vote for the two major party candidates, Clinton defeated Bush by seven percentage points—53.5 percent to 46.5 percent. Clinton's seven-point lead in the *two-party* vote came close to Franklin Roosevelt's two-party vote lead in 1944 (53.8 percent to 46.2 percent). It also approached, though it fell short of, the two-party vote lead that Bush had over Michael Dukakis in 1988—53.9 percent to 46.1 percent.

The Perot Factor

1. The 19.7 million votes (18.9 percent) polled by Ross Perot was the largest percentage received by a minor party or independent candidate

since Theodore Roosevelt ran as the candidate of the Progressive (Bull Moose) party in 1912. And it was the largest percentage ever received by a third party or independent candidate who had not already served as president of the United States.

2. The two-party vote determined the outcome in the electoral college because Ross Perot—despite polling 19.7 million popular votes—did not come close to receiving a plurality in any state. The closest Perot came to winning some electoral votes was in Maine, where he ran 8.4 points behind the winner in Maine, Bill Clinton. In every other state, Perot lagged behind the statewide winner by eleven percentage points or more.

Sectional Patterns

1. In the presidential race, the most Democratic region was the Northeast, where Clinton out-polled Bush by 47 percent to 35 percent. Along the East Coast, for example, Clinton carried every state from Maryland to the Canadian border—a feat that not even Franklin D. Roosevelt had been able to achieve. In the Midwest, the outcome was closer. There, Clinton ran ahead of Bush, 42 percent to 37 percent.

Table 2.9. *How Groups Voted in 1992[a]*

	Clinton (%)	Bush (%)	Perot (%)
All (100)	44	37	19
Men (46)	41	37	21
Women (54)	47	36	17
Whites (87)	40	39	21
Blacks (8)	83	11	7
Hispanics (3)	62	24	14
Didn't complete high school (6)	56	27	18
High school graduate (25)	44	36	21
Some college (29)	43	36	21
College graduate (24)	41	39	20
Postgraduate (16)	50	35	15
Age 18–24 (11)	47	31	22
25–29 (11)	41	35	24
30–39 (25)	42	38	21
40–49 (24)	44	37	19
50–59 (13)	42	39	19
60 and Up (16)	50	37	12

Table 2.9. *(continued)*

	Clinton (%)	Bush (%)	Perot (%)
Family income			
Less than $15,000 (14)	59	22	19
$15,000–29,999 (24)	46	34	20
$30,000–49,999 (30)	42	37	21
$50,000–74,999 (20)	41	41	18
$75,000 or more (13)	38	46	16
Protestants (56)	34	45	21
Catholics (27)	42	37	21
Jews (4)	78	10	11
Family financial situation compared with 1988:			
Better (25)	25	60	15
Worse (34)	62	13	25
About the same (41)	42	41	18
Democrats (39)	78	10	13
Republicans (34)	11	72	18
Independents (28)	39	31	30
Liberals (22)	69	13	18
Moderates (50)	49	30	21
Conservatives (29)	18	64	17
1988 votes:			
Bush (53)	22	58	20
Dukakis (27)	83	5	12
Didn't vote (15)	50	24	26
First-time voters (11)	48	29	23
Union households (19)	56	23	22
Nonunion households (81)	42	39	19
Reagan voters in 1984 (44)	21	58	21

Source: Voter Research and Surveys exit polls for 1992 in *National Journal*, November 7, 1992, p. 2543.

[a]Does not always add to 100 percent due to rounding.

2. The Democrats' Clinton-Gore ticket, the first all-southern ticket since 1828, made inroads into previous Republican strength in presidential voting in the South. In 1988, Bush led Dukakis by 17.4 percentage points in the South; in 1992, Bush's lead in the region was cut to less than two percent. Moreover, Clinton carried four southern states— Arkansas, Georgia, Louisiana, and Tennessee—and came close to carrying two more, North Carolina and Florida.

3. Nevertheless, Bush ran most strongly in the once heavily Democratic South. In the eleven states of the former Confederacy, Bush led Clinton—42.6 percent to 41.2 percent. Outside the South, Clinton led Bush by a sizable margin—43.7 percent to 35.6 percent.

4. The Clinton tide extended across most sections of the country. In terms of states won and lost, however, there were important centers of Bush strength in four areas—most of the Southeast, Indiana, a string of six states in the center of the country running from Texas to the Canadian border, and four of the eight Rocky Mountain states.

5. One of the most striking regional trends was the improved showing by the Democrats in the West, a region where Ronald Reagan carried many of the states by landslide margins in the 1980s. Clinton won decisive victories in California, Oregon, and Washington; and, among the eight Rocky Mountain states, Clinton was the winner in four—Colorado, New Mexico, Montana, and Nevada.

6. Despite Clinton's generally strong showing in the West, there was a substantial difference between the voting patterns in the Pacific Coast region and the pattern in the Rocky Mountain area. In the three Pacific Coast states, Clinton ran ahead of Bush, 46 percent to 32 percent. In the Rocky Mountain states, by contrast, Bush won narrowly, with 38.6 percent to Clinton's 36.9 percent—with nearly one vote in every four in the Rocky Mountain region (24.5 percent) going to Perot.

Social Groups

1. Clinton ran well among some traditionally Democratic groups among whom the Democrats had suffered heavy losses to Reagan in the 1980s. Among members of union households, Clinton led Bush 56 percent to 23 percent; he also ran ahead of Bush among Hispanic Americans, 62 percent to 24 percent. In addition, exit polls showed Clinton doing well among two groups that had remained Democratic in 1984 and 1988: Clinton was backed by 83 percent of Black voters and by 78 percent of Jewish voters (Table 2.9). Despite the attacks on his draft record, Clinton also won the votes cast by veterans of the nation's armed forces, by 41 percent to 37 percent.[21]

2. The contribution made by Black voters to the Democratic presidential victory was particularly noteworthy. One in every twelve Americans (8 percent) who went to the polls was Black. This large group voted 83 percent for Clinton, and only 11 percent for Bush. The exit polls suggested that African Americans gave Clinton a margin of about 6 million votes, more than his 5,805,000 margin of victory.

3. Among some groups that had been key components of the Roosevelt New Deal coalition, however, there were again signs of how much change had occurred in American voting patterns since 1950. In the 1930s and 1940s, Roman Catholic voters regularly gave top-heavy majorities to Franklin D. Roosevelt and Harry S Truman. In 1992, Clinton won a plurality among the votes cast by Roman Catholics. But Clinton's edge over Bush among Catholic voters—42 percent to 37 percent— was no greater than his lead in the U.S. electorate as a whole. Among White southern Protestants, another group who used to give large victory margins to Roosevelt, Bush had a decisive advantage over Clinton in 1992, winning 53 percent to 30 percent.[22]

4. One other group—White voters who attend church on a weekly basis—turned in a large vote for Bush. This "churched" portion of the electorate is huge, one-third (33 percent) of all the voters who went to the polls in 1992. It also includes millions of the White southern Protestants whose voting proclivities have just been noted. Nevertheless, among this segment of the voting public, Bush ran ahead of Clinton by 53 percent to 31 percent. (Perot's vote was 16 percent.)[23] As Everett Carll Ladd has noted, in 1992 it was, to a considerable extent, church-going White voters who kept the Republican party in the presidential race.[24]

5. Among Black voters, by contrast, support for the Democratic presidential ticket was at least as high among Blacks who went to church on a weekly basis as among those who did not. Blacks who said they attended religious services weekly gave 85 percent of their votes to Clinton, while Blacks who called themselves "Born-Again Christians/ Fundamentalists" gave 86 percent. As noted, the Clinton vote among all Blacks was 83 percent.[25]

6. As in the 1980s, there was a substantial difference in the way women and men voted in the 1992 presidential contest. Among male voters, Clinton had a modest lead over Bush. Among women who voted, Clinton led Bush by eleven percentage points. If all voters had voted the way American women cast their ballots in 1992, Clinton probably would have won the election by more than 11 million votes, instead of by 5.8 million.

7. Taken together, quite a number of the salient voting patterns of 1992 showed how greatly the lines of electoral cleavage in America had changed since the old New Deal Democratic coalition was formed. A "gender gap," a heavy Republican vote among southern White Protestants, only a modest Democratic victory margin among Roman Catholics, an overwhelming preference for the Democratic party among Black voters, and a pronounced difference among White voters between those who attend church regularly and those who do not—these voting pat-

terns would have startled an electoral analyst in the days of Franklin Roosevelt. But by the 1980s and the early 1990s, they had become staples of American politics.

Party Loyalty and Defection

1. Despite the Clinton victory, the major change in party identification that took place in the mid-1980s was once again strongly evident in the returns. Among those who voted, self-described Democrats outnumbered Republicans by only a moderate margin—39 percent to 34 percent (Table 2.9). As recently as 1980 (and in spite of Ronald Reagan's presidential victory that year), the exit polls suggested that 43 percent of the voters considered themselves Democrats, compared with 28 percent who said they were Republicans.[26]

2. The proportion of actual voters who identified with the Republican party was probably higher in 1992 than in any other election since the first part of the 1940s. By the beginning of the 1990s, the Democratic party had clearly lost the large advantage in party identification that it had enjoyed for more than four decades.

3. Nevertheless, although the number of Republican identifiers grew substantially in the eight years before the 1992 election, in 1992 the Republican vote splintered badly at the presidential level. For the first time since the Johnson landslide over Goldwater in 1964, the Democrats mobilized a higher percentage of their partisans than did the Republicans. To be sure, both Democratic and Republican identifiers defected from their party's ticket. But Clinton held on to 78 percent of the votes cast by Democrats, while Bush polled only 72 percent of the votes of Republicans (Table 2.9).

4. Clinton also out-polled Bush among voters who considered themselves independents. Here again, it was the first time since 1964 that the Democratic nominee ran ahead of the Republicans among independents.

5. Ross Perot showed substantial strength among all three types of voters—Democrats, Republicans, and independents. But he drew more deeply from Republican ranks than from Democratic identifiers. Perot polled 13 percent of the vote among Democrats and 18 percent of the vote cast by Republicans. Among independents, the Perot total rose to 30 percent (Table 2.9).

Control of Government

1. In many of the contests for public offices other than the presidency, Democratic candidates did well in 1992. But Republican candi-

dates also showed substantial strength, enough to leave the Republican party in a position to be highly competitive in subsequent elections in 1994 and 1996.

2. The Democrats made a net gain of two in the nation's governorships, leaving them with thirty governors to the Republicans' eighteen. Two governors in 1992 were independents. Republican gains in 1993 and, especially, 1994 brought the number of Republican governors up to thirty in January 1995. It was the first time the GOP controlled a majority of the nation's governors mansions since 1970.

3. Despite the Democratic presidential victory for Bill Clinton, in the battle for control of the House of Representatives, the Republicans strengthened their position in 1992. Republicans made a net gain of nine seats in the House. That still left the Democrats with a majority in the House of 259 to 175 (plus one Socialist from Vermont). Republicans had hoped for larger gains, however; the 1992 results followed a post–1990 census reapportionment that moved nineteen House seats from Democratic areas in the Northeast and Midwest to more Republican areas in the South and West. Two years later, in the midterm Republican election victory of 1994, the continuing impact of this reapportionment helped the GOP significantly. For the first time since the 1952 elections, a Republican majority was elected to the U.S. House.

4. The new House of Representatives elected in 1992 was also more representative of the American people. One-fourth of the new House that assembled in January 1993 were new members—men and women who had not served in the preceding Congress. Compared with the 102nd Congress, the new 103rd Congress was more diverse, had more members of minority groups, was younger, and had fewer lawyers. There were many more women in the House—forty-seven in the new House compared with twenty-eight in the old. There were also thirty-eight African Americans, compared with twenty-five in the old House, and seventeen Hispanic Americans, compared with ten in the previous House.

5. In the Senate, the balance of power between the parties remained the same at the end of 1992—fifty-seven Democrats, and forty-three Republicans.[27] Like the House, the Senate became somewhat more diverse. Four more women were elected to the Senate, joining the two who served in that body before 1992. One of the new senators, Carol Mosely Braun of Illinois, was the first African American woman to serve in that chamber. And in Colorado the victory of Ben Nighthorse Campbell, running as a Democrat, sent the first Native American to the Senate in more than sixty years.

6. The 1992 elections left the Democratic party with a majority in the Senate, but it also left the Democrats with many more seats than the Republicans to defend in the next battle for control of the Senate—the midterm congressional elections of 1994. One-third of the U.S. Senate seats (or thirty-four seats) were to be filled in the midterm elections of 1994. Of those thirty-four seats, twenty-two were held by Democrats and only twelve were held by Republicans. (When Senator Lloyd Bentsen of Texas gave up his Senate seat to become Secretary of the Treasury in the new Clinton administration, the Democrats promptly lost Bentsen's Senate seat to a Republican, in a special election held on June 5, 1993.)[28] In 1994 the Republicans captured a Senate majority for the first time in eight years, 52 to 48. The day after the elections Senator Richard C. Shelby of Alabama switched from the Democratic party to the Republican party, raising the Republican margin to 53–47.

7. Perhaps the most important point about the 1992 election was that for two years there would be no more "divided government," and fewer excuses for legislative or executive inaction. For the first time in twelve years, the presidency and the Congress would be controlled by the same party—the Democrats. How well the Democrats were perceived as *governing* would go a long way toward determining how their party would fare in future elections. As it turned out, divided government returned to Washington just two years later, as the Republicans won control of the House and Senate.

THE 1992 RESULTS—
WHY THE OUTCOME WAS DIFFERENT
FROM 1984 AND 1988

Nevertheless, in 1992, supporters of the Democratic party had reason to derive a measure of satisfaction from the results. The Democrats had done something they had done only once before in the previous twenty-five years—they had won the elections at virtually every level of government. The question remains, however: *Why* were the returns in 1992 different from those of earlier years, particularly 1984 and 1988? A number of factors appear to have made the political environment of 1992 different from the election years of the 1980s.

"It's the Economy. . . ."

First and foremost was the state of the economy—and, probably even more important, the way the voters *perceived* the state of the economy. During 1992, surveys of voter attitudes toward the economy were con-

Table 2.10.   Voters' "Family Financial Situation" Compared with Four Years Earlier, 1984–1992

Year	Worse (%)	Better (%)	About the Same (%)
1992	34	25	41
1988	17	44	39
1984	19	41	40

Source: For 1992, Voter Research and Surveys exit polls, *National Journal*, November 7, 1992, p. 2543; for 1988, Cable News Network-*Los Angeles Times* exit polls, *National Journal*, November 12, 1988, p. 2955; for 1984, *Los Angeles Times* and ABC News-*The Washington Post* exit polls, *National Journal*, November 10, 1984, p. 2132.

ducted fourteen times between January and Election Day by CBS News and the *New York Times*. In each of those fourteen polls, the persons interviewed were asked: "How would you rate the condition of the national economy these days: Is it very good, fairly good, fairly bad, or very bad?" In none of the fourteen surveys did the number of people who rated the economy as "very good" or even "fairly good" exceed 23 percent. And, in the last of the fourteen polls—conducted during a four-day period that ended November 1, just forty-eight hours before Election Day—37 percent of the respondents said the economy was "very bad," and 40 percent said it was "fairly bad."[29]

This CBS News and *New York Times* question asked prospective voters how they felt the economy was doing generally. The question did not necessarily require a response regarding how the interviewee felt he or she was faring personally—how the economy was affecting his or her own economic well-being. On Election Day, however, voters leaving the polls were asked how their own family's "financial situation" was in 1992, compared with how it had been four years earlier. The responses to this question provide a revealing picture of how members of the electorate felt they had been affected by economic trends during the Bush years (Table 2.10).

A large number (34 percent) said that, compared with four years earlier, their family's financial situation was "worse." Moreover, this group of people who felt they had lost ground economically since the preceding election was much larger in 1992 than it had been in the elections of the 1980s, when the Republican party was returned to power. In 1988, seventeen percent of the voters said their family's financial situation was worse than it had been four years earlier. In 1984, the number reporting that their financial situation had slipped was 19 percent.

Those who had lost ground financially were in no mood to reelect the incumbent. As has been noted, they voted nearly five to one for Clinton over Bush (62 percent to 13 percent), and another 25 percent voted for Ross Perot (Table 2.9).

The World Changes

A second development that greatly altered the political landscape between 1988 and 1992 was the disintegration of the Soviet Union and the apparent end of the Cold War. Both in 1984 and in 1988, many voters reported that they had greater confidence in the Republicans than in the Democrats on two vital issues—the maintenance of a strong national defense, and the provision of competent leadership in foreign policy. Moreover, at the grassroots level, Republican electoral strategists often found that taking a strong position of anticommunism worked well for them.

After an extensive analysis of public opinion surveys conducted in 1988, Patricia A. Miranda concluded that doubts about Michael Dukakis as a potential commander-in-chief and foreign policy leader—and a preference for George Bush on those same dimensions—were important factors that led to the Republican victory in 1988.[30] Four years later, with the Cold War apparently over, foreign policy and national defense issues were much less salient than they had been in 1988, and the Republican party had largely lost one of its most effective campaign themes.

Even in 1992, foreign policy and national defense concerns were a pro-Republican issue. Voters who said that "foreign policy" was one of the issues that "mattered most" to them "in deciding" how to vote went for Bush over Clinton by eleven to one (87 percent to 8 percent). But in 1992, only 8 percent of the electorate cited foreign policy as an issue that "mattered most in deciding" how to vote.[31] In 1988, the number of voters for whom "national defense" was an important concern was 23 percent.[32]

The Democrats Moderate the Message

A third factor that made 1992 different from 1984 and 1988 is that, in 1992, the Democratic party changed the message they tried to transmit to the voters—by changing their platform, by changing the issues they emphasized, and by changing their presidential candidate. In 1985, in the aftermath of Ronald Reagan's landslide victory over Walter Mondale, a group of moderate and conservative Democrats—many of them from the South—formed the Democratic Leadership Council. The avowed goal of the DLC was to move the Democratic party closer to "the center."

One of the Council's cofounders, Senator Sam Nunn of Georgia, declared: "The perception is that the party has moved away from mainstream America. We want to move it back to the mainstream."[33] Another early supporter, Lawton Chiles, then a Democratic Senator from Florida, struck the same theme: The national Democratic party has "got to get back where our state parties are . . .we know where the middle is. . . ."[34] But it was Bill Clinton, then the Governor of Arkansas and an early chairman of the DLC, who stated the group's objective in the most pragmatic terms. The goal of the DLC, he said, was to "define a new middle ground of Democratic thinking on which someone can run for president and be elected."[35]

In 1988, supporters of the DLC had only limited success changing the issue stances and the image of the Democratic party. A DLC member who ran for the Democratic nomination for president, Senator Al Gore of Tennessee, was eliminated from the race early in the primary season. But in 1992, things were different. Arkansas Governor Bill Clinton announced his presidential candidacy in a speech that contained twelve separate references to the needs of the "middle class."[36] And, of course, Clinton won the Democratic nomination and selected as his vice presidential running mate Senator Al Gore, another DLC supporter. When the 1992 Democratic party platform was drafted, Clinton, as the prospective Democratic presidential nominee, and the DLC exercised considerable influence on the platform planks that were adopted.[37]

The 1992 Democratic platform was, as Douglas B. Harris has pointed out, very different indeed from the Democratic platforms of the 1980s with respect to a series of issues.[38] Harris analyzed the Democratic platform planks of 1984, 1988, and 1992 concerning a number of issues. He also analyzed the 1988 Republican platform planks on the same issues. The issues covered included crime, welfare, affirmative action, foreign policy, and the degree to which government programs were emphasized as the way to solve social problems—as opposed to an emphasis on the responsibility of individual citizens. After a detailed examination of the four platforms, Harris concluded: The 1992 Democratic platform was directed at a "new audience. Where mentions of the middle class were rare in the 1984 and 1988 [Democratic] platforms (and especially dwarfed by mentions of minorities and the poor), the middle class was the featured social group in the New Democratic platform of 1992."[39]

Harris adds: "The 1992 Democratic platform represents a DLC inspired departure from traditional Democratic positions. Through textual examination of [the three Democratic and one Republican] platforms, it is evident that the Democrats in 1992: (1) changed their party's targeted audience; (2) drastically altered the party's official positions on a number of issues; and (3) were 'closer' to the Republican platform of 1988 in many ways than to their own 1984 and 1988 platforms."[40]

Other changes in 1992 also suggested that the message the Democratic party tried to send to the voters that year was different from the message conveyed in earlier election years. In 1988, the Democratic presidential nominee, Michael Dukakis, was an opponent of the death penalty. In 1992, the new Democratic nominee, Bill Clinton, supported the death penalty. To at least some voters, the choices that were offered when considering whether to vote Democratic or Republican in 1992 must have seemed different than in the 1980s.

The Perot Factor

A fourth factor that differentiated 1992 from 1984 and 1988 was a major change in the political landscape—the emergence of Ross Perot in 1992. Moreover, this Perot phenomenon seemed to hurt the Republican presidential ticket more than it hurt the Democrats. Perot's candidacy appears to have done special damage to the Bush campaign in at least two ways. First, as has been noted, Perot attracted a higher percentage of Republican identifiers (18 percent) than Democratic identifiers (13 percent); he also won a larger proportion of those who had voted for Bush in 1988 (20 percent) than he won from the 1988 Dukakis voters (12 percent) (Table 2.9). But Perot also may have hurt Bush's campaign even more in another way. For month after month in 1992, Perot emphasized weaknesses in the American economy, including the budget deficit. Indeed, until Clinton emerged in the polls as a potentially strong candidate in mid-July, Perot was probably a far more effective critic of George Bush's economic leadership than was Clinton. Then, even after July, Perot continued to emphasize a point that was the Democrats' main campaign theme—that the American economy was in bad shape under a Republican administration. Throughout the 1992 campaign year, Perot helped to focus extensive media attention on the economy. It was not an issue focus that was helpful to George Bush.

The Racial Factor: Jackson and Wilder Decide Not to Run

Other key developments during the campaign season also appeared to benefit the Democrats in 1992. The decision of the Reverend Jesse Jackson, and then of Governor Douglas Wilder, not to seek the Democratic presidential nomination in 1992 probably made it easier to hold the Democratic electoral coalition together. Jackson had sought the presidency both in 1984 and 1988; and his candidacy had generated much excitement and considerable support among some White voters as well as among Black voters. But the Jackson candidacy was also a candidacy that made some White voters less willing to vote Democratic—both during the primary season and during the general election campaign.

Thomas Byrne Edsall and Mary D. Edsall have argued that the impact of racial issues and racial divisions frequently tended to splinter the Democratic electoral coalition from 1968 to 1988.[41] With Jackson out of the race, the 1992 Democratic primary campaigns were less divisive than they had been in 1984 and 1988; and the Democratic presidential nominee was less likely to be perceived as "making too many concessions" to Jackson during the general election campaign.

The absence of Jackson and Wilder in 1992 may have helped the Democratic party in another way as well. As noted, Clinton received most of the votes cast by Black voters in the Democratic primaries. This enabled him to emerge as the near certain Democratic presidential nominee fairly early in the primary season. It also may have made it easier for the Democrats to unify their party and to begin preparing for the upcoming fall campaign.

The Democrats' Ultimate "Southern Strategy"

Another factor that made 1992 different from 1984 and 1988 is that, in 1992, the Democrats came up with their own, and ultimate, "southern strategy." As noted, the 1992 Democratic ticket was the first all-southern presidential and vice presidential major-party ticket since Andrew Jackson ran with John C. Calhoun in 1828. This choice of ticket helped make the Democratic presidential slate strongly competitive in the South for the first time since Jimmy Carter ran in 1976. Clinton and Gore carried Arkansas, Tennessee, Louisiana, and Georgia; and they came close to winning in both North Carolina and Florida. The all-southern ticket may also have helped produce Democratic victories elsewhere—as in Kentucky, a state that after 1952 has gone Democratic only when the Democratic party has nominated a southerner for president. Although the Republicans won most of the South in 1992, they had to expend many resources defending their supposed base.

The Democrats Out-campaign the Republicans

Another factor that may have made 1992 different from recent previous elections is harder to establish objectively, but it may have played an important role in the outcome of the election. In 1984 and 1988, and also in 1980, the Republican candidates often seemed to be on the attack; it was the Republicans' electoral strategies that most frequently seemed to be defining the terms of the campaign debate. In 1992, by contrast, Clinton and Gore often appeared to be dominating the terms of the campaign dialogue. And it seemed to be the Republican candidates who were reacting to, rather than controlling, the flow of events. A judgment on these matters inevitably must be subjective. But a case can be made that in 1992, in terms of the technical skill with which the two major-party campaigns were conducted, for the first time in many years the Democrats out-campaigned the Republicans.

Republican Schism: Buchanan Challenges Bush

One of the unexpected developments of the election year was a full-fledged challenge to President Bush from within his own party. Although challenger Patrick Buchanan did not win any primaries or caucuses, his presence weakened the president. Buchanan's criticisms of the president hurt Bush's image and Bush had to allocate resources toward his nomination campaign. Furthermore, Buchanan's prime-time speech at the Republican Convention, witnessed by the whole country, resonated with conservative themes that were pleasing to conservatives but were less well received by many other voters.

Buchanan's extended challenge was in sharp contrast to the Republican nomination process of 1984. In 1984, President Ronald Reagan did not face any opponents for the Republican nomination. In 1988, however, Vice President George Bush was challenged by five other candidates for the Republican presidential nomination. Of these, Senator Robert Dole of Kansas and Pat Robertson, a minister and television broadcaster from Virginia, showed considerable early strength in Iowa, New Hampshire, and South Dakota. But on Super Tuesday, March 8, 1988, Bush swept all sixteen primaries. Dole withdrew from the race on March 29 and Robertson suspended his candidacy on May 11, 1988. By contrast, in 1992, Buchanan maintained his candidacy to the end, drawing over 26 percent of the vote in the June 2 California primary.

The President Loses the Confidence of the Public

Another factor which worked strongly against President Bush in 1992 was his declining support among the public. Not only was his support low, but the overall trend reflected a record decline. In March 1991, just after American forces, dispatched to the Persian Gulf by President Bush, forced Iraq's Saddam Hussein to withdraw from Kuwait, Bush's approval rating, buoyed by a wave of patriotic feeling, soared to 89 percent in the polls. Only a year later, in February 1992, with the administration plagued by economic recession and broad voter dissatisfaction, Bush's popularity had plunged to 39 percent in one poll.[42] In mid-October, Bush's approval rating was only 34 percent (Table 2.6).

President Reagan's approval ratings were not without their own ups and downs. But Reagan did not reach the depths of Bush's lowest numbers, and he was in an upward trend in both 1984 and 1988. Reagan's approval rating reached its nadir during his first term, 35 percent in January 1983. But from the Grenada invasion of October 1983 to the November 1984 election, Reagan's approval ratings did not drop below 53 percent.[43] Reagan and his vice presidential running mate Bush thus entered the 1984 campaign in a position of strength.

In his second term, Reagan's approval ratings were over 60 percent for the first two years. But when the Iran-contra affair became public in November 1986, Reagan's approval rating plummeted from 63 to 47 percent in little more than a month. During 1987 and the first half of 1988, Reagan's approval was generally under 50 percent. In June 1988, however, following Reagan's summit meeting with Soviet Premier Gorbachev in Moscow, the president's popularity began to improve. By August, immediately after the Republican Convention, Reagan's approval rating stood at 53 percent.[44]

STRATEGIC FACTORS
AND SITUATIONAL FACTORS
IN 1992

Each of the foregoing factors were, in the terminology of the pioneering electoral analysts at the University of Michigan, "short-term factors" that influenced the national election of 1992.[45] They were issues or developments that arose in that one election year—1992; and it was almost certain that some of these factors would not be repeated in the next presidential election year.

Some of the developments that brought about change in 1992 were *situational factors*—changes in the total environment within which the election campaign had to be fought. An example of a situational factor would be the weakening of the economy from 1990 to 1992.

Other factors that brought about change in 1992 were *strategic factors*—things which the Democrats or the Republicans (or Ross Perot) did or did not do, strategies taken or strategies missed. An example of a strategic factor was the decision by leaders within the Democratic electoral coalition to move their party "toward the center," to take more moderate issue stands.

This conceptual framework, which distinguishes between situational factors and strategic factors, can be broadened. It could perhaps also be applied to other presidential election years. But, in any event, in 1992, two distinct groups of short-term factors can be classified as follows:

Situational Factors in 1992	*Strategic Factors in 1992*
Economy weakens in 1991 and 1992.	Democrats change their message, take more moderate issue positions.
Soviet Union disintegrates and the Cold War ends.	Ross Perot decides to run—twice.
	Jackson (and Wilder) decide not to run.
Bush's approval ratings decline	Democrats nominate an all-southern ticket.
	Democrats out-campaign the Republicans.
	Buchanan challenges Bush for the nomination.

There were, in sum, a number of short-term factors that made 1992 different from 1984 and 1988; and in 1992, most, if not all of them, worked to the Democrats' advantage.

CONCLUSION: 1992 AND BEYOND

All of the foregoing lines of speculation still leave two major unanswered questions. What was the fundamental nature of the verdict handed down by the American electorate in 1992? And, amid the large number of elections that make up the total "population of elections,"[46] how is the 1992 election to be classified? The famous elections typology developed by scholars at the University of Michigan—maintaining elections, deviating elections, and realigning elections—might be applied. But there are conceptual difficulties in deciding which major party was the normal majority party in 1992, in Michigan's terms. By 1992, the Republicans appeared normally to be the stronger party in presidential elections. But the Democratic party maintained a nominal advantage in terms of the party identification of the American electorate.

There is, however, another famous typology of elections that might shed light on the nature of the electoral verdict in 1992. And it has the added merit of being a simpler typology. V. O. Key, Jr. once classified presidential elections into three broad types: (1) Votes of Lack of Confidence; (2) Reaffirmations of Support by Votes of Confidence; and (3) Realignments. As Key wrote:

> In the quest for an understanding of electoral decision, one category of elections appears quickly from an inspection of presidential elections. On occasion the electorate votes a party out of

power in a decisive manner; it expresses clearly a lack of confidence in those who have been in charge of affairs. The mandate to the incoming party may be vague, and, indeed, it may be difficult to read into the vote a bill of explicit dissatisfactions with the party that has been cast out of office. Yet the election clearly expresses a widespread unhappiness with past performance . . . the party in power, in comparison with the preceding election, loses voting strength in most counties of the nation. Though the data are lacking, the odds are that the decline in strength also permeates most social and economic classes.[47]

In 1992, the loss of strength by the Republicans was less precipitous than the loss by the party that controlled the presidency in some of the "Lack of Confidence" elections cited by Key. In addition, it is clear that a very important reason why Bush's voting strength dropped sharply between 1988 and 1992 was because there were *two* other significant candidates—Clinton and Perot—to whom people could give their votes. Even so, the drop in the Republican presidential vote between 1988 and 1992 was very large. In just four years the Republican share of the total presidential vote dropped by sixteen percentage points—from 53.4 percent in 1988 to 37.4 percent in 1992. Moreover, the total vote for President Bush on November 3 was very close to the percentage of Americans who said they "approved of the job George Bush [was] doing as President"—thirty-six percent—as the general election campaign got under way in September 1992.

In Key's terms, then, the 1992 electoral verdict appears fundamentally to have been an expression of "a lack of confidence in those who have been in charge of affairs."[48] In Key's terms, also, the mandate given to the Democratic candidates who won the election appears to have been anything but clear. Perhaps the only clear mandate to the new winning party—in this as in most elections—was the mandate to take on the risks of governing. How well the Democrats were perceived as managing the government would go a long way toward determining whether *they* received a "Vote of No Confidence" or a "Vote of Confidence" in November 1994 and November 1996.

NOTES

Milton Cummings would like to thank Margaret Brassil and Pamela Winston for their invaluable research assistance.

1. Theodore H. White, *The Making of the President 1960* (New York: Atheneum House, 1961), p. 258.

2. Everett Carll Ladd, with Charles D. Hadley, *Transformations of the American Party System: Political Coalitions from the New Deal to the 1970s*, 2nd ed. (New York: Norton, 1978), p. 262.

3. Angus Campbell, "Interpreting the Presidential Victory," in *The National Election of 1964*, ed. Milton C. Cummings, Jr. (Washington, D.C.: Brookings, 1966), pp. 256–281, at 271–273.

4. Milton C. Cummings, Jr., *Congressmen and the Electorate: Elections for the U.S. House and the President, 1920–1964* (New York: The Free Press, 1966), pp. 206–224.

5. James L. Sundquist, *Dynamics of the Party System: Alignment and Realignment of Political Parties in the United States*, rev. ed. (Washington, D.C.: Brookings, 1983), pp. 269–297.

6. Sectional partisan trends in U.S House races are analyzed in Cummings, *Congressmen and the Electorate*, pp. 206–224; Charles O. Jones, "Inter-Party Competition for Congressional Seats," *Western Political Quarterly* 17 (September 1964): 461–476; and Harvey L. Schantz, "Inter-Party Competition for Congressional Seats: The 1960s and 1970s," *Western Political Quarterly* 40 (June 1987): 373–383.

7. Before 1958, and the admission of Hawaii and Alaska to the Union, there were thirty-seven nonsouthern states.

8. Dukakis carried ten states, plus the District of Columbia, which had a total of 112 electoral votes. However, in one state that Dukakis carried, West Virginia, one of the Democratic electors voted for Lloyd Bentsen for president instead of voting for Dukakis.

9. The data concerning the percentage of Democratic identifiers who voted for the Democratic presidential ticket in 1976 and 1988 were provided by the Gallup poll.

10. "The West" is defined here as the eight Rocky Mountain states of Arizona, Colorado, Idaho, Montana, Nevada, New Mexico, Utah, and Wyoming; plus California, Oregon, and Washington State.

11. Gerald M. Pomper, "The Presidential Election," in *The Election of 1988*, ed. Pomper (Chatham, N.J.: Chatham House, 1989), pp. 129–152, at 132.

12. This narrative account of the 1992 campaign draws heavily on Milton C. Cummings, Jr. and David Wise, *Democracy Under Pressure: An Introduction to the American Political System*, 7th ed. (Fort Worth: Harcourt Brace Jovanovich College Publishers, 1993), pp. 325–339.

13. *Newsweek, Special Election Issue*, November/December 1992, p. 72.

14. *New York Times*, July 17, 1992, p. A16.

15. *Newsweek, Special Election Issue*, November/December 1992, p. 34.
16. Ibid., p. 37.
17. Ibid., p. 39.
18. *Washington Post*, October 30, 1992, p. A1.
19. *Washington Post*, October 31, 1992, p. A1.
20. Richard M. Scammon and Alice V. McGillivray, comps. and eds., *American Votes 20* (Washington, D.C.: Congressional Quarterly, 1993), pp. 7 and 11.
21. Voter Research and Surveys exit polls; reported in *Newsweek, Special Election Issue*, November/December 1992, p. 10.
22. Voters Research and Surveys exit polls; cited in Everett Carll Ladd, "The 1992 Vote for Bill Clinton: Another Brittle Mandate?," *Political Science Quarterly* 108 (Spring 1993): 1–28, at 4.
23. Ibid., *loc. cit.*
24. Ibid., p. 5.
25. Ibid., p. 4.
26. The party identification data cited for 1980 come from exit polls of 12,782 voters conducted by CBS News and the *New York Times*; reported in *National Journal*, November 8, 1980, p. 1878.
27. In 1992, two Senate contests were decided after Election Day in special elections, held November 24 in Georgia, won by the Republicans, and December 4 in North Dakota, won by the Democrats.
28. The newly elected Republican senator from Texas, Senator Kay Bailey Hutchison, brought the number of women in the Senate to seven in 1993.
29. Surveys by *CBS News* and the *New York Times*. Cited in Ladd, "The 1992 Vote for Bill Clinton," p. 15.
30. Patricia A. Miranda, *The Latent Demands of the American Electorate in the 1988 Presidential Election and the Implications of These Demands: The Americans Talk Security Surveys* (Master's thesis, Johns Hopkins University, 1989).
31. Voter Research and Surveys exit polls, *National Journal*, November 7, 1992, p. 2544.
32. Cable News Network-*Los Angeles Times* exit polls, in *National Journal*, November 12, 1988, p. 2854.
33. Quoted in Dan Balz, "Southern and Western Democrats Launch New Leadership Council," *Washington Post*, March 1, 1985, p. A2.
34. Quoted in Tom Sherwood, "Robb Leads Democrats on Texas Blitz," *Washington Post*, July 2, 1985, p. A8.
35. Quoted in David Broder, "'Mainstream' Democratic Group Stakes Claim on Party's Future," *Washington Post*, May 3, 1991, p. A15.

36. Governor Bill Clinton, "Announcement Speech," Old State House, Little Rock, Arkansas, October 3, 1991, in Governor Bill Clinton and Senator Al Gore, *Putting People First: How We Can All Change America* (New York: Times Books, 1992), pp. 187–198.
37. See L. Sandy Maisel, "The Platform Writing Process," *Political Science Quarterly* 108 (Winter 1993–94): 671–698.
38. See Douglas B. Harris, "The Democratic Leadership Council and the Democratic Party Image: A Case Study and Test of Competing Theories of Party Competition," paper prepared for delivery at the 1994 Annual Meeting of the Midwest Political Science Association, Chicago, Ill., April 14–16, 1994.
39. Ibid., p. 14.
40. Ibid., pp. 13–14.
41. Thomas Byrne Edsall, with Mary D. Edsall, *Chain Reaction: The Impact of Race, Rights, and Taxes on American Politics* (New York: Norton, 1991).
42. Gallup/*USA Today*/CNN poll, February 19–20, 1992.
43. *Gallup Report*, December 1983, p. 18; June 1984, p. 11; and Gallup poll, press release.
44. *Gallup Report*, September 1987, pp. 17–18; and Gallup poll, press release, October 9, 1988.
45. Angus Campbell, Philip E. Converse, Warren E. Miller, and Donald E. Stokes, *The American Voter* (New York: Wiley, 1960); Philip E. Converse, "The Concept of a Normal Vote," in *Elections and the Political Order*, ed. Angus Campbell, Converse, Warren E. Miller, and Donald E. Stokes (New York: Wiley, 1966), pp. 9–39.
46. The phrase, "population of elections," is V. O. Key's. See Key, "The Politically Relevant in Surveys," *Public Opinion Quarterly* 24 (Spring 1960): 54–61, at 55.
47. V. O. Key, Jr., *Politics, Parties, and Pressure Groups*, 5th ed. (New York: Crowell, 1964), p. 522.
48. Ibid., *loc cit.*

CHAPTER 3

Sectionalism in Presidential Elections

HARVEY L. SCHANTZ

Sectional rivalries have frequently been reflected in presidential election balloting. The elections preceding the Civil War are only the most prominent examples of regional conflict in presidential elections. Earlier contests, from 1804 to 1816, found New England to be the sole enclave of the waning Federalist party, while in the 1820s and 1830s the Jacksonian wing of the Democratic-Republican party flourished in the southern regions. After the Civil War there was a period of relatively national voting patterns, artificially brought about by Reconstruction laws in the South. By 1892, though, traditional southern-northeastern differences returned and were exacerbated for awhile by western protest voting. Through the early decades of the twentieth century sectional voting patterns in presidential elections prevailed, and the South was unique in its vote well into mid-century.

These presidential voting patterns comported nicely with sectional interpretations of U.S. history and politics. During the 1920s, preeminent historian Frederick Jackson Turner emphasized the importance of the section to the United States.[1] Along with the already gone frontier, "the Section" was a "fundamental factor in American history." "The greater sections" of the United States, according to Turner, "are the result of the joint influence of the geologists' physiographic provinces and the colonizing stocks that entered them."[2]

"Geological foundations" led each section to develop unique economic capacities and interests. And, according to Turner, "these differences between sections in economic interests mean also differences in political interests." Sectional political interests are reflected in the "political affiliation of the mass of voters" in the various regions. These affiliations are long-term and form the basis of "a geography, a habitat, of political habit."[3]

Sectional interpretations of presidential elections are found in the 1920s to 1940s writings of two prominent political scientists, Arthur N. Holcombe and Cortez A. M. Ewing. In his 1924 book, *The Political Parties of To-Day*, Holcombe presented a theory and history of U.S. political parties that was based on sectional politics. "National politics," wrote Holcombe, "is inseparable from sectional politics." His theory, he claimed, was a "realistic" one, written from the point of view of "ambitious and realistic party leaders." In Holcombe's view, the task of such a leader is to assemble a "combination of interests" large enough to win the presidency and control the Congress.[4]

A winning combination of interests cannot be based on the transient issues of the day, but rather "upon permanent sectional interests, above all upon those of an economic character." Sectional economic power is found in "the primary producers, especially the agricultural interests, the manufacturing interests, and the mining interests." Party leaders must identify and "appeal" to these sectional interests in order to "build up" their winning combination.[5]

The opportunities to attract and bind sectional interests to a combination are provided by the constitutional grants of power, especially the economic ones, accorded the national government. They include in particular, the power to levy taxes, including tariffs, the power to regulate interstate and foreign commerce, and the power to coin and regulate the value of money. The issues of foreign policy and war have not proven to be "well adapted to the purposes of ambitious party leaders."[6]

Throughout American history control of Congress and the presidency has been held by those "ambitious and realistic party leaders" capable of attaching sufficient interests. Holcombe was particularly impressed with the hegemonies of the Jacksonian Democrats, during the period 1829–1861, and the supremacy of the conservative Republicans, from 1896 to the 1910 midterm election.[7] Other political party combinations were more short-lived or failed to control all the branches of government as completely.

In *Presidential Elections,* published in 1940, Ewing presented a statistical portrait of sectional and state voting trends in the nineteen presidential elections from 1864 to 1936. His focus included patterns of partisan support and competition, the roles of third parties, voter turnout, and the translation of popular votes into electoral votes. Although popular and electoral votes are accrued state by state, Ewing's analysis of presidential balloting was explicitly tied to a sectional interpretation of American politics: "Though the state is the intermediate unit in the electoral college process, the great political movements that elect and defeat candidates for the presidency are surprisingly sectional in scope. The larger clashes in the electoral college are therefore intersectional rather than intrasectional." According to Ewing, "there emerges a picture of American politics, the outlines of which are not clear if too close scrutiny is given to the political behavior of particular states."[8]

The sectional classification of the states used by Ewing differed somewhat from the geographical emphasis of Turner and the economic emphasis of Holcombe. "The sections set up in this study," wrote Ewing, "are not strictly geographical, economic, social, or racial; they are essentially political." In contrast to Holcombe's twelve sections, Ewing divided the states into East, Border, South, Middle West, and West.[9]

Presidential elections from 1864 to 1936 reflected sectional conflict, mainly involving an alliance of the East and Middle West against the South. "As the period under discussion opened, the sections were locked in mortal combat," wrote Ewing. The conflict had moral roots in the slavery issue, but also reflected eastern support for high tariffs which the South opposed. By the time that the issues of the Civil War era passed, the Middle West shared with the East a substantial stake in the new "industrial order."[10]

By the New Deal era of the 1930s, sectional conflict played a less pronounced role in national politics. Political coalitions began to be viewed in terms of social classes and group affiliations rather than sectional blocs. These changes were reflected in more nationally uniform voting patterns, though the South continued to be an independent-minded voting bloc.

Holcombe and Ewing picked up on these changes. In a 1933 book, Holcombe argued that the United States had passed from a time of "rustic politics" to an era of "urbane politics." In this new party politics "there will be less sectional politics and more class politics."[11] Ewing noted that the electoral "break in 1932 was too general a political phenomenon to be explained from the standpoint of geography." He saw the changes as perhaps explained by the increasingly national economy and "the mutuality of problems and the human disposition to react to those problems, in whatever section they may arise, in a manner conducive to individual and social welfare."[12]

The discussion of sectionalism and its demise was continued by V. O. Key, Jr. and E. E. Schattschneider, the two leading mid-century students of American parties and politics. Both emphasized sectional interpretations of American politics in their earlier work.[13] But by the 1950s, Key and Schattschneider pointed to a wearing away of regional differences in the partisan division of the presidential vote. Both scholars described an evolving party system in which sectional peculiarities in partisan predilections would continue, however irregularly, to give way to a more nationally uniform division of the vote, beginning with presidential elections and working down to contests for state and congressional offices. Key referred to this process as "the erosion of sectionalism."[14] Schattschneider called it "the nationalization of politics."[15] In addition, Schattschneider emphasized that we could expect increasingly uniform swings in the presidential vote throughout the country, as the process of nationalization proceeded.[16]

Key and Schattschneider emphasized different reasons for the electoral changes. Key felt that "the weakening of sectional blocs comes fundamentally from the multiplication of interests within regions." The growth of economic diversity within an agricultural region, including manufacturing and finance, is part of the urbanization process: "The processes of urbanization created the raw materials for party cleavages more nearly along class lines than was the politics of sectionalism."[17]

Schattschneider explained that the change from sectional to national voting patterns was due to a "profound change in the agenda of American politics."[18] The new policy initiatives of the Democratic party in 1932 brought to the fore political combinations that were national, rather than sectional.

This chapter examines the sectional dispersion of the presidential vote from 1824 to 1992, documenting sectionalism and testing the erosion of sectionalism thesis. Specifically, it measures and analyzes the deviations of the regions from the national vote distribution, and the deviations of the regional vote swings from the national movement. It thus studies two important indices of what Schattschneider called the "nationalization of American politics." It emphasizes Key's term "erosion of sectionalism" for two important reasons. First, the concept of nationalization of the electorate has been defined differently by various students of voting behavior.[19] Second, we wish to emphasize that *section* is our unit of analysis, rather than state, congressional district, county, or individual voter.[20]

The electoral analyses illuminate longitudinal patterns of sectionalism in presidential elections, the track record of individual regions *vis-à-vis* the national vote and the national vote swing, and the New Deal transition from an era of sectionalism to one of a national party system. This chapter also considers the implications of the data for the evolving party battle in an era featuring a national party system.

DATA AND METHODS OF ANALYSIS

This study measures sectional dispersion in presidential elections from 1824 to 1992, a total of forty-three elections. It considers the regional dispersion in the vote distribution and the vote swing. These two analyses are each divided into two broad time frames, 1824–1852 and 1856–1992.

The first broad era is from 1824 to 1852, from the earliest available popular votes to the election prior to the Republican party. Our unit of analysis is region, and for these eight elections, following the lead of William G. Shade, we have divided the United States into six sections: South Atlantic, Southwest, Border, New England, Middle Atlantic, and Old Northwest.[21] Our computations are based on the Jacksonian Democratic (1824–1828) or Democratic share of the two-party vote, since these parties won a plurality of the popular vote in six of these eight elections.[22]

The second broad time frame examines presidential elections from 1856 to 1992, a total of thirty-five elections. In all of these elections, with the exception of 1912, the Republicans and Democrats were the two leading political parties. For these elections, we have divided the United States into eight commonly accepted and politically important sections: South, Border, New England, Middle Atlantic, Midwest, Plains, Rocky Mountains, and Pacific Coast.[23] Our computations for these years are based on the Republican share of the two-party vote, since Republicans have won a plurality of the popular vote in nineteen of the last thirty-five presidential elections.[24] Election returns for all forty-three elections are from Congressional Quarterly Inc.[25]

For each election, we calculate (1) sectional deviations from the national vote distribution[26] and (2) sectional deviations from the national vote swing.[27] For both indices of nationalization, each year we compute the average of the absolute regional deviations, yielding a mean regional deviation.[28] On each index, a high average deviation indicates a sectional pattern in presidential elections, while a low mean deviation indicates a nationalized pattern. An average deviation of zero, each region paralleling the national vote distribution, or vote swing, would indicate a regionally uniform pattern—a complete erosion of sectionalism in presidential elections.

SECTIONAL DISPERSION OF THE PRESIDENTIAL VOTE

The data on sectional dispersion of the presidential vote are presented in Tables 3.1 and 3.2. Table 3.1 presents regional deviations from the

Democratic national two-party vote from 1824 to 1852. Table 3.2 presents regional deviations from the national Republican percentage of the two-party presidential vote in each election from 1856 to 1992. In both tables, the first data column presents the national percentage for each year, and in each succeeding column the deviation of the sectional vote from the national figure is given for the specified section. In each table, the last column presents the average of the absolute sectional deviations, the mean deviation, for each election. The last columns for Tables 3.1 and 3.2, along with the summarizing least-squares regression lines, are graphed in Figures 3.1 and 3.2, respectively.

1824–1852: The Second Party System

The 1824–1852 time span is frequently called the second party system.[29] It was an era in which the Jacksonian wing of the Democratic-Republican party came to dominate the presidency. In the election of 1824, Andrew Jackson ran as one of four Democratic-Republican candidates, winning a plurality of the popular vote but losing in the U. S. House to John Quincy Adams. Four years later, Jackson won the presidency as the only Democratic-Republican candidate, ousting John Quincy Adams who was running on the National-Republican ticket. In 1832, Jackson was the Democratic candidate, winning reelection over Henry Clay, the National-Republican standard-bearer. The five remaining presidential elections of this time span, from 1836 to 1852, were essentially contests between Democrats and Whigs, with the Whigs achieving their only successes in 1840 and 1848.

During the years of the second party system there was an overall steep decline in sectional diversity in presidential election balloting. This is shown by Equation 3.1 in which we regress the election mean deviation (y) on the year (x):

EQ. 3.1

1824–1852, 8 observations: $y = 20.89 - 3.18x$; $r = -.86$.[30]

Thus, on average, the mean regional deviation fell by more than three points in any election.

Electoral Eras. The years of the second party system, as Figure 3.1 shows, were characterized by a sectionally diverse vote pattern from 1824 to 1836, and a much more nationally uniform vote from 1840 to 1852. In the first four elections, the average sectional deviation varied between 24.2 (1824) and 13.3 (1828), averaging 17.7 percentage points.

On the other hand, between 1840 and 1852, the average sectional deviation varied from 2.6 (1848) to only 1.2 (1844), with a mean of 1.8.

Another way of demonstrating two distinctive electoral eras is by regression analysis. If we divide the time series into two parts, we obtain the following summary equations:

EQ. 3.1A

$$1824\text{--}1836, 4 \text{ observations: } y = 20.02 - 1.53 \text{ x}; r = -.41;$$

EQ. 3.1B

$$1840\text{--}1852, 4 \text{ observations: } y = 1.39 + 0.29 \text{ x}; r = .61.[31]$$

Comparison of the intercept values of these equations, 20.02 versus 1.39, demonstrates that sectionalism in presidential elections was of a completely different order in the two sets of elections. The lion's share of the decline in diversity occurred between the 1836 and 1840 contests, but between 1824 and 1836 diversity declined over 1.5 percentage points, on average, per election, as indicated by the slope in Equation 3.1A. From 1840 to 1852, regionalism was higher in the later two elections, as indicated by the positive slope; nevertheless, these four elections were the ones with the closest regional outcomes in U.S. presidential election history.[32]

Our analysis is in general accord with commentaries on presidential elections during the second party system that find a sectional (1824–1832) and national (1840–1852) period, with 1836 frequently cited as the transitional election.[33] As Shade wrote, "The presidential elections from 1824 to 1852 fall into two groups . . . the election of 1836 was a transitional one . . . The elections of the first phase were distinctly sectional . . . while Phase II witnessed a uniformity of voter behavior throughout the country."

Our calculations differ from earlier ones, though, in that we find 1840, rather than 1836, to be the beginning of the national vote pattern. This difference in the calculations stems from our isolating the William H. Harrison (Whig) vote, rather than considering it along with the polls for the two other Whig candidates.[34] Our finding is completely consistent with the interpretation of Richard P. McCormick, the leading student of the second party system, who wrote that "In the successive contests for the presidency between 1824 and 1836 strong sectional loyalties shaped the responses of political leaders and voters in each region to the opposing candidates."[35] There are no transitional calculations for sectionalism in 1836 because the Hugh L. White and Daniel Webster

Table 3.1. Sectional Deviations from Jacksonian Democratic or Democratic Percentage of National Two-Party Vote, Presidential Elections, 1824–1852

Year	National Democratic Percentage[a]	South Atlantic	Southwest	Border	New England	Middle Atlantic	Old Northwest	Average Sectional Deviation
1824	57.2	30.0	31.2	2.6	-57.2*	19.8	4.5	24.2
1828	56.2	19.7	31.9*	-1.4	-24.4	-0.2	-2.3	13.3
1832	59.2	24.2	34.0*	-10.0	-13.2	2.2	-5.2	14.8
1836	58.1	41.9*	41.9*	-6.9	5.6	-5.6	-10.1	18.6
1840	47.0	-1.1	0.6	-2.7*	-1.7	2.0	-0.6	1.5
1844	50.7	0.0	3.5*	-1.2	-1.7	-0.1	0.4	1.2
1848[b]	47.3	0.7	2.7	0.2	-1.5	-5.2	5.3*	2.6
1852[b]	53.7	3.8*	2.6	-1.8	-2.4	-1.0	0.6	2.0
Average Deviation		15.2	18.6	3.4	13.5	4.5	3.6	
Times Most Deviant		2	4	1	1	0	1	
Times Above National Democratic Percentage		6	8	2	1	3	4	

aFor 1824 and 1828 the Jackson vote is used in computations. For remaining years, the Democratic vote is used.
bExcluded from analysis is the vote in California (1852), and in Iowa (1848, 1852).
*Indicates most deviant section for that year.

Figure 3.1.   Sectional Mean Deviation from Jacksonian Democratic or Democratic Percentage of National Two-Party Vote, Presidential Elections, 1824–1852

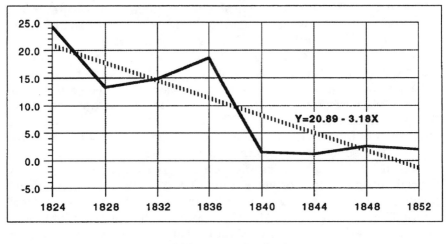

— Values   ''' Predicted

votes are either included (yielding a national calculation), or not included (yielding a sectional calculation). But all analysts agree that 1836 was a midway point, from a personalized multicandidate politics to an organized two-party presidential contest.[36]

During the second party system the most sectional election was in 1824. In that election and in 1828, the two leading candidates were John Quincy Adams and Andrew Jackson. They were clearly sectional candidates, both among the political elite and electorate, with Jackson popular in the South Atlantic and Southwest and Adams popular in New England.[37] In 1828, sectionalism moderated; Jackson appeared on New England ballots for the first time, and his overwhelming strength compared to Adams' subsided in the South Atlantic and especially the Middle Atlantic, which now included New York balloting.

Sectional voting patterns persisted in the two elections of the 1830s. The 1832 election was largely a contest between Democratic incumbent Jackson and National-Republican candidate Henry Clay. In 1832, Jackson gained strength versus the National-Republicans in all the regions except the Border, and although he gained impressively in New England, these two sections were markedly weak ones for "Old Hickory." Jackson was still overwhelmingly strong in both southern regions. In 1836, with Vice President Martin Van Buren as the Democratic standard-bearer, sectionalism was very high. The major reason for this was that Van Buren's chief opponent, Whig William H. Harrison, was not on the ballot in the South Atlantic and Southwest states as these states supported southern Whig Hugh L. White.

The election of 1840 ushered in an era of national voting patterns and close competition between the parties. "The campaign of 1840," wrote McCormick, "brought the second American party system at last to fruition. In every region of the country, and indeed in every state, politics was conducted within the framework of a two-party system, and in all but a handful of states the parties were so closely balanced as to be competitive."[38] These points are clearly reflected in Table 3.1, which shows that the Democratic percentage of the national two-party vote was close to 50 percent from 1840 to 1852 and that sectional deviations from the national percentages were minimal during these years.

Both the Whigs and Jacksonian Democrats campaigned vigorously throughout the nation for votes from 1840 to 1852. They argued over ideological positions, domestic policy (including a national bank and internal improvements), and tariffs, as well as other questions of foreign policy.[39] However, the most sectionally charged issue, slavery, "did not dominate the agenda prior to the 1850s."[40] Thus, sectional antipathy between New England and the South was not reflected in voting results.

The historical antagonism between New England and the southern regions had been reflected in the early years of the second party system. Adams was the favorite of New England and Jackson was the champion of the South. But by the 1840s, with the absence of Adams and Jackson, both Democrats and Whigs were drawing substantial strength in all sections, thereby masking the sectional conflict. In this sense, "because their ultimate alignments bore no direct relationship to the realities of sectional antagonism," McCormick labelled the Whigs and Democrats of this era "artificial" national parties.[41]

Sectional Vote Patterns Over Time. During the second party system, as indicated by the average deviation row in Table 3.1, three sections, the Border states, the Old Northwest, and the Mid-Atlantic, closely tracked the national presidential vote, whereas the other three sections, New England, the South Atlantic, and the Southwest, deviated markedly from the national vote.[42] All substantial deviation occurred in the first four elections, from 1824–1836, however. Furthermore, between 1840 and 1852, there were only minor differences in the average deviations of the six sections, as all toed the national line. The Southwest was the most deviant region in four of the eight elections from 1824 to 1852. The South Atlantic, which tied the Southwest in 1836, was most deviant twice. The Middle Atlantic was the only section never to be most deviant.

These sectional trends reflected the differential appeal of the presidential candidates in the early elections of the second party system and the nationally oriented agenda of the later period. Thus, during the 1824 to 1832 time period, huge pro-Democratic deviations in the South Atlantic and Southwest are a reflection of Jackson's appeal in those two regions and his weakness in New England. The great negative deviations in New England from 1824 to 1832 indicate Adams' strength in those six northern states, as well as his southern weakness. For the most part, the other regions did not have a viable sectional favorite for whom to vote so they split their vote between the candidates.[43] From 1840 to 1852, there was little deviation in any of the regions, Adams and Jackson were gone, and voters responded to the national agenda the parties offered.

1856–1992: Republicans versus Democrats

Since 1856, the quest for the presidency has essentially been a contest between the Republicans and Democrats. In the thirty-five elections from 1856 to 1992, Republicans won twenty-one times, including twice when the Democrats had a popular vote plurality, and the Democrats won fourteen times. Furthermore, only once, in 1912, did a third party place second in a presidential election.

Political scientists frequently divide these years into party systems: the third party system, the Civil War system, from 1856 to 1892; the fourth party system, the industrialist system, from 1896 to 1928; the fifth system, the New Deal system, from 1932 to 1968; and the sixth party system, with no agreed upon title, from 1968 to the present.[44] Each of these systems dealt with unique issue agendas and electoral alignments. We will study these alignments with respect to sectionalism.

Since reaching an all-time peak in 1856, sectionalism in presidential elections has receded. Sectionalism since 1856, as explained earlier, is measured and presented graphically in Table 3.2 and Figure 3.2. The overall trend in Figure 3.2 is a decline in the regional diversity of the vote since 1856. If we regress the election mean deviation (y) on the year (x), the equation that describes this relationship is as follows:

EQ. 3.2

1856–1992, 35 observations: $y = 10.88 - .26x$; $r = -.60$.[45]

Thus, on average, over four elections the mean regional deviation fell by more than one percentage point.

Electoral Eras.   Viewing the trend line in Figure 3.2, we find four distinct eras. In the two elections leading up to the Civil War, sectionalism was rampant. The deviation for 1856 was 24.4 and for 1860, 17.6, for a mean of 21.0 points.[46] Sectionalism was much lower in the seven elections from 1864 to 1888. In these years, the average sectional deviation varied from a high of 6.2 (1868, 1876) to a low of 4.3 (1864) and averaged 5.4 percentage points.

In the period 1892–1924, the differences from section to section were again relatively large. Since 1928, by contrast, there has been much less difference between the regions. In the nine presidential elections from 1892 to 1924, yearly dispersion varied between 6.2 in 1916 and 12.2 in 1924, averaging 8.8 percentage points from the national vote. In the seventeen presidential elections from 1928 to 1992, yearly regional differences ranged from a low of 2.7 in 1976 and 1984 to a high of 6.2 in 1932, and averaged 4.0 percentage points from the national distribution of the two-party vote.

Another way of demonstrating distinctive electoral eras is by regression analysis. If we divide the time series into three parts, we obtain the following summary equations:

EQ. 3.2A

$$1864–1888, \text{ 7 observations: } y = 5.13 + .08x; r = .24;$$

EQ. 3.2B

$$1892–1924, \text{ 9 observations: } y = 9.02 - .05x; r = -.06;$$

EQ. 3.2C

$$1928–1992, \text{ 17 observations: } y = 5.23 - .16x; r = -.72.[47]$$

The intercept value and the small slope of equation 3.2B show that sectionalism was moderately high from 1892 to 1924. In the other two stretches, 1864–1888 and 1928–1992, sectionalism was comparatively low. Since 1928, furthermore, sectionalism has declined steadily.

These findings are for the most part consistent with numerous interpretations of the American party system, which emphasize the disastrous levels of sectionalism prior to the Civil War, the sectional vote pattern during the fourth party system, and the transition from a sectional to a national party system in the New Deal era—even though the South continued to be a markedly deviant region until the Eisenhower elections of the 1950s. Less generally recognized is the highly national vote pattern from 1864 to 1888.

Figure 3.2. Sectional Mean Deviation from Republican Percentage of National Two-Party Vote, Presidential Elections, 1856–1992

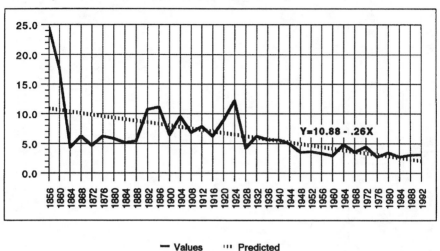

— Values   ''' Predicted

The 1856 election marked a great break with the past as the Republican party entered a presidential candidate for the first time and placed second, while the Whig party was a poor third in the balloting. The elections of 1856 and 1860 were the two most sectional of the contests between the Democrats and Republicans.[48] In 1856, the Republican party did not contest the South and Border sections, while it garnered almost two-thirds of the New England two-party vote. In 1860, the Republicans did gain, however, almost 20 percent of the two-party vote in the Border states. Nevertheless, sectionalism remained disastrously high.

National voting patterns dominated from 1864 to 1888. In a very real sense, for the first four of these elections, it was a forced homogeneity, since the South was not in the Union in 1864 and was controlled by Reconstruction governments for the subsequent three contests. In the 1880s, however, sectionalism did not rise, because the Border, New England, and Plains states moved toward the national vote. Outside the South, during these years, Civil War antagonisms were pushed off the agenda by economic issues, and newer voters, including many immigrants, replaced an older generation.[49]

The movement to and from the sectional party system of 1892–1924 was both marked and quick. In the post–Civil War era, the two largest interelection movements were the 1892 incline and the 1928 decline in regionalism. The three high-water marks of post–Civil War sectionalism were 1892, 1896, and 1924.[50] While it is commonly understood that the

Table 3.2. Sectional Deviations from Republican Percentage of National Two-Party Vote, Presidential Elections, 1856–1992

Year	National Republican Percentage	South	Border	New England	Middle Atlantic	Midwest	Plains	Rocky Mountains	Pacific Coast	Average Sectional Deviation
1856	42.2	-42.2*	-42.0	23.2	6.2	8.6	b		b	24.4
1860	57.5	-54.9*	-38.9	13.4	6.3	-2.8	0.3		-6.4	17.6
1864	55.0		-0.9	8.3	-4.4	0.1	9.2*		2.9	4.3
1868	52.7	-4.2	-11.4*	11.3	-2.3	1.9	10.0		-2.6	6.2
1872	55.9	-2.3	-9.1*	9.1*	0.7	-0.2	9.1*		1.7	4.6
1876	48.5	-8.1	-7.4	8.0	0.8	2.7	13.6*		2.5	6.2
1880	50.0	-11.7	-6.9	7.1	1.2	3.5	14.7*	1.4	0.1	5.8
1884	49.9	-9.5*	-3.9	5.6	1.6	2.2	8.1	6.6	3.3	5.1
1888	49.6	-11.8*	-2.1	6.1	2.0	2.0	8.4	7.9	2.7	5.4
1892	48.3	-18.3	-2.8	5.5	1.8	1.4	17.6	32.5*	5.6	10.7
1896	52.2	-16.3	-2.7	19.5	9.0	2.8	1.1	-34.1*	-3.3	11.1
1900	53.2	-16.6*	-3.5	8.4	4.8	2.2	4.4	-7.6	3.8	6.4
1904	60.0	-29.5*	-8.5	3.0	2.0	5.1	12.5	2.1	13.2	9.5
1908	54.5	-21.6*	-4.3	9.4	4.6	2.1	3.2	-0.9	8.6	6.8
1912	35.6	-19.9*	1.4	11.3	4.4	4.8	-0.5	5.0	-14.9	7.8
1916	48.4	-22.4*	-1.5	4.1	6.9	3.7	1.2	-8.4	1.2	6.2
1920	63.8	-27.1*	-9.7	4.7	6.6	3.9	9.3	-1.9	7.8	8.9
1924	65.2	-35.9*	-13.5	5.3	4.8	6.7	11.2	1.8	18.3	12.2
1928	58.8	-11.1*	-0.3	-5.3	-0.9	2.8	4.1	2.5	6.9	4.2
1932	40.8	-22.2*	-3.9	8.8	6.6	3.2	-1.8	-1.2	-2.1	6.2
1936	37.5	-18.3*	0.5	8.6	3.1	2.2	3.2	-3.6	-5.6	5.6
1940	45.0	-23.4*	-0.8	2.0	2.6	4.0	8.3	-0.6	-2.8	5.6

Year										
1944	46.2	-20.2*	0.4	1.3	1.9	3.7	7.6	1.2	-2.7	4.9
1948	47.7	-13.0*	-5.3	-0.3	3.6	2.1	1.1	-1.5	1.4	3.5
1952	55.4	-7.2	-3.7	0.9	-0.2	1.3	8.6*	4.9	1.6	3.6
1956	57.8	-7.2*	-3.8	4.3	2.6	1.7	1.9	2.5	-2.5	3.3
1960	49.9	-2.2	1.1	-6.0*	-1.6	1.6	5.9	3.7	0.7	2.9
1964	38.7	10.9	-2.2	-11.6*	-5.6	-0.4	1.8	4.7	0.8	4.8
1968	50.5	2.3	1.0	-10.3*	-2.2	0.7	3.4	7.7	0.6	3.5
1972	61.9	8.7	3.1	-9.0*	-2.0	-2.1	-1.9	4.2	-4.5	4.4
1976	49.0	-3.8	-1.8	-2.0	-0.3	2.3	0.8	8.5*	2.1	2.7
1980	55.4	-1.8	-2.5	-2.8	-1.9	-0.4	2.4	12.4*	3.2	3.4
1984	59.3	3.3	0.2	-2.9	-3.9	-0.9	-1.4	7.6*	-1.4	2.7
1988	54.0	4.8*	-0.7	-3.9	-3.0	-0.4	-3.5	4.6	-2.9	3.0
1992	46.6	4.2	-0.8	-5.0*	-3.0	-0.2	2.1	4.6	-4.5	3.1
Elections Analyzed		33	35	35	35	35	34	29	34	
Average Deviation		15.2	5.8	7.1	3.3	2.5	5.7	6.4	4.3	
Times Most Deviant[a]		19	2	6	0	0	5	5	0	
Times Above National Republican Percentage		6	7	24	22	27	29	20	21	

*Indicates most deviant section for that year.
[a]Does not add up to thirty-five because of ties.
[b]Excludes Iowa and California.

election of 1896 marked the beginning of the latest sectional era in presidential elections, as Key noted, "1892 severely jarred the old party alignments."[51] In 1892, the Democratic proportion of the vote in the Mountain states, and to a lesser degree in the Plains states, dropped greatly as the Populist party ran strongly in these regions. The weakness of the Democrats in these sections greatly increased the sectionalism of the two-party presidential vote.

The election of 1896 has been given many interpretations. Nevertheless, at bottom, according to Everett Carll Ladd, the Democratic standard-bearer William Jennings Bryan "ran as a sectional candidate, strongly appealing to the popular hinterland distrust of the Northeast. . . ."[52] This appeal is reflected in the flip-flop of the Mountain states from their 1892 pro-Republican position to one strongly supportive of the Democrats and in the larger than usual pro-Republican deviations in New England and the Middle Atlantic states.

The 1924 contest was the most sectional since the Civil War.[53] In the major party battle, it was the best year ever for the Republicans, as Calvin Coolidge won 65.2 percent of the two-party vote.[54] But his appeal did not extend to the South and Border states, where the Republicans netted only their baseline two-party support of the era—about 30 percent in the South and an even split in the Border states. This resulted in larger than usual pro-Democratic deviations for these two regions. At the same time, however, the strong Progressive vote in the Pacific, and the attendant weakness of the Democrats there, led to a marked pro-Republican deviation in the Pacific Coast region. The Progressive vote also contributed to larger than usual pro-Republican deviations in the two-party vote in the Plains states and in the Midwest. Between these peaks of sectionalism—1892, 1896, and 1924—regional diversity was much lower. Nevertheless, it rested on a much higher plateau than the years immediately preceding or succeeding.

Closer inspection of the elections in the current post-sectional era reveals both rises and declines in sectionalism. The 1928 election was a forerunner of the convergence in presidential election vote patterns, which emerged most fully in the post-World War II era. But first, sectional differences increased as the short-term factors of 1928—"rum and Romanism"—receded, the South returned to its Democratic moorings, and the northeastern regions moved back to their relatively Republican position.

This reversion to earlier voting patterns by the South and New England is reflected in the Roosevelt elections. In the presidential contests between 1932 and 1944, the South continued its tradition of deviating markedly from the national vote. Dixie lagged an average of more than twenty-one points behind the national Republican percentage in these four elections. In each of the last two FDR elections, the South accounted for over one-half of the total regional deviation from the national vote. Thus, long after the other regions had settled into a national party system, the South remained isolated from the national vote distribution. These southern election returns, of course, reflected the depth of southern regional consciousness, with its roots in war and military occupation; in Key's words: "Southern sectionalism bears the imprint of the trauma of history."[55]

In the contests of the 1930s, on the other hand, New England was substantially more Republican than the national vote—by an average of 8.7 points. But the magnitude of the New England deviation dropped markedly as the national Republican percentage increased in 1940 and 1944.

In the years after World War II, when Key and Schattschneider were writing about the erosion of sectionalism, there were consistently low average regional deviations from the national vote. From 1948 to 1960, the South underwent a sharp movement toward the national vote distribution, as southern fidelity to the Democratic party was shaken by that party's support for Black civil rights, and southern industrialization provided an increasing business constituency for the Republicans.[56]

The ideological elections of 1964 and 1972 were accompanied by a moderate increase in sectionalism, as the South moved to a sharply Republican position, and New England veered sharply Democratic, *vis-à-vis* the national vote. Throughout American history, as David Mayhew has shown, New England and the Deep South states have been at opposite poles in presidential elections.[57]

In the last five presidential elections, the process of regional convergence has continued, with the average regional deviations from the national vote dipping to twentieth-century lows of 2.7 percentage points in both 1976 and 1984.[58] Only the strong Republican vote in the Rocky Mountain states prevented the average sectional deviation from falling to minute proportions in these two elections.

Sectional Vote Patterns Over Time.   Since 1856, the Midwest has been the most accurate barometer of the national vote percentage. In the last thirty-five presidential elections, the five Great Lakes states have, on average, deviated only 2.5 points from the national two-party vote. Along with the Midwest, the Middle Atlantic states and Pacific Coast states have never been the most deviant region in a presidential election outcome. The extent to which these regions track the national vote may very well rest upon the diverse settlement and residential patterns of these states. All have attracted migrants from the chief competing political cultures, Yankee and Southerner.[59]

The South, by contrast, has been the most individualistic of the sections in presidential elections. Actually, for some time, the South was in a league unto itself; but, in recent years, it has come to mimic national trends more closely. Overall, for the last thirty-five presidential elections, the South has an average deviation of 15.2 percentage points from the national two-party vote. In nineteen of these thirty-five elections, most recently in 1988, it boasted the largest sectional deviation from the national percentage.

Since 1956, the mantle of isolation has been passed from the South to New England and from there to the Rocky Mountains. New England was the region furthest from the national vote in a four-election sequence, from 1960 to 1972, and again in 1992. The Mountain states were most deviant in 1976, 1980 and 1984. The Mountain West, according to George F. Will, is "today the way the South used to be before it became more homogenized with the rest of the nation."[60] The Rocky Mountain states, according to Will, resent the control Washington, D.C. has over the great expanse of public land in its borders. This, the argument continues, leads to strongly anti-Washington and pro-Republican leanings in the region.[61]

In addition to their magnitudes, the sectional deviations also have a direction toward one party or the other. Although the measurement of sectional convergence is based on arithmetic absolutes, the direction of sectional predilections supplies meaning to the calculations.

The bastions of the Republican party since the Civil War era have been the Plains states and the Midwest; twenty-nine and twenty-seven times, respectively, these regions were above the national Republican percentage of the two-party vote. By contrast, the South outpaced the nation as a whole in support of the GOP six times, and the Border states did so seven times. Each of the other four regions was above the national Republican percentage in twenty to twenty-four elections.

As with the data on the magnitude, there have been notable changes in the direction of regional deviations since the 1930s. Most spectacular and important have been the movements in New England and the South. In 1932 and 1936, New England was the weakest region for the Democratic Roosevelt. But, by 1940, this was changing, and in 1960 "Kennedy's victory marked the first time that New England, seedbed of the GOP a century earlier, was the *strongest* Democratic region in the country!"[62] It has been, with two exceptions, ever since. Meanwhile, the South, the most Democratic region in every election from 1900 to

1956, was the most Republican region in 1964, 1972, and 1988. These changes, as Kevin Phillips pointed out, turned the Civil War and early New Deal voting patterns on their heads.[63] Another noteworthy voting trend has been the evolution of the Mountain states into a Republican bastion, outpacing the nation in ardor for the GOP in every election since 1952, after having been a region of questionable Republican support. In all, three erstwhile Republican strongholds, New England, the Middle Atlantic, and the Midwest, have become more Democratic, and the South and Rocky Mountains have veered in the other direction, as compared to the post-World War II national presidential vote.

Overall, then, our major findings document substantial sectionalism in earlier times and confirm the assertions of Key and Schattschneider regarding the erosion of sectionalism. Defining sectionalism as the mean deviation of the regions from the national Republican percentage of the two-party vote, we find a large, irregular decline in dispersion beginning with 1928. The five most nationally uniform elections since the time of the Whigs were 1960, 1976, 1984, 1988, and 1992.

SECTIONAL DISPERSION
OF THE PRESIDENTIAL VOTE SWING

The data on sectional dispersion from the national presidential vote swing are presented in Tables 3.3 and 3.4. Table 3.3 presents sectional deviations from the Jacksonian Democratic national two-party vote swings from 1828 to 1852. Table 3.4 shows regional deviations in the national Republican two-party vote swings from 1860 to 1992. In both tables, the first data column gives the national change for each year, and each succeeding column presents the deviation of the regional swing from the national movement for the specified region.[64] The average of the eight absolute regional deviations, the mean deviation, is shown in the last column. The last columns of Tables 3.3 and 3.4, along with the summarizing least-squares regression lines, are graphed in Figures 3.3 and 3.4, respectively.

1824–1852: The Second Party System

The overall trend in Figure 3.3 is a decline in the regional dispersion of the vote swing during the second party system, from 1828 to 1852. If we regress the election swing mean deviation (y) on the year (x), the equation that describes this relationship is as follows:

Figure 3.3.   *Sectional Mean Deviation from Jacksonian Democratic or Demo-cratic Vote Swing, National Two-Party Vote, Presidential Elections, 1828–1852*

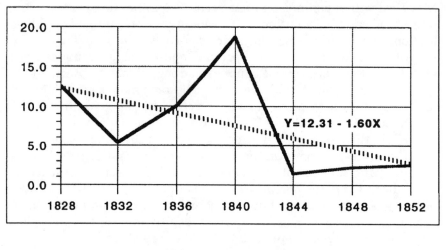

— **Values**   ''' **Predicted**

EQ. 3.3

     1828–1852, 7 observations: y = 12.31 − 1.60x; r = −.53.[65]

Thus, on average, the mean regional deviation of the vote swing fell by 1.6 percentage points.

Electoral Eras.   Figure 3.3 shows that the sectional dispersion of the vote swing was moderately high from 1828 to 1836, peaked greatly in 1840, and was very low from 1844 to 1852. In the three presidential elections from 1828 to 1836, the yearly average deviation ranged from 5.3 in 1832 to 12.5 in 1828 and averaged 9.3. It stood at 18.7 in 1840, but from 1844 to 1852 it ranged between 1.4 in 1844 and 2.5 in 1852, averaging only 2.0.

    Dividing these years into two periods yields the following summary equations:

EQ. 3.3A

     1828–1840, 4 observations: y = 8.13 + 2.33x; r = .54;

EQ. 3.3B

     1844–1852, 3 observations: y = 1.48 + 0.55x; r = .97.[66]

Table 3.3. *Sectional Deviations from Jacksonian Democratic or Democratic Vote Swing, National Two-Party Vote, Presidential Elections, 1828–1852*

Year	National Democratic Swing[a]	South Atlantic	Southwest	Border	New England	Middle Atlantic	Old Northwest	Average Sectional Deviation
1828	-1.0	-10.3	0.7	-4.0	32.8*	-20.0	-6.8	12.5
1832	3.0	4.5	2.1	-8.6	11.2*	2.4	-2.9	5.3
1836	-1.1	17.7	7.9	3.1	18.8*	-7.3	-4.9	10.0
1840	-11.1	-43.0*	-41.3	4.2	-7.3	7.1	9.5	18.7
1844	3.7	1.1	2.9*	1.5	0.0	-2.1	1.0	1.4
1848[b]	-3.4	0.7	-0.8	1.4	0.2	-5.1*	4.9	2.2
1852[b]	6.4	3.1	-0.1	-2.0	-0.9	4.2	-4.7*	2.5
Average Deviation		11.5	8.0	3.5	10.2	6.9	5.0	
Times Most Deviant		1	1	0	3	1	1	

[a]For 1824 and 1828, the Jackson vote is used in computations. For remaining years, the Democratic vote is used.
[b]Excluded from analysis is the vote in California (1852), and in Iowa (1848, 1852).
*Indicates most deviant section for that year.

The intercept values of these equations, 8.13 versus 1.48, show that sectionalism was considerably higher in the first era. The whole decline in sectionalism occurred from 1840 to 1844, for in each era sectionalism inclined, as shown by the positive slopes.

The yearly dispersions of the sectional vote swings are presented in Table 3.3. The table shows that the moderately high levels of dispersion in the first three elections were paced by New England's distinctiveness. In the last three elections, 1844 to 1852, all regions very closely tracked the national vote swing.

The pattern that protrudes most noticeably from Table 3.3 is the high dispersion in 1840, 18.7, and the dramatic drop to only 1.4 in 1844.[67] The major contributors to the 1840 dispersion were the huge vote swings in the South Atlantic and Southwest, two regions in which Jackson won all of the two-candidate vote in 1836 but which had a strong two-party poll for the Whig candidate in 1840. The disperse vote swing of 1840 moved all regions very close to the national vote percentage (Table 3.1). A national vote pattern prevailed from 1840 through the end of the second party system.

The Sections Over Time.   As with the data on the vote distribution, the Border, Old Northwest, and Middle Atlantic regions ranked one, two, and three, in their closeness to the national movement. In the seven elections from 1828 to 1852, New England was most deviant three times, the Border states were never most deviant, and each of the other four regions was most deviant once (Table 3.3).

New England was the most deviant region by a wide margin in the first three elections as a result of a pronounced pro-Democratic trend. Jackson did not appear on ballots in this region in 1824, so his 1828 candidacy led to a large pro-Jackson deviation. The New England trend toward Jackson continued in 1832. In 1836, the Democrats, with Jackson's successor Van Buren as their standard-bearer, captured over 60 percent of that region's two-party vote.

1860–1992: Republicans versus Democrats

Since 1860, sectionalism in presidential election vote swings has slowly diminished. This is detailed in Table 3.4 and graphed in Figure 3.4. If we regress the election swing mean deviation (y) on the year (x), the equation that describes the relationship is as follows:

EQ. 3.4

$$34 \text{ observations: } y = 6.45 - .12x; r = -.37.[68]$$

Figure 3.4. Sectional Mean Deviation from Republican Vote Swing, National Two-Party Vote, Presidential Elections, 1860–1992

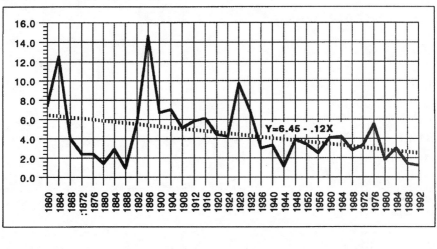

— Values   ''' Predicted

In the thirty-four elections, from 1860 to 1992, dispersion in the national vote swing declined an average of .12 of a point per election, as indicated by the slope.

Electoral Eras.   The decline in the diversity of the vote swing has been far from linear. Figure 3.4 reveals peaks of sectionalism in 1864 (12.5), 1896 (14.6), and 1928 (9.7), along with relative stability from 1868 to 1888, 1900 to 1924, and 1936 to the present. In the six elections from 1868 to 1888, diversity of the vote swing averaged 2.3 and ranged from 4.0 in 1868 to 0.9 in 1888. In the eleven elections from 1892 to 1932, diversity ranged from the 1896 peak to 4.2 in 1924 and averaged 6.9 points. In the fifteen presidential elections from 1936 to 1992, diversity varied from 1.1 in 1944 to 5.5 in 1976, with a mean of 3.0.

Further understanding of these eras of sectionalism is obtained from the following regression equations:

EQ. 3.4A

1868–1888, 6 observations: $y = 3.40 - .43x$; $r = -.73$;

EQ. 3.4B

1892–1932, 11 observations: $y = 8.08 - .23x$; $r = -.26$;

Table 3.4. Sectional Deviations from Republican Vote Swing, National Two-Party Vote, Presidential Elections, 1860–1992

Year	National Republican Swing	South	Border	New England	Middle Atlantic	Midwest	Plains	Rocky Mountains	Pacific Coast	Average Sectional Deviation
1860	15.3	-12.7*	3.1	-9.8	0.1	-11.4	b		b	7.4
1864	-2.5		38.0*	-5.1	-10.7	2.9	8.9		9.3	12.5
1868	-2.3		-10.5*	3.0	2.1	1.8	0.8		-5.5	4.0
1872	3.2	1.9	2.3	-2.2	3.0	-2.1	-0.9		4.3*	2.4
1876	-7.4	-5.8*	1.7	-1.1	0.1	2.9	4.5		0.8	2.4
1880	1.5	-3.6*	0.5	-0.9	0.4	0.8	1.1		-2.4	1.4
1884	-0.1	2.2	3.0	-1.5	0.4	-1.3	-6.6*	5.2	3.2	2.9
1888	-0.3	-2.3*	1.8	0.5	0.4	-0.2	0.3	1.3	-0.6	0.9
1892	-1.3	-6.5	-0.7	-0.6	-0.2	-0.6	9.2	24.6*	2.9	5.7
1896	3.9	2.0	0.1	14.0	7.2	1.4	-16.5	-66.6*	-8.9	14.6
1900	1.0	-0.3	-0.8	-11.1	-4.2	-0.6	3.3	26.5*	7.1	6.7
1904	6.8	-12.9*	-5.0	-5.4	-2.8	2.9	8.1	9.7	9.4	7.0
1908	-5.5	7.9*	4.2	6.4	2.6	-3.0	-9.3	-3.0	-4.6	5.1
1912	-18.9	1.7	5.7	1.9	-0.2	2.7	-3.7	6.9	-23.5*	5.8
1916	12.8	-2.5	-2.9	-7.2	2.5	-1.1	1.7	-14.4	16.1*	6.1
1920	15.4	-4.7	-8.2*	0.6	-0.3	0.2	8.1	6.5	6.6	4.4
1924	1.4	-8.8	-3.8	0.6	-1.8	2.8	1.9	3.7	10.5*	4.2
1928	-6.4	24.8*	13.2	-10.6	-5.7	-3.9	-7.1	0.7	-11.4	9.7
1932	-18.0	-11.1	-3.6	14.1*	7.5	0.4	-5.9	-3.7	-9.0	6.9
1936	-3.3	3.9	4.4*	-0.2	-3.5	-1.0	5.0	-2.4	-3.5	3.0
1940	7.5	-5.1	-1.3	-6.6*	-0.5	1.8	5.1	3.0	2.8	3.3
1944	1.2	3.2*	1.2	-0.7	-0.7	-0.3	-0.7	1.8	0.1	1.1
1948	1.5	7.2*	-5.7	-1.6	1.7	-1.6	-6.5	-2.7	4.1	3.9
1952	7.7	5.8	1.6	1.2	-3.8	-0.8	7.5*	6.4	0.2	3.4

Year										
1956	2.4	0.0	-0.1	3.4	2.8	0.4	-6.7*	-2.4	-4.1	2.5
1960	-7.9	5.0	4.9	-10.3*	-4.2	-0.1	4.0	1.2	3.2	4.1
1964	-11.2	13.1*	-3.3	-5.6	-4.0	-2.0	-4.1	1.0	0.1	4.2
1968	11.8	-8.6*	3.2	1.3	3.4	1.1	1.6	3.0	-0.2	2.8
1972	11.4	6.4*	2.1	1.3	0.2	-2.8	-5.3	-3.5	-5.1	3.3
1976	-12.9	-12.5*	-4.9	7.0	1.7	4.4	2.7	4.3	6.6	5.5
1980	6.4	2.0	-0.7	-0.8	-1.6	-2.7	1.6	3.9*	1.1	1.8
1984	3.9	5.1*	2.7	-0.1	-2.0	-0.5	-3.8	-4.8	-4.6	3.0
1988	-5.3	1.5	-0.9	-1.0	0.9	0.5	-2.1	-3.0*	-1.5	1.4
1992	-7.4	-0.6	-0.1	-1.1	0.0	0.2	5.6*	0.0	-1.6	1.2
Elections Analyzed		32	34	34	34	34	33	28	33	
Average Deviation		6.0	4.3	4.1	2.4	1.9	4.9	7.7	5.3	
Times Most Deviant[a]		14	4	3	0	0	4	5	4	

*Indicates most deviant section for that year.
[a]Does not add up to thirty-four because of ties.
[b]Excludes Iowa and California.

EQ. 3.4C

1936–1992, 15 observations: y = 3.37 − .06x; r = −.21.[69]

Once again we find, as indicated by the intercept values of these equations, that sectionalism was higher from 1892 to 1932, roughly the years of the fourth party system, than it was in the preceding or succeeding years. The slopes indicate that the drop-off in sectionalism was steepest in the post-Civil War era, declining .43 of a point on average each election. The period since the New Deal, though, has been the longest time without a substantial peak in sectionalism.

As with the data on the vote outcome, the vote swings show the most diversity in the Civil War era (1864) and at the beginning (1896) and ending (1928) of the fourth party system.[70] The diversity in 1864, which did not include voting in the South due to secession, was largely composed of a massive deviation in the Border states, as the GOP increased its sectional poll there by over 35 percent of the two-party vote. The great increase in and high level of regional diversity in the 1896 vote swing is consistent with general understanding of the Bryan-McKinley election as the instigator of the longest sectional era in U.S. politics. Table 3.4 shows that this increase was largely due to the plummeting of the GOP vote in the Rocky Mountains and to a strong GOP movement in New England. In the elections examined in Table 3.4, the third highest level of and second largest increase in the regionalism of the presidential vote swing occurred in 1928. In this election, the South, and to a lesser degree the Border states, strongly countered the national Democratic movement. The difference between the highly sectional vote swings of 1896 and 1928 is that the earlier one had, on average, a slight regional moving away from the national norm, while in the later election most regions moved toward the national vote distribution. Thus, 1896, building upon 1892, resulted in a highly regional vote outcome, while 1928 saw a significant erosion of sectionalism.

In the last fifteen elections, since 1936, the average sectional deviations around the national vote swing have been, with five exceptions, relatively uniform, varying between 2.5 and 4.2 percentage points. The national vote swing was most nationalized in 1944, when the average regional deviation was only 1.1 percent. In 1944, there was a minimal movement of each region toward the Republicans, as the New Deal Democratic peak continued to recede. Furthermore, in 1944, Franklin Roosevelt was running in a fourth consecutive election; with such a well-known incumbent present in a series of elections we would expect minimal sectional repositioning.

The diversity of the vote swing was at its second lowest level, 1.2, in 1992. In the George Bush-Bill Clinton contest, the Republican share of the two-party vote declined in every section. All the regions, except the Plains, were spectacularly close to the national vote swing in 1992.[71]

Both 1980 and 1988 were also years of historically low regional variation around the national two-party vote swing.[72] In 1980, there was a Republican trend, generally moderate, in every region, while eight years later the moderate trend, in every region, was to the Democrats.

The 1976 election was marked by a level of regional dispersion, 5.5 points, appropriate to the core years of the sectional era. The prime cause was the sharp movement of the South and Border states to support favorite son, Democrat Jimmy Carter. This movement, however, as Table 3.2 shows, had the impact of reducing the regional dispersion of the vote outcome to only 2.7.

The Sections over Time. Once again, the Midwest is the region closest to the national voting pattern. Over the thirty-four elections during the period 1860 to 1992, the swing in the Midwest averaged only 1.9 percentage points away from the national vote change. The Middle Atlantic region was not far off the mark either; its average deviation was just 2.4 points. These two regions were also the only ones never to have the largest deviation from the national vote swing.

On average, the Rocky Mountains had the largest deviation from the national vote swing, at 7.7 percent. The South was runner-up, averaging 6.0 points away from the national movement. But the South was the most deviant region in fourteen elections, while the Rocky Mountains were furthest from the national swing only five times. The reason for this disparity between the two measures of isolation is the tremendous vote swings in the Rockies that occurred in 1892, 1896, and 1900. In 1892, the Rockies abandoned the Democrats in favor of the Populist alternative, leading to a large increase in the GOP percentage of the two-party vote. In 1896, though, the Mountains left the Republicans on a "cross of gold," moving sharply to the Democrats. In 1900, two-party competition returned to this region. The Mountain states were also the most deviant section in 1980 and 1988, as they moved sharply to the Republicans in 1980 and away from the GOP eight years later.[73]

The modal pattern, however, is for the South to be the region furthest from the national movement. Dixie opposed national trends in 1904 and 1908. In 1928, the South moved strongly counter to the national Democratic movement. More recently, third-party politics and an odyssey to the Republican party led the South to be the most deviant region five times, between 1944 and 1972. In 1948, southern support for J.

Strom Thurmond led to an increased Republican share of the two-party vote. Twenty years later, George Wallace's candidacy provided a third-party outlet for southern discontent with the Democrats, and the Republican gain in the two-party vote was least in the South. In 1944, 1964, and most greatly, 1972, the South veered toward the Republicans. In 1976, the South abandoned the GOP in favor of Georgian Jimmy Carter and, in 1984, the South moved toward the Republicans.

The secular trend of New England toward the Democratic party led it to be the most deviant region three times, in 1932, 1940, and 1960. In 1928, New England moved sharply to the Democrats, but in 1932, without Al Smith as the Democratic standard-bearer and having already moved away from traditional voting patterns, New England lagged behind the national Democratic trend. However, in 1940, with the country moderating its Democratic leanings, New England barely budged. In 1960, New Englanders abandoned the GOP in droves to support favorite son John F. Kennedy, outpacing the rest of the nation in this movement.

During the Eisenhower years the Plains states were most isolated from national trends. In 1952, this region showed tremendous enthusiasm for Ike, but by 1956 their excitement waned, as they became preoccupied with trouble on the farm.[74] In 1992, the Plains were once again the most isolated region, as Republican support declined by less than two points in the two-party vote in these states.

One has to go all the way back to 1924 to find an election in which the Pacific states were most distant from the national trend. The Pacific Coast was most isolated from the national swing in 1912, 1916, and 1924. The reason was California's strong Progressive vote in both 1912 and 1924, abandoning the GOP in 1912, and the Democrats in 1924.

Our examination of regional vote swings in presidential elections documents eras of sectionalism and confirms Schattschneider's prediction of greater universality in political trends. Specifically, we have found less regional diversity around the national vote movement since 1936 than in the earlier years of the century. The diversity of the vote swing was very low from 1868 to 1892, especially in the three elections of the 1880s, hitting an all-time low of 0.9 in 1888. The four lowest diversity levels of the twentieth century were 1944, 1980, 1988, and 1992.

THE TRANSITION
FROM THE SECTIONAL TO NATIONAL ERA:
1928–1936

The movement from the sectional era to a more uniform national system was not simultaneous for both our measures. The data on vote outcomes indicate a regional peak and ebb, in 1924 and 1928, respectively, whereas the data on the vote swing show the erosion of sectionalism taking place in 1936, after a peak in diversity from 1928 to 1932.

The Herbert Hoover-Al Smith contest was crucial. The regional dispersion of the vote swing was massive in 1928, the highest in the twentieth century. In 1928, the regions moved to a temporarily more uniform voting posture—the most uniform since the time of the Whigs and until 1948. During the convulsions of 1928–1932, New England and the South zigzagged massively in opposite directions *vis-à-vis* the national vote swing. The South first moved toward and then away from the Republicans. New England, meanwhile, had a trend toward the Democrats in 1928, then swung relatively to the Republicans in 1932. These two regions contributed mightily to the sectional pattern of vote swings in 1928 and 1932.

The emphasis here on 1928 is closer to Key's interpretation than to Schattschneider's regarding the formation of the national party era. "In New England, at least," wrote Key, "the Roosevelt revolution of 1932 was in large measure an Al Smith revolution of 1928, a characterization less applicable to the remainder of the country."[75] Regarding New England, we agree with Key, but we also note that 1928 was a harbinger of the post-World War II movement of the South toward the national vote distribution.[76]

Schattschneider, by contrast, views an abrupt dawn of the national party system—"the Revolution of 1932."[77] For Schattschneider, the 1928 vote pattern is extremely sectional:

> In the election of 1908 in twenty-nine states in the North and West (not counting Arizona and New Mexico), the Democratic percentage of the major party vote deviated a total of 283.8 points from 50 per cent. In 1928 the total deviation was 312.1. By 1944, however, this figure had declined to 124 points.[78]

Schattschneider failed to see the nationalizing electoral influence of 1928 for at least two reasons: (1) he excluded the South from his calculations, thereby disregarding its convergence with the national vote distribution in 1928; and (2) he measured deviation from 50 percent rather than from the national vote, thereby seeking more two-party competition, not more sectional convergence. On the latter point, our regional data in Table 3.2 show 1928 to be lower in mean regional deviation from the national vote than either 1908 or 1944. But 1928 has more regional deviation from 50 percent than 1908, and a lot more than 1944.[79] A paradox of all this is that, in 1928, the South was the section closest to 50 percent, 47.7 percent Republican—the most nationalized region by

Schattschneider's measure—yet according to him, the South was the most sectional of the regions!

CONCLUSION

Sectionalism is central to many traditional and valued analyses of U.S. political parties and voting. Such leading political scientists as Arthur N. Holcombe, Cortez A. M. Ewing, E. E. Schattschneider, and V. O. Key, Jr. have used sectionalism as a central concept to further our understanding of U.S. elections. Building on their writings, as well as on the work of more contemporary scholars, this chapter has measured and analyzed sectionalism in presidential elections from 1824 to 1992.

This study has documented alternating periods of sectional and national voting patterns. The 1820s and 1830s contests involving the Jacksonian Democrats and their opponents featured a sectional party system, but the subsequent struggle between the Whigs and Democrats from 1840 to 1852 was remarkably nationally uniform. Sectionalism increased dramatically in the Civil War era, ripping apart the political system. Voting patterns during Reconstruction and its aftermath were surprisingly national. But the years of the industrializing political system, from the 1890s through the 1920s, were highly sectional. Since the New Deal era, there has been an "erosion of sectionalism in presidential elections."

An impact of the erosion of sectionalism is that popular vote pluralities have a greater potential to translate into overwhelming electoral college majorities. If voting percentages are rather uniform throughout the country, it follows that a plurality of the popular vote will probably mean victory in most states. Without large sectional bases safe for each of the parties, the potential for electoral college sweeps is always there. This is borne out by isolating electoral college percentages for the last century. From 1892 to 1924, no party ever received more than 82 percent (1912) of the electoral college votes. But from 1928 to 1992, a party exceeded this percentage of the electoral college vote ten times. The erosion of sectionalism is a key correlate of these overwhelming electoral college victories.

The erosion of sectionalism has by no means completely eroded individual regional predispositions in contemporary presidential elections. The two northeastern regions have lagged most in their GOP allegiance. The Mountain states have been the most consistently Republican section—although the Democrats won four of these states in 1992. The South, even with a moderate Democratic presidential candidate from the South, as demonstrated in 1992, today votes more Republican than the nation as a whole.

The last of these trends is most compelling, for the South is the largest section, currently holding 147 electoral votes or more than half of those needed to win the presidency. Recent Republican victories, from Nixon to Bush, have been based on a "southern strategy."[80] Likewise, the three most recent Democratic presidents—Johnson, Carter, and Clinton—were sons of Dixie. (It must be pointed out, however, that Clinton is the first Democrat elected president while losing most of the southern states, capturing five of the eleven.) Thus, in a complete turnabout from New Deal era presidential campaigns, both political parties strongly contest the South.

After the 1988 election, in which Republican Bush was elected, some academics and political practitioners argued that the Democratic party should abandon the South and pursue a northern tier strategy.[81] The envisioned liberal coalition would build upon relative Democratic strengths in the East, Heartland, and Pacific Coast. In the waning days of the 1988 presidential campaign, in fact, this was the essence of Michael Dukakis's strategy.[82]

Analysts differ over the sectional strategies used by the Democrats in 1992. Jerome Mileur has argued that the Democrats followed a northern tier stragegy: "The party's all-southern ticket . . . only skirmished in Dixie, and instead marched north to victory."[83] Carey McWilliams, on the other hand, argues that the nomination of an all-confederate state ticket is highly significant: "The 1992 nominations were a strong symbolic gesture to the South, part of a successful effort to dent that now-Republican bastion."[84] Strategies aside, it appears that the only Democrat presently able to win the presidency is a southern Democrat.

Having noted some of the regional patterns in current presidential election returns, we must still emphasize that the twentieth century has witnessed a decline in their diversity. The erosion of sectionalism has by no means been a linear movement. Individual candidacies, third parties, and political issues intrude upon and jar the process of secular change.[85] But there is no doubt that the trends we have discerned confirm the propositions set forth by Key and Schattschneider in the mid twentieth century.

NOTES

1. Ray Allen Billington, "Frederick Jackson Turner: Universal Historian," in Frederick Jackson Turner, *Frontier and Section: Selected Essays of Frederick Jackson Turner,* ed. Billington (Englewood Cliffs, N.J.: Prentice-Hall, 1961), pp. 1–9, at 7–8.
2. Frederick Jackson Turner, "The Significance of the Section in

American History," in *Frontier and Section,* pp. 115–135, quotations, pp. 115, 135. Originally published in 1925.

3. Frederick Jackson Turner, "Sections and Nation," in *Frontier and Section,* pp. 136–153, quotations, pp. 137, 144. Originally published in 1922; third quotation, "Significance of Section," p. 134.

4. Arthur N. Holcombe, *The Political Parties of To-Day: A Study in Republican and Democratic Politics,* 2nd ed. (New York: Harper and Brothers, 1925), quotations, pp. 40, 13. "Ambitious . . . leaders" is repeated numerous times throughout the book. On the last point, see pp. 14–15, 39–40, quotation, p. 84.

5. Holcombe, pp. 41, 53, 38.

6. Holcombe, pp. 14–38, quotation, p. 18.

7. Holcombe, pp. 83–92.

8. Cortez A. M. Ewing, *Presidential Elections: From Abraham Lincoln to Franklin D. Roosevelt* (Norman: University of Oklahoma Press, 1940), quotations, pp. 165, 213.

9. Ewing, quotation, p. viii; also see pp. 8–13.

10. Ewing, pp. 45–47, 213–218, quotations, pp. 216, 47.

11. Arthur N. Holcombe, *The New Party Politics* (New York: Norton, 1933), esp. Chapter 1, quotations, pp. viii, 11.

12. Ewing, *Presidential Elections,* pp. 149, 190–191.

13. V. O. Key, Jr., *Politics, Parties, and Pressure Groups* (New York: Crowell, 1942), Chapter 2; and E. E. Schattschneider, *Party Government* (New York: Holt, Rinehart and Winston, 1942), pp. 111–123.

14. V. O. Key, Jr., *American State Politics: An Introduction* (New York: Knopf, 1956), pp. 26–28, 50–51; *Politics, Parties, and Pressure Groups,* 5th ed.(New York: Crowell, 1964), pp. 245–248; and, for a more discursive treatment focusing on the South, "The Erosion of Sectionalism," *Virginia Quarterly Review* 31 (Spring 1955): 161–179.

15. The usual reference is E. E. Schattschneider, *The Semisovereign People: A Realist's View of Democracy in America* (Hinsdale, Ill.: Dryden Press, 1960), Chapter 5, esp. pp. 86–96. But these thoughts, expressed almost verbatim, appeared four years earlier in "United States: The Functional Approach to Party Government," in *Modern Political Parties,* ed. Sigmund Neumann (Chicago: University of Chicago Press, 1956), pp. 194–215, esp. pp. 206–215.

16. Schattschneider, *Semisovereign People,* p. 93; "Functional Approach," pp. 211–212.

17. Key, *Politics, Parties, and Pressure Groups,* pp. 245–253, quotations, pp. 246, 249. This and all further references are to the 1964 edition of this book.

18. Schattschneider, *Semisovereign People*, pp. 88–89, quotation, p. 88, emphasis deleted. Also see "Functional Approach," pp. 207–208.

19. See William Claggett, William Flanigan, and Nancy Zingale, "Nationalization of the American Electorate," *American Political Science Review* 78 (March 1984): 77–91, at 80–84.

20. Most studies of the nationalization of the presidential vote have generalized about regional trends, but performed calculations using state level data. To do so, however, is to measure state diversity, not sectionalism. Relevant studies on the presidential vote distribution include Key, *State Politics*, pp. 26–27, *Politics, Parties, and Pressure Groups*, pp. 246–247; Schattschneider, *Semisovereign People*, pp. 89–90, "Functional Approach," pp. 208–209; David R. Mayhew, *Two-Party Competition in the New England States* (Amherst: Bureau of Government Research, University of Massachusetts, 1967), esp. p. 11, Figure 3; and Everett Carll Ladd, *American Political Parties: Social Change and Political Response* (New York: Norton, 1970), pp. 176–177. Ladd did, however, present a series of graphs depicting the regional distribution of the presidential vote; on pp. 95, 99, 174, and 235.

Paul Allen Beck and Frank J. Sorauf measured diversity in presidential election outcomes at the state level and also interpreted it at that level; see Beck and Sorauf, *Party Politics in America*, 7th ed. (New York: HarperCollins, 1992), pp. 60–61.

Paul Kleppner measured the diversity in the presidential vote for the years 1848 to 1900 at both the state and sectional level; see Paul Kleppner, *The Third Electoral System, 1853–1892* (Chapel Hill: University of North Carolina Press, 1979), esp. p. 23, Table 2.2.

There are fewer studies of diversity in the presidential vote swing. Schattschneider, quoted approvingly and extensively by Ladd, generalized about regional level diversity while performing calculations with state level data; see Schattschneider, "Functional Approach," pp. 211–212, *Semisovereign People*, p. 93; and Ladd, pp. 234–235. Pomper measured and discussed diversity in state changes from the previous four-election state mean in presidential elections; see Gerald M. Pomper, "Classification of Presidential Elections," *Journal of Politics* 29 (August 1967): 535–566, at 542, 547–551, and Pomper, with Susan S. Lederman, *Elections in America: Control and Influence in Democratic Politics*, 2nd ed. (New York: Longman, 1980), pp. 89–91.

21. South Atlantic: Fla., Ga., N.C., VA. (S.C., had no popular voting for president until after the Civil War); Southwest: Ala., Ark., La.,

Miss., Tenn., Tex.; Border: Dela., Ky., Md., Mo.; New England: Conn., Me., Mass., N.H., R.I., Vt.; Middle Atlantic: N.J., N.Y., Pa.; and Old Northwest: Ill., Ind., Mich., Ohio, Wisc. See William G. Shade, "Political Pluralism and Party Development: The Creation of A Modern Party System, 1815–1852," in *The Evolution of American Electoral Systems*, Kleppner et al. (Westport, Conn.: Greenwood, 1981), pp. 77–111, at 83.

22. In studies of this sort there is no entirely satisfactory way of dealing with the vote for third parties or independent candidates. To account for any possible significance they may have had on sectional voting patterns, we conducted parallel calculations for each of the two major candidates using the leading four-candidate (1824, 1836) or three-candidate (1832, 1848) vote. When relevant, these findings are discussed in the notes.

23. South: Ala., Ark., Fla., Ga., La., Miss., N.C., S.C., Tenn., Tex., Va.; Border: Ky., Md., Mo., Okla., W.V.; New England: Conn., Me., Mass., N.H., R.I., Vt.; Middle Atlantic: Dela., N.J., N.Y., Pa.; Midwest: Ill., Ind., Mich., Ohio, Wisc.; Plains: Iowa, Kan., Minn., Neb., N.D., S.D.; Rocky Mountains: Ariz., Colo., Id., Mont., Nev., N.M., Utah, Wyo.; and Pacific Coast: Alaska, Calif., Hawaii, Ore., Wash.

24. We conducted parallel calculations for the Republican and Democratic percentages of the three-party vote utilizing 1856, 1860 (four-party), 1892, 1912, 1924, 1968, 1980, and 1992 electoral returns.

25. Congressional Quarterly Inc., *Guide to U.S. Elections*, 2nd ed. (Washington D.C., 1985), pp. 329–366; Richard M. Scammon and Alice V. McGillivray, comps. and eds., *America Votes*, Vol. 18 (Washington, D.C.: Congressional Quarterly Inc., 1989), p. 7; and "Official 1992 Presidential Election Results," *Congressional Quarterly Weekly Report* 51 (January 30, 1993): 233. The Alabama vote was corrected for 1972, as was the resulting national total. Calculations excluded the vote in the District of Columbia.

26. Key and Ladd also employed the national vote percentage as the baseline from which to calculate (state) deviations; Key, *State Politics*, p. 27; Ladd, *American Political Parties*, p. 177. Mayhew also used the national vote percentage (*Two-Party Competition*, esp. p. 13), but also calculated the standard deviation of state election results (esp. p. 11), thus employing the state mean as a baseline. Beck and Sorauf's (*Party Politics*, p. 61) standard deviation calculations are also based on the state mean. Kleppner's (*Third Electoral System*, p. 23) variance calculations are based on the state and sectional means. Although we do not present the figures, our results are not substantially changed by substituting the regional mean for

the national percentage in the calculations. Schattschneider (*Semi-sovereign People*, pp. 89–90, "Functional Approach," p. 208) employed 50 percent of the major party vote as the baseline from which to calculate state deviations. In doing so, however, he may have measured competitiveness, rather than dispersion; see Claggett *et al*, "Nationalization," p. 81.

27. Although he confined his analysis to the direction of the vote swing, this is the reasoning used by Schattschneider for state level data (*Semisovereign People*, p. 93, "Functional Approach," pp. 211–212). Schattschneider's reasoning was adopted by Ladd (*American Political Parties*, pp. 176, 234). Pomper defined vote change in any election as the movement from the average vote in the four previous presidential elections. He then calculated the dispersal of the fifty individual state vote changes around the national trend, defined as the fifty-state mean. See Pomper, "Classification of Presidential Elections," pp. 542 (for definition of the average state vote), and 547–551 (for dispersion of vote change); also Pomper, with Lederman, *Elections in America*, pp. 89–91.

28. A variety of techniques have been used to measure state dispersion in individual presidential elections over an extended period. Key (*State Politics*, pp. 26–27, *Politics, Parties, and Pressure Groups*, pp. 246–247) employed the range and its variations, as well as an illustrative graphic. Schattschneider (*Semisovereign People*, pp. 89–90, "Functional Approach," p. 208) gave total state deviations from 50 percent of the two-party vote. Mayhew (*Two-Party Competition*, p. 11) presented the standard deviation of the Democratic percentage of the total vote in the states. Beck and Sorauf (*Party Politics*, p. 61) presented the standard deviation of the national election winner's percentage of the total vote for each state. Ladd (*American Political Parties*, p. 177) calculated the standard deviation of state deviations from the Democratic percentage of the national two-party vote. Kleppner (*Third Electoral System*, p. 23) presented the state and sectional variance.

To measure dispersal of state changes from the four-election average vote, Pomper used the standard deviations of the fifty state changes from the mean state vote change (Pomper, "Classification," pp. 547–551, Pomper, with Lederman, *Elections in America*, pp. 89–91).

On the greater interpretability of the average deviation than the standard deviation, see William H. Flanigan and Nancy H. Zingale, "Summarizing Quantitative Data," in *Analyzing Electoral History: A Guide to the Study of American Voter Behavior*, ed. Jerome M.

Clubb, Flanigan, and Zingale (Beverly Hills, Calif.: Sage, 1981), pp. 201–234, at 218–221.

29. Richard P. McCormick, *The Second American Party System: Party Formation in the Jacksonian Era* (Chapel Hill: University of North Carolina Press, 1966); and Walter Dean Burnham, "Party Systems and the Political Process," in *The American Party Systems: Stages of Political Development,* ed. William Nisbet Chambers and Burnham (New York: Oxford University Press, 1967), pp. 277–307, at 292–295.

30. (1824 = 0, 1828 = 1, . . . 1852 = 7). This regression line reduces almost three-quarters of the variance of the yearly deviations as indicated by the coefficient of determination, $r^2 = .73$

31. (1824 = 0, 1828 = 1, . . . 1836 = 3), $r^2 = .17$; (1840 = 0, 1844 = 1, . . . 1852 = 3), $r^2 = .37$.

32. Ladd, *American Political Parties,* p. 99; McCormick, *The Second American Party System,* pp. 13–14.

33. McCormick, "Political Development and the Second Party System," in *The American Party Systems,* pp. 90–116, at 97–102, 111–112; Ladd, *American Political Parties,* pp. 98–99; and Shade, "Political Pluralism and Party Development," *passim,* quotations, pp. 82, 88. We should note that Shade finds regional voting patterns, but rejects a sectional interpretation of the 1820s and 1830s; see Shade, p. 84.

34. In 1836, Democrat Martin Van Buren defeated three Whigs, William H. Harrison (36.6 percent of the total vote), Hugh L. White (9.7), and Daniel Webster (2.7). White was popular in the southern regions as was Webster in Massachusetts. The other researchers aggregate the votes of the three Whig candidates, but we work with the Harrison vote. Since electoral votes are designated to candidates, not to parties, our two-person calculations are more realistic. Furthermore, aggregating the Whig vote hides the sectional fissures within their 1836 ticket and therefore does not reflect the transitional nature of those years. The average sectional deviation in Table 3.1 for 1836, based on the vote of the two-leading candidates, is 18.6. Calculated on the total of the Van Buren, Harrison, White, and Webster votes, the average deviation for the Harrison vote is 19.3, but for the Van Buren vote it is 2.1. Studies that do not distinguish in their calculations between the votes of the three Whig candidates and therefore find a national vote distribution in 1936 include McCormick, "Political Development and the Second Party System," p. 98, Table 1; Ladd, *American Political Parties,* p. 99, Figure 3.9; Shade, "Political Pluralism and Party Development," p. 83, Table 3.1; and Joel H. Silbey, *The American Political*

Nation, 1838–1893 (Stanford, Calif.: Stanford University Press, 1991), p. 29, Table 1.4.

35. McCormick, "Political Development," p. 111.
36. McCormick, *Second Party System*, pp. 340–342, "Political Development," pp. 97–102; Ladd, *American Political Parties*, pp. 84–85; Shade, "Political Pluralism" pp. 82–88; and Silbey, *American Political Nation*, pp. 24–32.
37. McCormick, "Political Development," pp. 97–98. In 1824, William H. Crawford won more popular and electoral votes than Jackson in the South Atlantic due to Crawford's success in Virginia.
38. McCormick, "Political Development," p. 102.
39. Silbey, *The American Political Nation*, pp. 72–89.
40. Ladd, *American Political Parties*, p. 100.
41. McCormick, "Political Development," pp. 111–112; *Second Party System*, pp. 14, 15, 353.
42. Using the median deviation, rather than the mean deviation, of the states from the national presidential vote, Mayhew (*Two-Party Competition*, pp. 12–14) termed this measure an "index of isolation."
43. McCormick, "Political Development," p. 98. Actually, in 1824 Clay was a respectable runner-up to Jackson in the Border region and the Old Northwest, and Crawford won a plurality in the South Atlantic. In 1836, White won a plurality in the Southwest and was very competitive with Van Buren in the South Atlantic.
44. Burnham, "Party Systems and the Political Process," esp. pp. 287–304; and idem, "Critical Realignment: Dead or Alive?," in *The End of Realignment?: Interpreting American Electoral Eras*, ed. Byron E. Shafer (Madison: University of Wisconsin Press, 1991), pp. 101–139, at 117. There is not complete general acceptance of a sixth party system; see Beck and Sorauf, *Party Politics*, pp. 173–176. For discussions of the utility of the party systems approach, see *The End of Realignment?*
45. (1856=0, 1860=1, . . . 1992=34). This regression line reduces over one-third the variance of the yearly deviations, as indicated by the coefficient of determination, r^2=.36.
46. Sectionalism in these two elections was actually much closer than this. The major difference between 1856 and 1860 in Table 3.1 is a result of our factoring in two new regions for 1860.
47. (1864 = 0, 1868 = 1, . . . 1888 = 6), r^2 = .06; (1892 = 0, 1896 = 1, . . . 1924 = 8), r^2 = .00; (1928 = 0, 1932 = 1, . . . 1992 = 16), r^2 = .52.
48. The sectional pattern obtained in the Republican percentages of the three-party (1856, 22.7) and four-candidate (1860, 21.1) balloting. But the Democratic percentages of these vote totals were much less

sectional, 7.1 in 1856 and 8.7 in 1860. This is mainly because southern and Border state deviations were greatly reduced as Democratic hegemony in the two-party vote in these sections was diluted by the 1856 Whig vote and 1860 support for the Southern Democrats and Constitutional Union parties.

49. See Kleppner, *Third Electoral System,* pp. 25–26, 32, 39–40; and James L. Sundquist, *Dynamics of the Party System: Alignment and Realignment of Political Parties in the United States,* rev. ed. (Washington, D.C.: Brookings, 1983), pp. 101–104.

50. We also analyzed the distribution of the three-party vote in 1892, 1912, 1924, 1968, 1980, and 1992. These data, along with the analyses of others, highlight important asymmetry in the distribution of the Democratic and Republican vote, especially in regard to comparisons between 1892 and 1896. The Democratic percentages of the three-party vote reflect the two-party pattern, with peaks in diversity in 1924 (12.6) and 1892 (11.1). In his study of state diversity of the Democratic percentage of the total vote from 1828 to 1964, Mayhew found 1892 to be even more diverse than 1896, and 1924 more heterogeneous than either of the 1890s' contests; see Mayhew, *Two-Party Competition,* p. 11.

   The Republican share of the three-party vote, however, does not peak in 1892 (5.7) or 1924 (7.3). Even this lower 1924 figure, though, is comfortably higher than any subsequent one presented in Table 3.2. Key's analysis of interquartile state ranges in the Republican percentage of the total presidential vote from 1880 to 1960 follows our general contours. He found 1892 only slightly more diverse than 1888; a peak in 1896; 1924 less diverse than even 1904; and 1924 more diverse than any subsequent election; see Key, *Politics, Parties, and Pressure Groups,* p. 246.

51. Key, *Politics, Parties, and Pressure Groups,* p. 257.

52. Ladd, *American Political Parties,* p. 172.

53. Ladd, p. 234.

54. In terms of the percentage of the total vote, the best Republican year was 1972, with 60.7 percent. In the Electoral College, the Republicans did best in 1984, winning 97.6 percent (525 of 538) of the electors.

55. Key, *Politics, Parties, and Pressure Groups,* p. 239.

56. Ladd, *American Political Parties,* p. 295.

57. Mayhew, *Two-Party Competition,* pp. 15–16; also, Everett Carll Ladd, with Charles D. Hadley, *Transformations of the American Party System: Political Coalitions from the New Deal to the 1970s,* 2nd ed. (New York: Norton, 1978), pp. 54–55.

58. This finding is not altered in the three-party calculations. In 1980, the diversity of the three-party vote was 3.0 for the Republicans and

3.5 for the Democrats. In 1968, reflecting the ideological era, it was 4.8 for the Republicans and 5.2 for the Democrats. And in 1992, it was 2.4 for the Republicans and 2.6 for the Democrats.

59. Kevin P. Phillips, *The Emerging Republican Majority* (Garden City, N.Y.: Anchor, 1970; originally published in 1969 by Arlington House); Key, *State Politics*, pp. 217–265.

60. George F. Will, *The New Season: A Spectator's Guide to the 1988 Election* (New York: Simon and Schuster, 1987), p. 48. Will defines the Mountain West as our eight Rocky Mountain states.

61. Will, pp. 48–49.

62. Kevin P. Phillips, *Mediacracy: American Parties and Politics in the Communications Age* (Garden City, N.Y.: Doubleday, 1975), p. 104.

63. Phillips, *Mediacracy*, pp. 5–8.

64. Looking at Table 3.4, for example, in 1892, the national movement was a 1.3 percent loss for the Republicans. In the South, with a negative 6.5, the vote shift was 7.8 percent away from the Republicans. In the Plains, with a positive 9.2, the movement was actually 9.2 minus 1.3, or 7.9 percent toward the Republicans. For an exchange of views regarding the utility of the vote swing as a measure of electoral change, see David Butler and Stephen D. Van Beek, "Why Not Swing? Measuring Electoral Change," *PS* 23 (June 1990): 178–184; and Richard Rose, "The Ups and Downs of Elections, or Look Before You Swing," *PS* 24 (March 1991): 29–33.

65. $(1828 = 0, 1832 = 1, \ldots 1852 = 6)$. This regression line reduces over one-fourth the variance of the yearly deviations as indicated by the coefficient of determination, $r^2 = .28$.

66. $(1828 = 0, 1832 = 1, \ldots 1840 = 3)$, $r^2 = .29$; $(1844 = 0, 1848 = 1, 1852 = 2)$, $r^2 = .94$.

67. The 1840 Democratic swing calculated on the 1836 four-candidate vote, including all three Whig candidates, is extremely low, 1.9. The 1840 Harrison vote swing calculated on the 1836 four-candidate vote total is 19.5. We feel the higher figure is more realistic. As we argued earlier, aggregating the Whig vote in 1836 hides the sectional divisiveness in that party.

68. $(1860 = 0, 1864 = 1, \ldots 1992 = 33)$. This regression line reduces 14 percent of the variance of the yearly deviations as indicated by the coefficient of determination, $r^2 = .14$.

69. $(1868 = 0, 1872 = 1, \ldots 1888 = 5)$, $r^2 = .53$; $(1892 = 0, 1896 = 1, \ldots 1932 = 10)$, $r^2 = .07$; and $(1936 = 0, 1940 = 1, \ldots 1992 = 14)$, $r^2 = .04$.

70. Third party intervention only changes this generalization with respect to comparisons between 1860 and 1864. Using the 1856 three-party and 1860 four-party votes, the dispersion of the Republican vote swing remains higher in 1864 (16.1) than in 1860 (4.6).

But the Democratic dispersion is greater in 1860 (15.0) than in 1864 (9.3). In 1860, the Democrats lost massively in the South and Border states, as the Southern Democrats and Constitutional Union parties did very well in these two regions. In 1864, the South did not vote due to Reconstruction. For the elections of 1892, 1896, 1912, 1916, 1924, 1928, 1968, 1972, 1980, 1984, and 1992 we calculated the diversity of the vote swings utilizing the Republican and Democratic percentages of the three-party vote of 1892, 1912, 1924, 1968, 1980, and 1992. For these data, the Republican vote swings were most heterogeneous in 1928 (7.6), 1896 (7.4), and 1916 (7.4). The Democratic vote swings were most diverse in 1896 (18.0), and 1928 (9.9).

71. In the South, the Democratic share of the 1992 three-party vote (41.4) was greater than the 1988 Democratic share of the two-party vote (41.2). The diversity of the three-party vote swing was also historically low in 1992, with a lowest ever (1.6) for the Republicans and a third lowest (2.1) for the Democrats.

72. Diversity was also low in the 1980 three-party vote swings, 2.0 for the Democrats and 2.1 for the Republicans. Democratic diversity was lower only in 1968 (1.8).

73. On Democratic presidential prospects in the Mountain states, see Jerry Hagstrom, *Beyond Reagan: The New Landscape of American Politics*, rev. ed. (New York: Penguin Books, 1989), pp. 69–72.

74. For example, Key, *Politics, Parties, and Pressure Groups*, p. 29; and Phillips, *Emerging Republican Majority*, p. 279.

75. V. O. Key, Jr., "A Theory of Critical Elections," *Journal of Politics* 17 (February 1955): 3–18, at 4.

76. As Phillips (*Emerging Republican Majority*, p. 197) notes, "Embryonic Southern Republicanism proved to be one of the first casualties of the Great Depression." Of course, in contrast to earlier patterns, beginning in 1964, Republicans have generally done better in the Deep South than in the Rim South. See, for example, Ladd, *American Political Parties*, pp. 297–301; Ladd, with Hadley, *Transformations*, pp. 151–166; and Phillips, *Emerging Republican Majority*, pp. 187–289.

77. *Semisovereign People*, pp. 86–96; "Functional Approach," pp. 206–215.

78. *Semisovereign People*, pp. 89–90; "Functional Approach," p. 208.

79. Regional mean deviations from 50 percent are not presented in this chapter but, according to our calculations, are 8.9 points for 1908, 9.2 in 1928, and 5.6 in 1944. This closely approximates Schattschneider's relative ranking of these elections.

80. Reg Murphy and Hal Gulliver, *The Southern Strategy* (New York: Scribner's, 1971).

81. C. B. Holman, "Go West, Young Democrat," *Polity* 22 (Winter 1989): 323–339; Jerome M. Mileur, "Dump Dixie—West is Best: The Geography of A Progressive Democracy," in *The Democrats Must Lead*, ed. James MacGregor Burns, Willliam Crotty, Lois Lovelace Duke, and Lawrence D. Longley (Boulder, Colo.: Westview, 1992), pp. 97–111; Rhodes Cook, "Democrats Search for Clues to Regain White House," *Congressional Quarterly Weekly Report* 47 (February 18, 1989): 346–349; and Cook, "History a Tough Opponent for Democrats in 1992," *Congressional Quarterly Weekly Report* 48 (April 14, 1990): 1146–1151.
82. Paul Taylor and David S. Broder, "Dukakis Electoral Strategy Set," *Washington Post*, October 16, 1988, pp. A1, A26.
83. Jerome M. Mileur, "The General Election Campaign: Strategy and Support," in *America's Choice: The Election of 1992*, ed. William Crotty (Guilford, Conn.: Dushkin, 1993), pp. 45–60, quotation, p. 52.
84. Wilson Carey McWilliams, "The Meaning of the Election," in *The Election of 1992*, ed. Gerald M. Pomper (Chatham, N.J.: Chatham House, 1993), pp. 190–218, quotation, p. 206.
85. V. O. Key, Jr., "Erosion of Sectionalism," esp. 164–165; and idem, "Secular Realignment and the Party System," *Journal of Politics* 21 (May 1959): 198–210.

CHAPTER 4

Alive!
The Political Parties after the
1980–1992 Presidential Elections

GERALD M. POMPER

The election of 1992 should make us wary of conventional wisdom. Did the "experts" predict the defeat of a president with a 90 percent popularity rating who led the only significant American military victory in half a century? Did they anticipate the presidency would be won by the governor of a small state who was accused of extramarital affairs? Conventional wisdom cannot answer these unexpected questions about the election: Why did substantial numbers of new voters turn out? Why did one-fourth of the membership of the House of Representatives turn over? Why did over one hundred million viewers turn on the televised presidential debates?

In this chapter, I want to dispute another common assertion, that American parties have become weakened, irrelevant, and impotent. To the contrary, I will argue that the parties are increasingly rooted in distinct voter coalitions, stronger organizationally, and clearly relevant to the policy issues facing the nation.

My argument runs counter to the concerns of some of our most eminent students—and supporters—of American political parties. Leon Epstein worries that "the relative *in*effectiveness of contemporary American parties is now our field's principal concern."[1] William Crotty foresees that "their impact will be reduced and their contributions to the governing system and the society nowhere as near as substantial as they have been in the past."[2]

The argument for the "decline of the parties" takes much of its evidence from electoral behavior, particularly the purported loosening of traditional party loyalties. Where voters once held fast to their partisan faith, they now are said to identify increasingly as independents[3] and to view the parties with indifference more than disdain. Voters "have come to see political parties as less relevant to what goes on in the everyday world of politics, and hence have become far more neutral toward them."[4] Ballot behavior parallels this apparent loss of affect. Close to one-fifth of the national electorate cast ballots in 1992 for a self-financed independent, Ross Perot; his surprising showing followed a series of presidential contests where substantial numbers of Democrats voted for Republican nominees Ronald Reagan and George Bush, and millions of voters split their tickets between presidential and congressional candidates.

Moreover, election campaigns assertedly have eliminated political parties. According to David Price, "Members are increasingly 'on their own' electorally and less dependent on the parties."[5] Campaigns are reportedly dominated by self-starting candidates, mass media that focus on their individualistic characteristics, and financial contributors who send their money directly to those who meet their particular ideological tests or promise to serve their particular economic interests. In this candidate-centered politics, party tides are contained within the privileged dikes of incumbency. In the absence of scandal, the advantages of office seemingly make the members of Congress almost invulnerable at the polls.

As a result, so goes the thesis of decline, parties have little to do with government. "All too often," according to William Keefe, "parties are nothing more than spectators to the campaign clashes of candidate organizations. As for the members of Congress, they have never been more independent; party is what they choose to make of it. . . . In the critical area of policy formation, majority party control often slips away, to be replaced by enduring, biparty alliances or coalitions of expediency."[6] David Broder laments that "we do not have two parties in Washington. We have 536. The president, the 100 senators and the 435 representatives are each a party of one."[7]

The thesis of the decline of parties in America seems convincing. Indeed, it is wrong on only two major points: the data and the theory. Let us examine each, beginning with the data on recent presidential election patterns, and then looking at the theory and practice of contemporary American party organizations.

VOTING COALITIONS FROM 1980 TO 1992

New, stable voter coalitions indicate that the parties may have passed successfully through an era of realignment. For nearly four decades, political scientists have argued the concept of "partisan realignment." Inspired by a pathbreaking article by V. O. Key,[8] scholars have created categories, found and disdained realignment in presidential elections since 1964, and even tried to dismiss the subject entirely. The arguments have recently been summed up in a series of disputatious papers that evolved from a special session at the meetings of the American Political Science Association.[9]

The arguments are partially matters of measurement and partially matters of definition. Some change occurs in every election—but how much change is necessary to constitute realignment? What is the proper level of data to be employed? While much of the original work was based on aggregate data, later research employed individual level data, based on surveys. One important problem has been that of temporal stability. A major element in Key's definition was that changes in electoral divisions persist over considerable periods of time. Persistence, however, can only be demonstrated retrospectively, considerably after the "critical" election(s). Since scholars and publications are more interested in the exciting present, research inevitably lacks the retrospective perspective that is needed to provide a full test of realignment.

We have now reached a point at which some retrospective evaluation may be possible on one aspect of realignment, the changes in voting coalitions that occurred as a result of the unsettling events of the 1960s. At the time, some political tracts already suggested that a basic change was under way in the nation's politics.[10] Since then, scholars have examined such phenomena as the development of race as an open electoral division, the emergence of the Reagan (Bush) Democrats, and the stress on social and moral issues in presidential elections.[11]

From the longer perspective of the 1992 election, we can take some measurements of the existence and degree of realignment. For this purpose, we use simple methods, previously developed, employing aggregate data.[12] The basic data we employ are the Democratic percentages of the presidential vote by state.

Correlation of Successive Elections

Periods of electoral stability evidence high correlations of the state-by-state vote from one election to the next. In periods of realignment, as the parties' coalitions change, the correlations first decrease and then

Figure 4.1. Realignment in Presidential Elections: Correlation of Democratic Vote in Successive Presidential Elections, 1956–1992

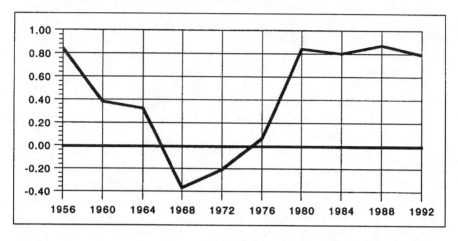

increase again as the new coalitions are stabilized. Illustratively, in the stable, post-McKinley period of Republican dominance from 1900 to 1924, the correlations in successive elections ranged from .87 to .96. In the transitional period of 1928–1932, the correlation dropped to .78. As the Roosevelt coalition took hold through 1948, these correlations reached extraordinarily high levels, none lower than .93.[13]

Using the same method, Figure 4.1 shows a similar pattern in recent presidential contests. The stability of the New Deal period continues into the 1956 election. Even though the Republicans won this and the preceding contest, the same state alignments existed, yielding a high correlation. Disruption in this coalition then occurred; the Democratic return to power with Kennedy and Johnson was on a different basis from the former coalition. Then, stability appeared to return, slightly with the Carter victory in 1976 and then strongly in the following four elections, from Reagan to Bush to Clinton.[14] Using this method, the period from 1976 to 1992 appears to constitute a time of relatively stable electoral coalitions, insofar as these coalitions are mirrored by statewide votes.

Correlation with Average State Vote

Another method used in the earlier research involved a longer time perspective. Each election was correlated with the average Democratic vote in the previous four elections. Thus, Truman's inheritance of the New Deal coalition was shown by the .95 correlation between his 1948 vote and the average Democratic tally from 1932 to 1944.[15] The radical disruption in electoral coalitions that occurred during the period 1960–1964, by contrast, is evident in much lower correlations, ranging between plus and minus .40, between the preceding four elections, and the votes of Democratic candidates from 1968 to 1976.

With the 1992 election, we now have sufficient elections to employ the same method in regard to the 1976–1988 period. The persistence of an electoral coalition is again indicated. The 1992 results are highly correlated with the previous four elections—a .80 coefficient correlating the 1976–1988 average with the two-party Democratic vote in 1992, and even higher, .87, using the three-candidate figures.[16]

Variation in State Votes

A similar pattern appears when we use another statistical method, employing standard deviations of the presidential vote across states. In any given election, individual states vary around the national average, and the standard deviation measures that spread. The upper line in Figure 4.2, graphing the 1976–1992 period, shows the standard deviation of the vote itself has changed little over this time; the states have retained their relative diversity.

Variation in State Vote Swings

More significant for our purposes is the change in the standard deviation of the state vote swings from one election to the next. A lowered standard deviation of state changes indicates a more stable political system, as states respond in similar ways to the political forces of the time. The lower line in Figure 4.2 shows the expected decrease. Shifts in the vote have become more uniform, indicating that political events have had similar effects across the nation during this period, reinforcing the new coalitions.

Correlation of Nonsuccessive Elections

A final method we can borrow from the earlier research is the correlation of nonsuccessive elections, arranged in a matrix. In a period of electoral stability, the state-by-state distributions of the vote will be similar throughout the period, resulting in high correlations of elections across time. For example, despite the passage of twelve years, Harry Truman's vote in 1948 strongly resembled that of his Democratic predecessor, Franklin Roosevelt, in 1936 (r=.90). In a period of electoral change, by contrast, nonsuccessive elections will show lower correla-

Figure 4.2. State Variation in the Democratic Presidential Vote, 1976–1992 (in Standard Deviations)

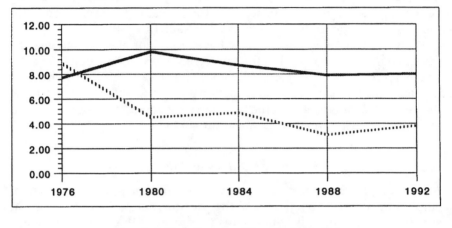

— **Diversity in Given Year**   ·· **Diversity of Vote Swing**

tions. Twelve years after Truman's victory, in 1960, John Kennedy won the presidency with a different Democratic coalition, the correlation to Truman's vote being only .21 (and .09 to Roosevelt's 1936 figures).

A new Democratic coalition appears in elections beginning with Jimmy Carter's victory in 1976, as detailed in Table 4.1. From that point through 1992, the Democratic candidates draw their support from similar bases, even when we compare both losers (Carter in 1980, Mondale and Dukakis) and winners (Carter in 1976, Clinton) and when we compare any pair of elections across the period. The correlations are not as high as in the elections of the New Deal period, to be sure, and the analysis is complicated by the large Perot vote in 1992.[17]

Still, there is considerable continuity in electoral patterns over this period, indicating the settling of the political system that is typical of a post-realignment period. Changes of this magnitude certainly indicate major change in voting alignments. We might well return, as William Mayer suggests, to Key's core concept, that realignments "set in motion major, long-term changes in the electoral order." If we keep our definition simple, "a realignment surely did occur between 1964 and 1972,"[18] leading to new and stabilized electoral coalitions of the present day.

THE CHARACTER OF POLITICAL PARTIES

Data aside, the thesis of party decline fails because it rests on a flawed theoretical foundation. The thesis depends on a view of parties as col-

Table 4.1. *Correlation of Democratic Vote in Presidential Elections, 1976–1992*

	1980	1984	1988	1992[a]	1992[b]
1976	.84	.62	.35	.71	.51
1980		.80	.54	.81	.67
1984			.87	.83	.84
1988				.65	.79

[a]Three-candidate vote
[b]Two-party vote

lectivities of voters. In this view, parties are weaker because fewer voters are strongly identified with the parties, and fewer are consistent supporters at the ballot box.

The problem with this argument is that parties are not properly considered as collections of voters. The appropriate conception of parties is quite different: "A political party is first of all an organized attempt to get power," as Schattschneider put it bluntly.[19] Voters are not members of the party organization, but rather its clientele. It is both confusing and inaccurate to think of voters as the party, even in the common usage of "party-in-the-electorate." As Anthony King dismisses this categorization, "It is rather as though one were to refer not to the buyers of Campbell's soup but to the Campbell-Soup-Company-in-the-Market."[20]

The long tradition of party theory has consistently focused on the parties as organizations,[21] while the newer and important research on voter partisanship properly constitutes a separate, although related, subject. As argued by the modern pathbreaking theorists such as Michels and Ostrogorski, basic issues of democracy involve the relationship of parties and the electorate, but conflating the two elements confuses our understanding.

We do better to think of the parties as seekers of voters, following Downs, Schumpeter, and Schlesinger. Downs defined a political party simply as "a coalition . . . a group of individuals who have certain ends in common and cooperate with each other to achieve them."[22] More bluntly, Downs employs a "self-interest axiom," that party politicians seek only "to attain the income, prestige, and power which come from being in office." As Schlesinger elaborated, this definition sparingly says only "that the political party is some kind of an organization. Yet the character of that organization—how it is arranged, what if any lines of authority it has, how disciplined it is, how much division of labor exists—is not part of this definition of party."[23]

To gauge parties we need first to recognize that a party is simply defined, like any other organization, as "a system of consciously coordinated personal activities or forces." And, in the words of Chester I. Barnard, "An organization comes into being when (1) there are persons able to communicate with each other (2) who are willing to contribute action (3) to accomplish a common purpose."[24]

An appropriate way to understand parties—and current trends in American politics—is to analogize from the way in which business entrepreneurs seek customers in the economic market to the way in which party entrepreneurs seek voters in the political market. In the automobile industry, we recognize the Ford and Toyota motor companies as the relevant organizations and car buyers as their market. In sports, we think of the New York Yankees and the Los Angeles Dodgers as organizations competing for the loyalties of fans. We should think similarly of Republicans and Democrats as competing for voter loyalties.

If parties are competitive organizations, like automakers and sports teams, we then should measure their strength in similar ways. In particular, we should determine their strength not by voter identification, but by their ability to compete. This view of party "must exclude the voter," writes Schlesinger. "Voters are choosers among parties, not components of them." Certainly, "It is a great advantage to a party to have large numbers of voters inclined in its favor. Yet the ultimate test of a party's strength, at least within the electoral context, lies in its ability to win elections, not in its identification among the electorate." Indeed, parties may need better organizations when they lose in voter identification. "This seeming paradox, parties growing stronger while they are growing weaker, is a paradox only if we make the error of equating partisan strength with partisan identification."[25]

The ability to compete is not the same as winning the competition. Even General Motors and the Dallas Cowboys sometimes lose. In a two-party system, defeat is even more inevitable amid the tides of electoral ebb and flow. Indeed, ability to compete may increase with the degree of competition. The American automotive industry probably has stronger organizations as a result of the competition of foreign manufacturers, just as athletic teams have been organizationally strengthened when new franchises have been added in the expansion of competition to new cities. Politically, state party organizations were weak in the erstwhile "Solid South," while they became stronger as Republicans became competitive in the former Confederacy.[26]

Seeing parties as organizations, we then can employ some basic tests of organizational strength. These standards are different from those applied by Max Weber to bureaucracies, for American parties surely fail his telltale tests of hierarchy and professionalism.[27] These particular and bureaucratic characteristics are variables, but not necessary elements in every organization. More modestly and more realistically, we can assess the character of an organization by these criteria: (1) recruitment of leadership; (2) command of resources; (3) structural articulation; (4) cohesion; and (5) defined mission.[28] We consider the Dallas Cowboys a strong organization, for example, because it is able to recruit its own leadership, commands large amounts of money, clearly articulates the roles of its players, works cohesively, and has a clearly defined mission.

Politics is different, but party organizations can be assessed, using different data, on the same criteria.[29] The political analogues are as follows: presidential nominations; campaign funds; party organizational continuity; policy unity; and party ideology. In the election of 1992, and in recent years, American parties have become stronger organizations on these criteria.

PARTY ORGANIZATIONAL DEVELOPMENTS

Recruitment of Leadership: Presidential Nominations

If a strong organization is able to select its own leadership, American parties would seem weak indeed, particularly in regard to their most important leaders, the presidential nominees. Particularly since the "reforms" of the parties, beginning with the McGovern-Fraser Commission after 1968, presidential nominations have apparently become contests among self-starting aspirants who succeed by assembling a personal coalition that appeals directly to the voters in a series of uncoordinated state primaries.

Some observers, like Epstein, accept the new "plebiscitary system" as no more than an extension of established state primaries which have made nominations "large-scale public rather than private organizational affairs."[30] Others, such as Austin Ranney, complain that "reform" got out of hand, confounding him and others, who "preferred a reformed national convention to a national presidential primary or a major increase in the number of state presidential primaries."[31] But the consequences go beyond personal disappointment. To Nelson Polsby, "What it takes to achieve the nomination differs nowadays so sharply from what it takes to govern effectively as to pose a problem that has some generality."[32]

In light of these analyses, recent nominations, particularly in 1992, evidence a trend toward increased party influence in the selection of national leadership. Since 1980, we have seen eight presidential nominations, all the choice of an established party leader, even in the face of strong insurgencies. These selections include two renominations of the sitting party leader, either without challenge (Reagan, 1984) or without significant challenge (Bush, 1992); one renomination against a strong challenge (Carter, 1980); three selections of the leader of the established dominant faction of the party (Reagan, 1980; Mondale; Bush, 1988); and two selections of the leader of a major party faction (Dukakis, Clinton).

These choices represent selection *of* leaders of the organized parties or its factions, even if the choice has not been made primarily *by* the formal party leadership (such as Democratic "super-delegates" and similar Republican officials). These decisions are quite different from the selection of such insurgents as Barry Goldwater in 1964 or George McGovern in 1972, which are the typical illustrations of the asserted decline of party. The reality is that now insurgents do have access to the contest for presidential nominations, but that they fail in that contest, as shown by the examples of Democrats Edward Kennedy in 1980, Gary Hart in 1984, and Jesse Jackson in 1988, and the virtual absence of any Republican insurgents throughout the period.

It is not completely extravagant to compare these choices to those that might occur in a U.S. parliamentary system. Is the selection of Reagan in 1980 that different from the British Tories' choice of Margaret Thatcher to lead the party's turn toward ideological free-market conservatism? Is the selection of Mondale as the liberal standard-bearer of the liberal Democratic party that different from the succession of leadership among British Labour? Within federal systems, with their diverse paths of recruitment, are the choices of Dukakis and Clinton much different from the selection of factional leaders with local bases of support in Canada and Australia?

The party basis of recruitment is particularly evident in the presidential nominations of 1992. There were notable insurgent candidates, Republican Pat Buchanan and Democrats Jerry Brown and Paul Tsongas, but they were soundly defeated by established party figures. George Bush was not only the incumbent leader, but also typified the career of a party politician, including service as a national Republican chairman who rose regularly in party ranks, securing his nomination as the heir of the retiring leader, Ronald Reagan. In a parliamentary system, he would be the ideal analogue to Britain's John Major.

Bill Clinton came to party leadership from the position of governor, reflecting the variety of career opportunities available in a federal system, but Arkansas was hardly a robust power base. Clinton's real base was the Democratic Leadership Council (DLC), which provided much of his program, his source of contacts and finances, and his opportunity for national exposure. The DLC, composed of party officials and office-holders, is an organized party faction. Clinton's success is a testament to the influence of that faction, far more than evidence of the decline of party and the substitution of unmediated access to the voters. Again, parliamentary analogues are plentiful, such as Labour's replacement of Neil Kinnock by John Smith.

The analogy is not complete, to be sure. American political leadership is still quite open, the parties quite permeable. (Other strong organizations are also permeable; for example, corporations are subject to take-overs by "outsider" stockholders.) Presidential nominations do depend greatly on personal coalitions and popular primaries are the decisive points of decision. Yet it is also true that leadership of the parties is still, and perhaps increasingly, related to prominence within the parties. On this first test, we find a significant degree of organizational strength.

Resources

Money is the measure of this second criterion of organizational strength. In 1992, continuing a trend of the 1980s,[33] the political parties were major sources of campaign spending, particularly in the presidential race and even in the face of the party-weakening provisions of election finance laws.

There were two large sources of party money in 1992: the direct subsidies provided by the federal election law, and the "soft money" contributions provided for state parties and organizational work. Together, these funds totaled $213 million for the major candidates and their parties.[34] Together, the parties received direct public grants of $22 million for their national conventions, spent another $20 million directly,[35] and spent half again as much as the public grants to the candidates in their "soft money." Moreover, and significantly, even the public funding provided directly to the candidates was closely coordinated with the parties. Underlining the significance of this party spending, the Republican and Democratic national campaigns in 1992 *each* spent twice as much money as did billionaire Ross Perot, whose candidacy is often seen as demonstrating the decline of the parties.

An enhanced party role is evident in other national elections as well. Beyond direct contributions and expenditures, the parties have developed a variety of ingenious devices, such as bundling, coordinated spending, and agency agreements, to again become significant players in the election finance game. Overall, in 1992, the six national party committees spent $290 million. (For comparison, total spending in all House and Senate races was $678 million, and total political action committee (PAC) contributions were $180 million.)[36] The proportion of funds from party committees rose regularly over the 1980s, although individual and PAC contributions are certainly greater, and likely to remain so, even under new legislation. Yet, Frank Sorauf shrewdly predicted, "The financial rebirth of the national parties offers hope of new influence for parties and a reversal of the much heralded 'decline' and 'decomposition' of the American parties."[37]

Structure

The structural viability of the parties, a third criterion of organizational strength, is quite evident. The national parties are now continuing institutions, with elaborate permanent headquarters (this institutionalization a marked response to earlier calls for party renewal programs).[38] They have large professional staffs who conduct party programs of candidate recruitment and training, opinion polling, research, campaign management, broadcasting, advertising, and finance. Campaign consultants and political action committees, which are often seen as replacements of the parties, are increasingly allied with the parties. The national parties, to be sure, do not dominate election campaigns, but the truth is that they never did. It is more accurate to say that the national parties have changed from the locus of "politics without power" to active participants in coalitional politics.[39]

State parties, it is now understood, rather than declining, have become stronger organizations. Even while electoral loyalty to the parties has dropped (and perhaps because it has dropped), the party organizations have been transformed and have actually "gained in organizational strength over a period when they were generally thought to be in decline."[40] That organizational strength was evident in the 1988 and 1992 presidential elections, when Democrats Dukakis and Clinton ran much of their campaigns through the state party organizations.

PARTY PROGRAMS

Cohesion: Party Voting in Congress

The fourth test of a strong party system is cohesion in pursuing its goals. The best recent evidence on this criterion can be found in the first congressional session under the Clinton administration. Until the 1992 election, divided government had become almost the normal state of American national government and some analysts had even concluded that a partisan division between the president and Congress made no substantial difference in the functioning of that government.[41] David Brady, however, suggests an empirical test of the effect of divided government: the direction of public policy in the Clinton presidency.[42]

There is already sufficient evidence to show both the viability of parties in Congress and the effects of single-party government. In the first year of the new administration, there were a series of party-line votes on such issues as family leave, economic stimulus, "motor-voter" registration, national service, handgun control, campaign finance, strategic defense and (three times) the broad economic policies incorporated in the national budget. Perhaps the most striking if less noted vote was the vote to cut off the filibuster on the "motor-voter" bill, where every Democrat voted for cloture. Those who remember when Strom Thurmond, or even Phil Gramm, bore the Democrat label must gape at southern Democrats uniting to end debate on a measure to extend voting participation.

Journalists concentrated on the close votes on the budget, which passed only by a single vote in both the House and Senate (where Vice President Gore broke a tie). If we look—more appropriately—at the entire picture, we see perfect party unity among the Republicans and Democratic party cohesion of 85 to 95 percent on a budget that included both higher taxes and lower spending. When it counts, party is clearly significant.

Brady suggests a quite specific test of party influence under Clinton—the impact of Representative Charles Stenholm, the median member of the House in roll call voting. In the debate on the first budget resolution, the first comprehensive measure presented by Clinton, Stenholm was marginalized; only twelve Democrats followed him to desert the party on the decisive, recommittal vote. Overall, Stenholm split his support, voting with the Democratic majority on party-line votes essentially half (48 percent) of the time—but only seven other Democrats fell to that level of party infidelity.[43]

Party made a difference in Congress (the North American Free Trade Agreement (NAFTA), which temporarily split the Democrats notwithstanding). Clinton won 86 percent of the test votes in the 1993 Congress (surpassed only by Eisenhower in 1953 and Johnson in 1965, but never topped by Reagan); party unity was more common than at any time in the four decades of roll call measurement by Congressional Quarterly, Inc.; the Southern Democratic-Republican conservative coalition shrank to its lowest level in the same period; and the average member of both houses of Congress voted with his or her party on 86 percent to

Figure 4.3. Party Unity in Congress, 1970–1993

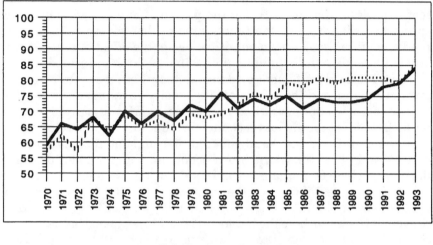

— Republicans ⋯ Democrats

Source: *Congressional Quarterly Weekly Report* 51 (December 18, 1993): 3479

89 percent of party-unity votes. Overall, in fact, only four members—one in each party in each chamber—voted more frequently against than with their parties.[44]

In these votes, we do not see hierarchical party discipline but rather some semblance of party responsibility. The president does not command loyalty, and must bargain vigorously, but his party still acts cohesively. As the *New York Times* reported, "Mr. Clinton's pitch is that Congress can rise or fall with him. It is a message that seems to be resonating with Democrats who say they feel pressure to help keep their party's hold on the White House and are only encouraged by Mr. Clinton's entreaties."[45] Gridlock is being dissolved, David Broder wrote early in the administration, by "the fact that Clinton, the congressional leaders, and the big majority of the freshmen are all Democrats, who have a clear common political interest in trying to make this economic package a success."[46]

Precise data are not yet available for the 1994 session of Congress, but the same party trends are already evident. While President Clinton lost many battles, the split between Democrats and Republicans remained and possibly intensified to the point of deadlock. Sharp partisan divisions were evident in committee votes on health care, as well as floor votes on campaign finance, education, crime control, and government spending. Only foreign trade, particularly the ratificaiton of the General Agreement on Tariffs and Trade (GATT), showed true bipartisanship.

The influence of party in Congress has increased with the advent of President Clinton and unified party control of the legislative and executive branches. The increased impact of party, however, reflects more than the current political lineup, for "the mid- and late 1980's witnessed the emergence of strong, policy-oriented majority party leadership in the House of Representatives," and parties increasingly affected congressional behavior.[47] Consequently, legislative cohesion, as measured by party unity in Congress and shown in Figure 4.3, has been slowly increasing since at least 1970—in both parties, in both House and Senate, and in both Republican and Democratic administrations. Once again, the evidence contradicts the wailing over the decline of party.

Mission: Ideology

Legislative cohesion is possible because contemporary parties also meet the fifth standard of strong organizations—a defined mission or, in political terms, a common ideology. Voters certainly see a difference between the parties. In 1992, a majority of the electorate chose either Democrats or Republicans as likely "to do a better job" regarding the nation's economy, foreign affairs, the problem of poverty, and "making health care more affordable." On only one issue, "keeping out of war," was the nation indifferent between the parties.[48] These attitudes reinforce the electorate's consistent attitude, unvarying even as party identification has fallen, that there are "important differences" in the parties' beliefs.

These mass attitudes accurately reflect the real differences that exist between the parties on the elite level. In research conducted nearly forty years ago, Herbert McClosky and his students demonstrated the large ideological differences among the two major parties' national convention delegates.[49] More recent work shows that these divisions persist among broader layers of party activists, such as contributors and campaign workers.[50] The point is even made, inadvertently, by Richard Herrera, who emphasizes the relative lack of cohesion among convention delegates. Nevertheless, his data show that Democratic delegates in 1988 were overwhelmingly liberal, although not always consistently so, and that Republicans were sometimes conservative, sometimes moderate, but almost never liberal.[51] There is a difference.

Party differences are far more significant than even these labels suggest. Party leaders at every level, from campaign activists to members of Congress, differ on significant policies and act on their different ideological commitments. The presidential candidates of 1992 are further testament to basic party differences. Bush was probably the most moderate Republican, and Clinton the most moderate Democrat, who could conceivably be nominated. Nevertheless, there were major differences in policy and ideology between them—reflecting their basic party identities.

A simple experiment can underline the point. Remove the labels from the Democratic and Republican platforms for 1992, and then read their positions on a series of issues, choosing from a long list including abortion, health insurance, education vouchers, regulation of the economy, and endangered species legislation. Would any political scientist, or most voters, have great difficulty in matching the party to the position?

Underlying these specific issues is a basic philosophical and historical disagreement between the major parties. Republicans are individualists; Democrats are communitarians. America tries to balance a commitment to individual liberty with a commitment to social equality, to balance the pursuit of our private interests with our search for a public community. We engage in a perpetual personal and national debate, asking, to paraphrase John Kennedy, *both* what we can do for ourselves and what we can do for others. In that debate, Republicans will be more likely to raise the banner of individualism: pursuit of individual goals will add up to the common good. Democrats will be more likely to raise the banner of community: pursuing the social good will be better for each of us individually.[52]

This philosophical difference leads to significant differences in the parties' attitudes toward power and politics. Republicans distrust government, even when they control it. They rely on the private sector, particularly the accumulation of private capital, to meet social needs. By contrast, the Democratic party, at least since the New Deal, has regarded government as a potentially benign force, which can take action—at the very least to stimulate the private sector—and, more ambitiously, to redistribute the national wealth. Only a Republican could give Reagan's 1981 Inaugural Address, proclaiming that "government is not the solution to our problem—government is the problem." Only a Democrat could give Clinton's 1993 speech, reiterating the party's call for "bold, persistent experimentation, a government for our tomorrows."

These basic ideological distinctions were evident in the 1992 election campaign and continue in the Clinton administration, on such issues as family leave, capital taxation, social spending, and education. Health care is exemplary. While the president and his wife developed a complex program involving government regulation, subsidies, and mandates, the Republicans looked to individualistic solutions such as private health insurance and tax credits. We can easily predict that future congressional roll call votes on health care, whenever they finally occur, will reflect these continuing philosophical differences—and the parties' continuing viability as organizations with distinct missions.

CONCLUSIONS: PARTIES IN THE MARKETPLACE

By conceptualizing parties as purposive organizations rather than as mass collectivities, we find considerable evidence of party strength in contemporary American politics. The parties now evidence significant recruitment of leadership, resources, structure, cohesion, and mission. As against the alleged decline of parties, we find them strengthened competitors in the electoral marketplace.

But a problem remains inherent in this conceptualization. Competitive organizations do not always survive. Parties, we must remember, are particular kinds of organizations, distinct from bureaucracies or interest groups, because of their orientation to a marketplace—of votes, not money. Market-oriented organizations eventually must show strength not only in their internal characteristics, but in their external support. Just as a corporation ultimately must win customers, so a party must win voters to be successful. Without profit, even the best-managed corporations go out of business. Without voters, even well-structured parties can fail and disappear—as did the Federalists and Whigs.

Our contemporary parties may face this possibility. They do have a problem, quantified in the data on partisan identification and personified by Ross Perot. The voters' weaker loyalties and lowered affect make it more difficult for the parties to sell their wares. "Independent entrepreneurs" such as Perot and new "product lines" of the mass media and political consultants could conceivably drive them from the marketplace.

Without an extended discussion at this point, we can point to a few indicators that the major parties are meeting these threats and will be able to maintain themselves in the electoral marketplace. There are at least the following signs of party strengthening in the electorate:

- Party identification, the proportion of strong identifiers, and affect toward the parties have all risen, after the decline of the 1970s.[53]
- There is strong continuity in the electoral coalitions of the parties during the period of 1976–1992, as elaborated in the first part of this chapter.
- In the election of 1992, strong party loyalty is evident in individual-level data. Clinton won not only all states carried by Dukakis in 1988, but the overwhelming proportion of Dukakis's

supporters (83 percent), and of self-identified Democrats (77 percent).[54]
- In 1992, only 23.9 percent of the congressional districts voted for different parties for president and the U.S. House, the lowest proportion in four decades.[55]
- Although the 1992 Perot vote may continue, the Texan's organization appears now to be becalmed, and its mass base lacks the distinctive demographic or ideological character needed for a long-term social movement to be successful.

Given the 1992 election, we should be wary of any bold predictions. The enduring features of American government, from separated institutions to ideological disparities, guarantee that the United States will never evidence the coherence of disciplined party rule. Yet we can see the emergence of stable voter coalitions and strengthened party organizations. Maybe, just maybe, and just in time, we can now observe an emerging "semi-responsible party government."[56]

NOTES

Gerald Pomper acknowledges, with thanks, the help and suggestions of Chris Bruzios, Malcolm Jewell, William Mayer, and Sarah Morehouse.

1. The Scholarly Commitment to Parties," in Ada Finifter, ed. *Political Science: The State of the Discipline* (Washington, D.C.: American Political Science Association, 1983), pp. 127–153, at 146.
2. Crotty and Gary Jacobson, *American Parties in Decline*, 2nd. ed. (Boston: Little, Brown, 1984), p. 283.
3. On this point, see the strong critique of Bruce Keith, et al., *The Myth of the Independent Voter* (Berkeley: University of California Press, 1992).
4. Martin P. Wattenberg, *The Decline of American Political Parties, 1952–1980* (Cambridge, Mass.: Harvard University Press, 1984), p. 126.
5. David E. Price, *Bringing Back the Parties* (Washington, D.C.: CQ Press, 1984), p. 56.
6. William J. Keefe, *Parties, Politics, and Public Policy in America*, 6th ed. (Washington, D.C.: CQ Press, 1991), pp. 82, 271.
7. *Washington Post Weekly Edition*, January 31–February 6, 1994, p. 23.
8. "A Theory of Critical Elections," *Journal of Politics* 17 (February 1955): 3–18.
9. In a vast literature, the most important books have been Walter Dean Burnham, *Critical Elections and the Mainsprings of American*

Politics (New York: Norton, 1970); James L. Sundquist, *Dynamics of the Party System*, rev. ed. (Washington, D.C.: Brookings, 1983); and Jerome M. Clubb, William H. Flanigan, and Nancy H. Zingale, *Partisan Realignment* (Beverly Hills, Calif.: Sage, 1980). The most recent debate is in Byron E. Shafer, ed. *The End of Realignment?* (Madison: University of Wisconsin Press, 1991).

10. See Kevin P. Phillips, *The Emerging Republican Majority* (New York: Arlington House, 1969); Richard Scammon and Ben Wattenberg, *The Real Majority* (New York: Coward-McCann, 1970).

11. Edward G. Carmines and James A. Stimson, *Issue Evolution* (Princeton, N.J.: Princeton University Press, 1989); John Kenneth White, *The New Politics of Old Values* (Hanover, N.H.: University Press of New England, 1988); Warren E. Miller, "Party Identification, Realignment, and Party Voting," *American Political Science Review* 85 (June 1991): 556–68.

12. Gerald M. Pomper, "Classification of Presidential Elections," *Journal of Politics* 29 (August 1967): 535–66; Pomper, with Susan Lederman, *Elections in America*, 2nd ed. (New York: Longman, 1980).

13. Pomper, with Lederman, pp. 229–31.

14. The Clinton vote in 1992 is the Democratic percentage of the two-party vote. Using the Democratic percentage of the three-candidate vote in 1992, the correlation to 1988 is .65. The District of Columbia is excluded from these calculations, to be consistent with the data before the 1964 election. Because the District casts an overwhelming Democratic vote, its extreme values would substantially increase the correlation coefficient.

15. Pomper, *Journal of Politics*, p. 566.

16. If the District of Columbia were included, the coefficients would be, respectively, .89 and .94.

17. The correlations would be considerably higher if the District of Columbia were included, as it is in calculations by Professor William Mayer of Northeastern University. In "Three Varieties of Electoral Change," a manuscript not yet published, he reports the following data:

Correlation of Democratic Presidential Vote, 1976–1992

	1980	1984	1988	1992*
1976	.92	.76	.61	.82
1980		.80	.63	.83
1984			.93	.92
1988				.83

*Clinton vote among three candidates.

18. Mayer, p. 15.
19. E. E. Schattschneider, *Party Government* (New York: Holt, Rinehart and Winston, 1942), p. 35.
20. "Political Parties in Western Democracies," *Polity* 2 (1960), p. 114, quoted in Denise Baer and David Bositis, *Politics and Linkage in a Democratic Society* (Englewood Cliffs, N.J.: Prentice-Hall, 1993), p. 108.
21. See Gerald M. Pomper, *Passions and Interests* (Lawrence, Kans.: University Press of Kansas, 1992), esp. Chapter 1.
22. Anthony Downs, *An Economic Theory of Democracy* (New York: Harper and Row, 1957), pp. 24, 28.
23. Joseph A. Schlesinger, "On the Theory of Party Organization," *Journal of Politics* 46 (May 1984): 369–400, at 375.
24. Chester I. Barnard, *The Functions of the Executive* (Cambridge, Mass.: Harvard University Press, 1938, 1968), pp. 72, 82; emphasis deleted.
25. Schlesinger, p. 377.
26. Cornelius Cotter, et al., *Party Organizations in American Politics* (New York: Praeger, 1984), pp. 31–35. Contrast the classic descriptions of V. O. Key, Jr., in *Southern Politics* (New York: Knopf, 1950), Chapters 2–13.
27. "Bureaucracy," in H. H. Gerth and C. Wright Mills, *From Max Weber: Essays in Sociology* (New York: Oxford University Press, 1946), pp. 196–198.
28. Major works on organizational theory include Barnard, *op. cit.*; Peter Blau and W. Richard Scott, *Formal Organizations* (San Francisco: Chandler, 1962); and James March and Herbert Simon, *Organizations* (New York: Wiley, 1958).
29. Some, but not all, of these criteria are employed in the leading textbook: Frank J. Sorauf and Paul Allen Beck, *Party Politics in America* 6th ed. (Glenview, Ill.: Scott, Foresman, 1988), p. 68.
30. Leon D. Epstein, *Political Parties in the American Mold* (Madison: University of Wisconsin Press, 1986), p. 108.
31. Austin Ranney, *Curing the Mischiefs of Faction* (Berkeley: University of California Press, 1975), p. 206.
32. Nelson W. Polsby, *Consequences of Party Reform* (New York: Oxford University Press, 1983), p. 89.
33. See Paul S. Herrnson, *Party Campaigning in the 1980s* (Cambridge, Mass.: Harvard University Press, 1988).
34. *Congressional Quarterly Weekly Report* 51 (May 15, 1993): 1197.
35. Anthony Corrado, *Paying for Presidents* (New York: Twentieth Century Fund, 1993), p. 102.

36. *Congressional Quarterly Weekly Report* 51 (March 20, 1993): 691; Federal Election Commission, *Record*, 19 (May, 1993): 22.
37. Frank J. Sorauf, *Money in American Elections* (Glenview, Ill.: Scott, Foresman, 1988), p. 132.
38. See Ranney, p. 45; Stephen Bailey, *The Condition of Our National Political Parties* (New York: Fund for the Republic, 1959).
39. Cornelius P. Cotter and John F. Bibby, "Institutional Development of Parties and the Thesis of Party Decline," *Political Science Quarterly* 95 (Spring 1980): 1–27.
40. Cotter et al., p. 102.
41. Particularly David R. Mayhew, in *Divided We Govern* (New Haven: Yale University Press, 1991).
42. "The Causes and Consequences of Divided Government: Toward a New Theory of American Politics?," *American Political Science Review* 87 (March 1993): 189–94.
43. *Congressional Quarterly Weekly Report* 51 (December 18, 1993): 3433.
44. Ibid., 3427–38.
45. Richard Berke, "Looking for Alliance, Clinton Courts the Congress Nonstop," *New York Times*, March 8, 1993, p. A1.
46. "Together at Last," *Washington Post Weekly Edition*, March 8–14, 1993, p. 4.
47. Barbara Sinclair, "The Congressional Party," in Sandy Maisel, ed., *The Parties Respond* (Boulder, Colo.: Westview, 1990), p. 227. See also Sinclair, *The Transformation of the U.S. Senate* (Baltimore: Johns Hopkins University Press, 1989); and David Rohde, *Parties and Leaders in the Postreform House* (Chicago: University of Chicago Press, 1991).
48. Martin Wattenberg, "The 1992 Election," paper presented at Annual Meeting of American Political Science Association, 1993, p. 30.
49. Herbert McClosky, Paul J. Hoffman, and Rosemary O'Hara, "Issue Conflict and Consensus Among Party Leaders and Followers," *American Political Science Review* 54 (June 1960): 406–27.
50. Christopher Bruzios, "Democratic & Republican Party Activists & Followers," *Polity* 22 (Summer 1990): 581–601.
51. "Cohesion at the Party Conventions: 1980–1988," *Polity* 26 (Fall 1993): 75–89.
52. See Orlando Patterson's insightful discussion, "Our History vs. Clinton's Covenant," *New York Times*, November 13, 1992, p. A29.
53. Steven Rosenstone and John Hansen, *Mobilization, Participation and Democracy in America* (New York: Macmillan, 1993), pp. 151–52.

54. See Gerald M. Pomper, ed., *The Election of 1992* (Chatham, N.J.: Chatham House, 1993), pp. 141, 138.
55. *Congressional Quarterly Weekly Report* 51 (December 4, 1993): 3320.
56. This artful phrase was suggested to me by William Mayer; it deliberately echoes E. E. Schattschneider, *The Semi-Sovereign People* (New York: Dryden Press, 1960).

CHAPTER 5

Presidential Elections and Policy Change: How Much of a Connection Is There?

DAVID R. MAYHEW

In analyses of American politics, it would be hard to find a more basic claim or assumption than that major policy changes owe to the outcomes of presidential elections. Old government policies are abandoned and new ones adopted because of election results. The idea is central to theories of "party government" and "electoral realignments," as well as to more conventional accounts of political processes by historians, political scientists, and journalists.

How true is the claim? Probably less than is commonly believed. Partly because most of us get excited by presidential elections, and partly because we see them as great democratic instruments, we tend to overestimate their causal power. Also, we tend to assume that causal power without actually showing it. In our studies, we zero in on the presumed independent variable—elections—without giving anywhere near the same systematic attention to the presumed dependent variable—policy change. The extreme case is the research design where we look only under the streetlight for lost coins and, sure enough, find them—a recurrent failing of "realignments" scholarship that takes cognizance of policy change only if it occurs just after an alleged "critical" election.

By these customary standards, this chapter is a backwards enterprise. I dwell on the dependent variable—policy change, of a sort, during American history—and only later speculate about what may be causing it. Moreover, presidential elections are made to compete here, at least in a thought experiment, against other potential causes. The causal discussion is organized under four rubrics—elections in general, the actions of political parties, the condition of the economy, and public moods—of which the first and second, though not the third and fourth, assign a prominent role to presidential elections. In general, the first two rubrics do not seem to outperform the second two as producers of policy change.

LAWMAKING SURGES

The policy change to be investigated here is of a particular kind—legislative "surges" that have produced a large share of the significant statutes enacted during American history. Four times since the 1790s, the national government has legislated in a striking surge pattern. In each case, exceptionally large numbers of major laws kept winning enactment year after year, Congress after Congress, under two or three presidents for a half decade or more. These surges of activity had beginnings and endings (although the boundaries are not always entirely clear). It is as if the system's volume could somehow be turned up to a pitch of accelerated change, stay there awhile, then be lowered again to a pitch of normal slow change.

There were also similarities in statutory content. In the laws of each of the four eras, there was a pronounced thrust toward enhancing the powers, activities, or reach of the national state. Among the means to those ends were increased public expenditure and taxation, new federal programs, direct coercion to the extreme of military occupation, government planning, regulation of the economy, and restructuring of the polity or society through such means as guaranteed individual rights. To be sure, not all the enactments of these eras worked. Many had unanticipated consequences or just failed. But there was substantial policy impact, even if it did not live up to the extraordinary levels of legislative ambition exhibited during these four strenuous times.

The first task here is to make the case for the existence of these four legislative "surges."[1] This will be done chronologically, era by era, in what I hope is sufficient, though not overwhelming, detail. Actual statutes will be emphasized, not catchphrases such as "the New Deal" or various statistics that are often taken to be indicators of legislative action. For the first three eras, the sources are standard secondary writings. For the fourth, the proximate source is David R. Mayhew, *Divided We Govern: Party Control, Lawmaking, and Investigations, 1946–1990*).[2]

1. The Civil War and Reconstruction Era: 1861 through 1875

Moves against slavery and in favor of civil rights provide the obvious theme of this first of the four "surge" eras, but, according to many interpretations, there also existed powerful companion themes of constructing a centralized American state and nourishing a nationwide capitalist economy. The laws of the time reflect these various aims. A sequence of unprecedentedly ambitious lawmaking extended through eight Congresses.

In the early years came moves to enact what amounted to an updated version of Henry Clay's Whig blueprint for an "American system." In early 1861, after the South had seceded from the Union, the lame-duck session of the Congress elected in 1858 enacted the Morrill Tariff Act. That measure initiated a Republican high-tariff regime that endured, despite temporary reductions in duties during the Democratic Cleveland and Wilson administrations, until the 1930s.[3] In 1862 came the Homestead Act, offering federal land to homesteaders for a nominal fee, the Morrill Land-Grant College Act, awarding federal land to the states to construct agricultural and engineering colleges, and the Pacific Railroad Act, providing land subsidies to build a transcontinental railroad. Funding the Civil War required banking measures that had an "American system" theme of centralized control: the Legal Tender Act of 1862 (fostering a national currency) and the National Banking Act of 1863 (creating a national, though not tightly centralized, banking system).[4]

Once the war had begun, Congress enacted certain anti-slavery measures that had had no chance of passage until that time—for example, bans on slavery in the western territories and in the District of Columbia. But in 1863, Lincoln bypassed Congress and the regular lawmaking process by abolishing southern slavery through executive order in his Emancipation Proclamation. Conventional legislative processes regained the initiative in this policy area in early 1865, when Congress approved the Thirteenth Amendment, which outlawed slavery and created the Freedmen's Bureau. After Lincoln's assassination, under President Andrew Johnson, the 39th Congress enacted the Civil Rights Act of 1866, the content of which prefigured the Fourteenth Amendment, approved that amendment later in the same year, and passed the First Reconstruction Act over Johnson's veto in March 1867. That measure imposed military rule on the South and revolutionized southern politics by enfranchising

Blacks and disfranchising many previously rebellious Whites. Three additional Reconstruction Acts followed in 1867 and 1868, as well as the Fifteenth Amendment, which guaranteed suffrage for Blacks, in February 1869.[5]

The Fifteenth Amendment is sometimes regarded as the concluding legislative measure of the Reconstruction era. In fact, during the two ensuing Congresses, substantial energy, commitment, and public attention were devoted to enacting five "Enforcement Acts" during 1870, 1871, and 1872, which mandated that the Attorney General take steps to make the earlier measures, particularly the Fifteenth Amendment, actually work in the South. The third of these acts is sometimes called the Klu Klux Klan Act because, in effect, it outlawed that organization. By 1875, these measures had largely failed, though some of them were to be drawn upon by the federal government much later during the civil rights revolution of the 1950s and 1960s. The Reconstruction era's last notable measure was the Civil Rights Act of 1875, a project promoted by Massachusetts Senator Charles Sumner as his long career ended, which won enactment during the closing lame-duck session of the Republican Congress that had been elected in 1872.[6]

2. The Progressive Era: 1906 through 1916

Moves to bring about government regulation of the economy, the polity, and the society keynoted lawmaking drives during the Progressive era. That much is generally agreed upon, notwithstanding scholarly dissensus otherwise about the aims and achievements of the era. Railroad regulation figured prominently during the early years, labor measures during the later ones, and regulation of parties and elections throughout. New instruments of government were created and funded. For purposes of periodizing, it may help to review events at the state level, where much of the significant reform action occurred. The period of roughly 1905 through 1914 is often cited as the time of high-volume lawmaking in the states, where ambitious reform programs were continually being enacted somewhere or other during those years. The principal instances include Wisconsin in 1903, a pacesetting session dominated by Governor Robert LaFollette, as well as 1905, Minnesota in 1905 and 1907, New York in 1907, Georgia in 1907 to 1909, California, New Jersey, and North Dakota in 1911, Massachusetts in 1911 to 1914, New York once again in 1913, and Ohio in 1913 to 1914.[7]

At the national level, President Theodore Roosevelt dramatically opened the Progressive era by winning congressional approval of the Hepburn Act of 1906, a plan to regulate railroad rates that, in the words of Jeffrey K. Tulis, "gave birth to the modern administrative state."[8] To pass it, Roosevelt needed to conduct an eighteen-month campaign to mobilize public opinion and assemble congressional support. Also enacted in 1906 were the Pure Food and Drug Act and the Meat Inspection Act. Roosevelt's last Congress of 1907–1909, which did little legislating, aside from the Tillman Act that banned corporate contributions in election campaigns, provides a gap in the sequence. This may be because the White House provided the national legislative agenda during these early Progressive years and, as a general rule, presidents almost never have much luck winning congressional approval of their domestic programs after six years in office (these were Roosevelt's seventh and eighth years).[9]

National lawmaking came to life again in 1909 under President William Howard Taft. Spurred by Democrats and insurgent Republicans, the Republican Congress of 1909–1911 passed the Mann-Elkins Act (another stab at railroad regulation), a measure establishing a postal savings system (an idea that had been around for about four decades), and the Sixteenth Amendment (authorizing a federal income tax). The Congress of 1911–1913, divided between a Republican Senate and a Democratic House, approved the Seventeenth Amendment that required popular election of U.S. Senators, mandated an eight-hour day for private-sector workers on federal contracts, established a federal Children's Bureau and the Department of Labor, and enacted the third and most ambitious of a 1907, 1910 and 1911 sequence of campaign-finance reforms. These measures, which among other things required disclosure of financial transactions by congressional candidates and placed a ceiling on candidate spending, had largely the same goals and enjoyed the same kind of reform backing as the more familiar series of campaign-finance laws enacted in the 1970s, although the instruments of the Progressive era, by comparison, lacked enforcement teeth.[10]

Woodrow Wilson's first Congress of 1913–1915 passed the Underwood Tariff Act, which lowered duties and used the new Sixteenth Amendment to inaugurate an income tax; the Federal Reserve Act; the Clayton Antitrust Act; a measure creating the Federal Trade Commission (FTC); and the La Follette Seamen's Act, which regulated maritime working conditions. A second major legislative drive under Wilson in 1916 generated the Federal Farm Loan Act; workmen's compensation for federal employees; a ban on interstate sale of goods produced by child labor (later struck down by the Supreme Court as unconstitutional); the Adamson Act, which mandated an eight-hour day for railroad workers; and the Revenue Act of 1916, which elevated the income tax to the status of chief revenue instrument of the federal government.

That year's energetic program was the last of the era. A few congressional initiatives came later—for example, the Eighteenth Amendment (prohibition of alcoholic beverages) in 1917 and the Nineteenth Amendment (women's suffrage) in 1919. But, as a general matter, the Progressive lawmaking impulse faded away at the national level during World War I, in 1917–1918.[11]

3. The New Deal Era: 1932 through 1938

The Roosevelt Years.   If seen as a sequence of lawmaking aimed at either recovery or reform, as those objectives were regarded at the time, the New Deal era arguably spanned four consecutive Congresses. The two Congresses during Franklin Roosevelt's first term in the White House (1933–1936) unquestionably stand out. The famous "hundred days" session of 1933 produced the National Industry Recovery Act, the Agricultural Adjustment Act (inaugurating the modern system of crop subsidies), the Emergency Banking Act, the Federal Emergency Relief Act, the Home Owners' Loan Act, the Securities Act, and measures creating the Civilian Conservation Corps (CCC), the Federal Deposit Insurance Corporation (FDIC), and the Tennessee Valley Authority (TVA). The 1934 session brought the Reciprocal Trade Agreements Act, which lowered tariff rates—not a state-expanding move—but arguably improved the government's planning capacity; the Taylor Grazing Act; the Indian Reorganization Act; and measures creating the Securities and Exchange Commission (SEC); the Federal Communications Commission (FCC); and the Federal Housing Administration (FHA).[12]

The strenuous "second hundred days" of 1935 generated the Social Security Act (setting up the modern U.S. pensions system), the National Labor Relations Act (establishing federal regulation of collective bargaining), the Public Utilities Holding Company Act, the Wealth Tax Act, the Banking Act of 1935 (centralizing monetary authority), and the Guffey-Snyder Coal Act (regulating the coal industry). The Emergency Relief Appropriation Act of 1935 enabled Roosevelt to create the Works Progress Administration (WPA), the New Deal relief agency run by Harry Hopkins. Measures enacted during the 1936 session included the Soil Conservation and Domestic Allotment Act and an act establishing the Rural Electrification Administration (REA) as an independent executive agency.[13]

The Congress of 1937–1938 greatly disappointed New Dealers, considering its immense Democratic majorities as Republicans fell to record lows of seventeen Senators and eighty-nine House members.

Many initiatives foundered, including TVA-like designs for other river systems and Roosevelt's plans to pack the Supreme Court and reorganize the executive branch. But at least six significant measures passed. These were the Wagner-Steagall Housing Act (a commitment to low-income public housing), the Farm Tenancy Act (a commitment, ultimately not implemented, to sharecroppers and tenant farmers), the Fair Labor Standards Act (the federal government's original minimum-wage law), the Agricultural Adjustment Act of 1938 (an important consolidating move for the commodity programs), the Robinson-Patman Act of 1938 (to curb alleged unfair price discrimination by chain stores), and an expensive antirecession pump-priming measure in 1938, based on Keynesian doctrine.[14] These enactments brought the era to a close. New Deal reform ideas kept percolating during Roosevelt's remaining years, but few had much success on Capitol Hill.[15]

The Hoover Years.   The start of this era still needs discussion. Although the choice of boundary date is unconventional, it arguably occurred in 1932, at a time when President Herbert Hoover faced a Republican Senate and a Democratic House. This extension of the New Deal "surge" era backwards derives from focusing on which laws of which types actually passed rather than, as is customary, on what Franklin Roosevelt, once elected to the presidency, asked for and received. At least five measures enacted in 1932 deserve mention. Hoover's proposed Reconstruction Finance Corporation (RFC), authorized by Congress that year, became the first alphabet agency of the Depression era. The Glass-Steagall Act permitted a more expansionary monetary policy. The Emergency Relief and Construction Act, engineered by Democrats and progressive Republicans, committed the federal government for the first time to countercyclical public works and relief spending. The prounion Norris-La Guardia Act, one of this century's key measures in the area of labor-management relations, outlawed yellow-dog contracts and curbed the use of antiunion injunctions by courts. Finally, the Revenue Act of 1932, which substantially raised taxes and shifted their incidence in a progressive direction through use of corporate, estate, and high-bracket income levies, came to serve as the federal government's basic revenue instrument of the 1930s. It required an uprising on Capitol Hill during the spring of 1932 for that "most progressive tax law of the decade" to pass: backbench Democrats and progressive Republicans rebelled against the leaderships of both parties to defeat a proposed national sales tax and substitute their own plan. As a producer of recovery and reform measures, as those causes were then understood, the Congress of 1931–1933 arguably ranks with that of 1937–1938.[16]

4. The Johnson-Nixon-Ford Era: 1963 through 1975–1976

Whether one examines gross indicators of congressional workload or lists of major statutes enacted, the early or mid-1960s through the mid-1970s stands out as the era of exceptional legislative productivity since World War II.[17] Best known is the burst of lawmaking during the mid-1960s, bearing the label of Johnson's Great Society. Hardly less striking in retrospect, although the Vietnam war, Nixon's use of "social issues," and the Watergate scandal overshadowed it at the time, is the record of enactments under Nixon and Ford during the period 1969–1976. The ideological direction was largely the same as under Johnson. In general, in the realm of domestic lawmaking, the entire era amounted to one long successful drive to enact a liberal agenda of increased spending, new federal programs, and increased regulation of the society, polity, and economy.[18]

The New Frontier and the Great Society. The era's boundary dates are not clear-cut. The Kennedy administration had won a few legislative victories earlier during the period 1961–1963, but, in general, the New Frontier domestic program stalled, hence the choice of 1963 as the era's opening date. Soon after Kennedy's assassination late that year, and partly because of the new sympathetic political environment created by that event, legislative output ratcheted upward. Within a year, the results included Kennedy's Keynes-inspired tax cut; the Economic Opportunity Act (Johnson's ambitious anti-poverty program); and the Civil Rights Act of 1964, which addressed public accommodations (the most far-reaching civil rights measure since the 1870s); as well as, for example, the Higher Education Facilities Act of 1963; the Wilderness Act of 1964; the Urban Mass Transportation Act of 1964; and the Food Stamp Act of 1964. November 1963 through November 1964—between the assassination and the presidential election—was arguably the most productive peacetime legislative year since 1935. Following Johnson's landslide victory in 1964, the hyperactive congressional session of 1965 went on to produce the Elementary and Secondary Education Act (the first broad-based federal funding of local schools), Medicare and Medicaid, and the Voting Rights Act, as well as many other measures addressing, for example, highway beautification, the arts and humanities, Appalachian development, pollution control, higher education, and subsidized housing.[19]

Late Johnson, Nixon, and Ford. After the Great Society, the story often tails off or becomes cloudy. But in fact, these initiatives under Johnson were just the beginning. In social welfare spending, for example, the country's remarkable post-World War II surge in actual outlays began in 1965 and lasted through 1976, peaking under Ford.[20] Contributing to that surge were many statutes enacted during Johnson's presidency (including major housing acts in 1966 and 1968), but also many passed after 1968 under Nixon and Ford during the period 1969–1976. These included the Food Stamp Act of 1970 (increasing that program's funding by an order of magnitude), Supplementary Security Income in 1972 (federalizing an income floor for the aged, blind, and disabled), the Comprehensive Employment and Training Act of 1973 (creating public sector "CETA jobs" for the unemployed), expansions of unemployment insurance in 1970 and 1976, the Housing and Community Development Act of 1974 (inaugurating federal "block grants"), the Higher Education Act of 1972 (creating "Pell grants" for lower income college students), and a series of Social Security hikes in 1969, 1971, and 1972, which raised benefits 23 percent, controlling for inflation. The Earned Income Tax Credit (EITC) for lower income workers—strictly speaking, a "tax expenditure"—came into existence in 1975 under Ford.[21] According to Robert X. Browning's count, a total of seventy-seven new social programs were initiated under Johnson and forty-four under Nixon and Ford.[22] Other spending initiatives during Nixon's time included federal "revenue sharing" with state and local governments and greatly increased funding authorizations for mass transit and water pollution control.[23]

In the regulatory realm, most of the era's initiatives occurred after Johnson's presidency. The "new social regulation" of American industry, according to David Vogel, took place during roughly 1964 through 1977; the peak reform years were 1969 through 1974, under Nixon and Ford. Two new federal regulatory agencies were established under Johnson and seven under Nixon and Ford.[24] In the area of consumer protection, enactments began with the Traffic Safety Act of 1966 (engendered by Ralph Nader) and the Fair Packaging and Labeling Act of 1966, continuing with, for example, the Truth-in-Lending Act of 1968, the Consumer Product Safety Act of 1972, and the Magnuson-Moss Act of 1974 (which empowered the FTC to set industry-wide rules barring unfair practices).[25] Key environmental measures included the National Environmental Policy Act (NEPA) of 1969, which called for "environmental impact statements"; the Clean Air Act of 1970, the Water Pollution Control Act of 1972, and the Endangered Species Act of 1973.[26] Workplace conditions were addressed in the Coal Mine Health and Safety Act of 1969 and the Occupational Safety and Health Act (OSHA) of 1970. Private pensions received detailed federal regulation for the first time in the Employee Retirement Income Security Act (ERISA) of 1974.[27]

Also, federal regulation of state and local governments set new records under Nixon and Ford—as in, for example, statutory requirements for clean air and water; the Equal Employment Opportunity Act of 1972, which banned discrimination in public employment; and the National Health Planning and Resources Development Act of 1974, which induced lower-level governments into new planning assignments.[28] When confronted by economic difficulties in the early 1970s, Congress reached for planning, not market, remedies—as in the Economic Stabilization Act of 1970, which authorized wage and price controls that Nixon later utilized, and the Emergency Petroleum Allocation Act of 1973, which called for the distribution of petroleum products by government formula. The Federal Election Campaign Act of 1974 brought campaign finance under strict, comprehensive regulation for the first time. Westerners who staged the "sagebrush rebellion" in the late 1970s were reacting to, among other things, two ambitious land-planning measures enacted under Ford—the National Forest Management Act (NFMA) of 1976 and the Federal Land Policy Management Act (FLPMA) of 1976. In the area of rights, the civil rights statutes of 1964 and 1965 were followed by the important Open Housing Act of 1968 and, among other initiatives, an unprecedented variety of women's rights measures enacted during the period 1971–1972, which included the Equal Rights Amendment to the Constitution (ERA), though not enough states finally ratified that initiative.[29]

The preceding highlights the lawmaking thrust of the 1960s–1970s era, which, to be sure, did not end abruptly. A 1977 measure to regulate strip mining, for example, continued the impulse. But, in general, further plans for expenditure and regulation fared poorly under President Carter during the period 1977–1980. Proposals for national health insurance and a consumer protection agency, for example, went nowhere despite sizable Democratic majorities in the House and Senate. Legislative production in general, and of major statutes in particular, fell off. The content shifted; under Carter, *de*regulation of industry arguably became the leading theme in statutes actually passed as trucking, airlines, railroads, banking and natural gas shed government controls. The program-building dynamism of the 1960s and early 1970s was no longer evident. The stage was set for Reagan.[30]

Assessment

These, then, are the four striking legislative surges of U.S. history. Obviously, they do not account for all important laws passed. Virtually any Congress enacts at least some significant legislation. Briefer bursts of lawmaking have occurred that one can categorize as expanding the reach of the national state—starting with basic statutory designs of government institutions and Alexander Hamilton's program to construct a national economy during the period 1789–1791. There was the so-called "billion-dollar Congress" of 1889–1891, under President Benjamin Harrison, run by Republicans, which passed the Sherman Antitrust Act, the Sherman Silver Purchase Act, the McKinley Tariff Act (raising duties), the Naval Act of 1890 (paving the way for the modern Navy), and the Dependent Pension Act of 1890 (greatly expanding the Civil War veterans' pension system).[31] Government size and scope mushroomed as a result of war-mobilization enactments under Wilson during the period 1916–1918 and Roosevelt during the period 1940–1945.[32]

Furthermore, not all major legislation sets out to expand the reach of the national state. Sometimes *dis*engagement of the state from the society or the economy requires major legislative action. That was true of, for example, Reagan's tax and domestic expenditure cuts in 1981, the deregulation moves under Carter, the Twenty-first Amendment repealing Prohibition in 1933, Secretary of the Treasury Andrew Mellon's steep tax cuts in the 1920s, Jefferson's measures to cut taxes, defense, and the national debt after he assumed the presidency in 1801, and Jackson's veto of the bill to recharter the Bank of the United States in 1832. (The latter may be the chief instance of a major American policy change—not just a preservation of the status quo—that derived from using the legislative process to block a bill rather than to pass one.)

Still, the four surges of 1861 through 1875, 1906 through 1916, 1932 through 1938, and 1963 through 1975–1976 seem to stand out for their programmatic ambition, length of time, and volume of major enactments. And it is probably no accident that all four of them exhibited drives to expand the reach of the national state, which is, after all, a kind of undertaking that is likely to require a great deal of strenuous legislative action.

CAUSES OF LEGISLATIVE SURGES

What can be said about the causes—or at least correlates—of the four major legislative surges outlined above? Chiefly at issue here is the causal force of presidential elections, but that factor can perhaps be explored most illuminatingly by placing it in a more general context. The causal discussion here will proceed under four rubrics, of which the first two afford a role for presidential elections.

1. Elections

Are legislative surges traceable in a more or less direct way to election outcomes? That is, have elections proximately preceded, or at least occurred at prominent junctures within, the legislative surges and arguably brought them about or spurred them on?

Realignment Elections.   This is to raise, for one thing, the subject of "electoral realignments"—the major reconfigurations in American popular voting patterns that are said to have taken place in or around 1800, 1828, 1860, 1896, and 1932. In the well-known literature on this subject, these elections are seen as boundary points between successive "party systems."[33] Such "realignments" evidently helped to spur the lawmaking surges during the periods 1861–1875 and 1932–1938. It is difficult to imagine the former surge without the Republicans' rise to power from 1854 to 1860 or the latter without the Democrats' sizable congressional gains in 1930 and 1932 and Franklin Roosevelt's landslide victory in 1932. The analogy between the Civil War and Reconstruction era Republicans and the New Deal era Democrats is perhaps the most attractive feature of realignment theory.

But aside from those two junctures, "electoral realignments" do not explain or illuminate legislative surges.[34] Consider American history since the 1870s. The surges of the Progressive era and the 1960s through the 1970s are not traceable to any electoral revolutions that "realignment" theorists include in their canon. And the realignment of 1896, historic though that may have been by virtue of its changes in popular voting patterns, its defeat of William Jennings Bryan's bid for the presidency, and its production of a new dominant Republican coalition, did not provoke any legislative surge. The new McKinley Republicans, possessing solid congressional majorities, might have been expected to repeat their party's lawmaking dynamism of a decade earlier under Benjamin Harrison, but they did not. Their legislative record during the period 1897–1901 was at best ordinary.[35] The leading enactments of that time seem to have been the Gold Standard Act of 1900, which upheld the gold standard that Grover Cleveland's Democratic administration had protected so tenaciously during the period 1893–1897, and the Dingley Tariff Act of 1897, which, following reductions under Cleveland, returned rates to high Republican levels (higher ones for dutiable imports, though lower ones for all imports, than in the party's McKinley Tariff Act of 1890).[36] The legislative doldrums experienced under McKinley decisively disconfirm any theory that posits a one-to-one relationship between electoral realignments and activist lawmaking.

Authorizing and Deauthorizing Elections. But a more commonsensical question can be asked about elections. Are there particular ones—besides the "realigning" ones already noted—that seemed to have helped authorize or deauthorize Congress to undertake legislative surges? There are obvious candidates for those roles, although, to be fair to the evidence, the search for them needs to be broad enough to accommodate congressional midterm elections as well as presidential contests. On the authorizing side, the post-Civil War midterm of 1866 was viewed by many contemporaries as a showdown referendum between President Andrew Johnson and Congress's radical Republicans, over how to deal with the conquered South; the latter won and Reconstruction ensued. The 1910 midterm election brought not only a generally Democratic tide but also a decisive defeat for the Republicans' conservative wing in state and district primaries; these results probably helped along the Progressive agenda in the next Congress. Woodrow Wilson and the Democratic party claimed a mandate for their brand of Progressivism after the 1912 election; lawmaking under the New Freedom banner ensued. The 1964 election contributed to the Great Society cause by producing Johnson's landslide mandate as well as a rare new two-to-one Democratic edge in the House; the energetic legislative session of 1965 followed. To be very contemporary, the 1994 midterm seemed to many at the time to authorize fulfillment of Newt Gingrich and the House Republicans' "Contract with America."

On the deauthorizing side, the Republicans' disastrous defeat in the 1874 midterm election is almost certainly part of the reason why the lawmaking of the Reconstruction era came to an end. And the 1918 and 1938 midterms, occasioning decisive Democratic losses under Woodrow Wilson and Franklin Roosevelt in their second terms, are often associated with the flagging reform impulses of Progressivism and the New Deal, although that argument should not be carried too far. World War I is more often cited as having put an end to Progressivism at the national level, and the New Deal was already suffering from conflict between Roosevelt supporters and increasingly powerful conservative forces on Capitol Hill in the two years leading to the 1938 election.

Particular elections help—midterm as well as presidential ones—but they leave a good deal unaccounted for. Notably left unexplained is the spurring of Progressivism at the national level by Theodore Roosevelt during the period 1905–1906; this is not ordinarily attributed to any electoral mandate (although it is possible that Roosevelt's record-setting landslide victory of 1904 has not been properly interpreted). Also, the move away from government activism under Carter during the period 1977–1980 does not seem to have stemmed from any deauthorizing election, presidential or congressional (although Reagan's victory in 1980 may be said to have ratified it).

Leadership Conversion.   Of course, the subject of electoral connections is not exhausted by pointing to particular elections and their alleged sweeping verdicts. Incumbent parties or politicians can accommodate major changes in public opinion by switching along with it, if they are alert. Major changes in government policy can thus occur without the stimulus of any party's election gains or losses, though those often contribute. In the 1870s, for example, Republican politicians dialed downward their support for Reconstruction on a schedule that evidently matched northern public opinion. During the period 1977–1978, Senate and House members seem to have gone along with what they saw as a swell of opinion against government spending and regulation. Some just changed their positions. In 1975, Republican Congressman John B. Anderson of Illinois had supported the controversial Naderite proposal to create a consumer protection agency; in 1977, apparently in response to new constituency sentiment, he came out against it. During those same years, liberal Democratic Senator Edward Kennedy surprisingly took on deregulation of industry as a new personal cause. Broad policy change can come about through conversion of incumbent members as well as membership change through election upheavals.[37]

2. Political Parties

Party Government.   To what degree can the laws of any surge be credited to one political party that controls government and monopolizes the legislative initiative and thus shapes an era? That is perhaps the leading question to ask about parties. By extension, it is also a question about elections, both presidential and congressional, since whether a party gets a chance to exercise such monopoly power owes to configurations of election results. If "party government" always functioned unambiguously in the United States, the answer to the question as posed would be obvious: legislative surges would always be entirely traceable to one party. But the reality is more complicated and it varies over time.

Without much doubt, the leading instance of a surge driven by one party was that of the Civil War and Reconstruction era. To be sure, serious disagreement occurred between "radicals" and moderates of the ruling Republican party and between President Andrew Johnson and Congress. In addition, because the southern states seceded from Congress in 1861, the lawmaking afterward has the flavor of a northern, not just a Republican party, surge. The absence of the Southerners permitted not only the anti-slavery measures, but also such Whiggish initiatives as the tariff and transcontinental railroad acts. Still, the Republican party won every presidential and congressional election between 1860 and 1874, and its leaders advanced all the important laws during that time.

Much more complicated was the record of the Progressive era. Parties or their leaders had lawmaking roles, but those varied over time and often departed from the "party government" model. Through 1908, at both state and national levels, reform-oriented executive leaders of the Republican party provided most of the era's programmatic impulse. The most prominent instances are Theodore Roosevelt as president and Governors Robert La Follette of Wisconsin and Charles Evans Hughes of New York. But Republicans supplied the chief opposition also—the Aldrich-Cannon regime on Capitol Hill and comparable conservative factions in the state legislatures. From 1909 through 1912, the progenitors of notable reform programs were typically cross-party coalitions of Democrats and progressive Republicans. That happened in the national government under President Taft as well as in, for example, Massachusetts, New Jersey (under Democratic Governor Woodrow Wilson), and North Dakota. After the 1912 election, the Democratic party took over as the successful proposer and carrier of legislative programs—in the national capital under President Wilson, but also in states such as New York and Ohio (under Governor James M. Cox).[38]

The New Deal was obviously engineered by the Democratic party or its leaders. It consisted largely of enactments initiated by Franklin Roosevelt or other liberal Democrats—Senator Robert F. Wagner of New York, for example, in the cases of the National Labor Relations Act of 1935 and the Wagner-Steagall Housing Act of 1937—and enacted by Congresses containing immense Democratic majorities. As a matter of electoral accountability, the Democrats certainly won credit for the achievements of the era. Still, the record was somewhat more muddled at the level of actual lawmaking. In fact, the 1930 election and the Great Depression revived the cross-party coalition of Democrats and insurgent Republicans who had won congressional victories—notably in initiating the progressive income tax—during the Taft and Wilson presidencies. That coalition put across, for example, the Revenue Act of 1932 and the Emergency Relief and Construction Act of 1932. Progressive Republicans (or former Republicans) took the lead on some key measures that year and also afterward. An example is Senator George Norris's role in enacting the Norris-La Guardia Act of 1932 (New York's

Fiorello La Guardia was also then an insurgent Republican) and establishing the Tennessee Valley Authority in 1933. Progressive Republicans receded in significance as the decade wore on, but after 1934, another development swerved the New Deal away from any single textbook model of "party government." President Roosevelt's policy initiatives increasingly divided his own party. By 1937, with the Republican party devastated and silent, congressional Democrats provided the president's chief opposition as well as his chief ranks of Capitol Hill support. The anti-Roosevelt Democratic faction included more than just conservative Southerners: one leader in the winning struggles against Roosevelt's court-packing and executive reorganization plans during the period 1937–1938 was, for example, Senator Burton Wheeler of Montana, who had accrued excellent progressive as well as Democratic party credentials. This was an odd brand of "party government."

No one would contest a general claim that the Democratic party was responsible for enacting Johnson's Great Society program in the mid-1960s. The major civil rights acts of 1964, 1965, and 1968 were something of an exception: on these measures the House and Senate roll calls pitted Northerners against Southerners, regardless of party, rather than Democrats against Republicans. Nevertheless, the Great Society's housing, health insurance, education, and antipoverty initiatives unquestionably offer a leading instance of party-based lawmaking. Yet, as the era's lawmaking impulse continued beyond 1968, the simplicity of rule by one party gave way. In general, the legislative initiative stayed with the Democrats—but now it was lodged in that party's congressional branch. Thus, for example, the National Environmental Policy Act of 1969 was advanced by Senator Henry Jackson of Washington, the Clean Air Act of 1970 by Senator Edmund Muskie of Maine, the 23 percent Social Security hike of 1972 by Congressman Wilbur Mills of Arkansas, the Equal Rights Amendment in 1972 by Senator Birch Bayh of Indiana, and the Earned Income Tax Credit of 1975 by Senator Russell Long of Louisiana. One Democratic legislative campaign after another succeeded. But the Nixon administration played a role also. Many spending and regulatory measures were championed by the White House—for instance, the major expansion of the food stamp program in 1970—or at least enjoyed Nixon's collaboration or acquiescence. At odds on many matters, Nixon and congressional Democrats shared a surprising joint responsibility for the era's domestic spending and regulatory record.

In summary, the clearest case for a "party government" model of lawmaking, notwithstanding the adversarial role played by President Andrew Johnson, is probably that of the 1861–1875 period. The New Deal is a good case. In the 1960s and 1970s, there was an approximation of "party government" under Johnson but bipartisan cooperation and conflict under Nixon. In the Progressive era, even though one party or the other promoted many legislative victories at various times at state and national levels, the overall pattern is exceptionally diverse.

Unified versus Divided Control. To ask a slightly different question about parties, to what extent have legislative surges occurred during times of unified party control of the national government—that is, times when one party, by virtue of election results possessed formal majorities in the Senate and House and also held the presidency? This is worth asking, since it is a common view in political science and, more generally, that such unified control is a necessary condition for major lawmaking. Otherwise, it has been argued by James L. Sundquist and others, "deadlock" or "stalemate" between the parties will occur.[39]

The surge of the 1861–1875 period offers a nearly pure case. Republicans controlled the presidency, the House, and Senate during those years, and they used that control to enact laws. The "nearly" qualification derives from taking account of President Andrew Johnson, in power during the period 1865–1869, whose connection to the Republican party was ambiguous and whose vetoes had to be overridden during those years for the program of the party's congressional majority to prevail. In general, they were and it did, at least at the level of passing laws; implementation proved more difficult.

The New Deal era presents another nearly pure case. Unified Democratic control of the government underlay all the legislative action beginning with the "hundred days" in 1933. The qualification owes to the era's initial burst of lawmaking in 1932 under Hoover, who, to be sure, blocked certain important initiatives but promoted or at least signed others.

The 1960s and 1970s are a mixed case. Unified Democratic control provided the setting for Johnson's Great Society and lasted until the 1968 election. But major legislative initiatives continued to pass under Nixon and even Ford, despite the shift in 1968 to divided control as Democrats kept their majorities in the House and Senate.

Various patterns prevailed during the Progressive era. Some major legislative programs were enacted under conditions of unified-control "party government." That was particularly true about Woodrow Wilson's presidential program during the period 1913–1916, as national party leader Wilson worked through Democratic party caucuses on Capitol Hill. At the state level, Democrats in control of governorships and legislatures enacted ambitious programs during those same years, for example, in New York and Ohio. Theodore Roosevelt won his program from a Republican Congress during the period 1905–1906 (though in fact his fellow partisans balked at times and he needed Democratic help), as did Governor Hughes from a Republican legislature in New York in 1907. Wisconsin's government was formally all-Republican when La Follette enacted his program in 1903 and 1905, as was California's when Hiram Johnson's program passed in 1911. But in fact this is misleading since the chief opposition to reform in these latter states, out of power because of losses in nominating processes, was also Republican. And many notable legislative programs at the state level—including those referred to above in North Dakota, Minnesota, Massachusetts, and New Jersey (under Woodrow Wilson as governor)—were enacted under circumstances of formally divided party control. Nationally, that was also the story under Taft during the period 1911–1913, when much lawmaking occurred despite a switch to divided control. During the Progressive era, major legislative programs were enacted in an impressive variety of formal party circumstances.[40]

"Party Voting" in Congress.　　One more question might be asked about parties. Does congressional "party voting," as political scientists define the concept, rise during times of legislative surges? The idea might be that that kind of party-versus-party confrontation is required to enact major laws. A "party voting" score, which can be calculated for the House or Senate for any Congress, reports the proportion of all roll calls on which a majority of Democrats opposed a majority of Republicans. The overall answer to the question is close to an unqualified no.[41] For the House, for example, between 1861 and 1984, the mean "party voting" score for Congresses during the four legislative surges was sixty; for other Congresses it was fifty-seven. There is a long-term decline in the statistic, it should be said, that makes simple averaging problematic. The best bits of evidence for a positive connection are that the 1861–1875 Congresses scored about four points higher, on average, than those of 1875–1891 (perhaps a fair comparison); and that the Congresses of 1931–1938 scored some nine points higher than those of the preceding Republican decade (1921–1930). Those results, which juxtapose the Civil War-Reconstruction and New Deal eras to neighboring periods of relatively low legislative productivity, show at least a modest relation between high "party voting" and legislative surges. But "party voting" did not stand out during the Progressive era, and it reached its nadir during Nixon's presidency, hitting an all-time low of 29 percent during the period 1969–1970. A fair inference is that "party voting" rises slightly during legislative surges where one party in fact produces the laws, but that it will not rise—it may even fall—during surges other-

wise. That would be understandable. The overall relation between the two variables, therefore, is weak or nonexistent. Confronted by just a time series on congressional "party voting," from 1861 to the present, one would have no way of knowing when the legislative surges took place. That holds for the Senate as well as the House. In very recent years—the late 1980s and early 1990s—congressional "party voting" has risen to heights not seen for many decades, without being accompanied by remarkable records of lawmaking.

Assessment of Parties.   Are parties, then, the producers of legislative surges? The historical trend is mixed and complicated. For the Civil War-Reconstruction and New Deal eras, yes is a plausible answer. The Progressive era presents the opposite extreme, for it is a good bet that ambitious lawmaking would somehow have occurred anyway—that the parties were secondary, even though they sometimes played prominent roles. Furthermore, in regard to party, the dominant impulse of the era was largely *against* parties. In the 1960s and 1970s, the Democratic party, or at least entrepreneurs within it, supplied most of the legislative dynamism, though the Nixon administration figured importantly too, and divided party control reigned after 1968. There is no clear trend in party role between the 1860s and the 1990s: the New Deal, for example, ranks higher in legislative achievement by one dominant party than does the Progressive era. Still, the pre–1900 data on party control, party voting, and legislative surges are compatible, at least, with the idea that parties were more central to governmental functioning in the nineteenth century than they have become in the twentieth. Possibly, they were.

Beyond that, there exists a plausible argument that conditions allowing a greater detachment of energetic lawmaking from single party control of the government have arisen since World War II. It is during these recent decades that elections have taken a turn toward candidate-specific (as opposed to party) appeals, and that both Congress and the presidency have adopted legislative practices that transcend, in a sense, parties. These include the annual presentation of "the president's program," and Congress's immensely improved staffing that permits countless legislative initiatives regardless of which parties control which branches. We may see more of the kind of ambitious cross-party lawmaking that took place under Nixon.

3. The Economy

There are at least two routes by which the state of the economy might be hypothesized to underpin legislative surges. The first does not involve elections in any clear way. The second may or may not involve elections, but when it does, they recede into the secondary role of transmitting economic signals to the government. Causal power, from this perspective, resides in the economy.

Underlying Economic Conditions.   The first route is a relatively static model in which basic underlying conditions in the economy might distinctively affect legislative action. Thus, it is sometimes argued that the lawmaking surge under Johnson and Nixon during the 1960s and 1970s required a high-growth economy as a base—that is, to provide the necessary slack for spending commitments and regulatory experiments. But lower the growth rate, bring on budgetary pressure, and the lawmaking would tail off as it indeed did in the mid-1970s. Possibly a similar prosperity-based argument could be made about the Progressive era. Unfortunately, the New Deal era presents an exactly opposite scenario: the uniquely dismal economy of the 1930s accommodated pathbreaking spending and regulatory drives by an activist government. The New Deal is a devastating disconfirmation of any theory that associates economic prosperity with lawmaking.

Economic Downturns.   Precipitous economic downturns offer the second possibility—as either provokers or dampeners of legislative surges. They might cause election upheavals that in turn cause legislative moves on Capitol Hill or, without that, they might cause alarm in the public that impinges in turn on elected officials. The leading instance is the Great Depression of 1929, which triggered huge electoral gains for the Democratic party that unquestionably set the stage for the legislative surge of the 1930s.

However, economic slumps seem to have helped close, rather than open, at least two of the surge eras—those of the Civil War-Reconstruction and the New Deal. The depression of 1873 was evidently one major cause of the Republicans' decisive loss of the House in 1874. The precipitous recession of late 1937 through early 1938 seems to have helped turn public opinion against further New Deal experiments; that in turn hobbled Roosevelt's legislative drive well before the 1938 election.

Some economic downturns, moreover, may not lead to legislative surges. The major depression of 1893, for example, instrumental as it probably was in elevating the Republican party to power for a generation, did not open, close, or figure in any of the prominent legislative surges of American history. Thus, economic slumps may encourage or discourage legislative surges, or they may have negligible impact. In general, sharp economic downturns delegitimize any governing party along with its economic policies; the opposition, whatever it stands for, comes to look like a good bet for power.[42]

4. Moods and Movements

Public Moods.   Another view of the causes of lawmaking surges would emphasize "public moods." Arthur M. Schlesinger, Jr. has argued that Americans periodically become caught up in moods of "public purpose"—a kind of secular revivalism. Large numbers of citizens throw themselves into public affairs for periods as long as a decade with the aim of reforming politics and society—and then tire of such efforts and recede into private pursuits like those associated with the quiet generations of the 1920s and 1950s. Schlesinger points to the Progressive era, the New Deal era, and the 1960s–1970s period as twentieth-century instances of activist eras. Obviously, the activist "moods" said to be exhibited during these eras map very well onto the century's three legislative surges.[43]

"Public moods" are more difficult to get an empirical handle on than are economic downturns or election results, but in fact, historians and other witnesses have often pointed precisely to "mood changes" as the reasons why legislative surges began or ended. All four endings have been given that interpretation: in each case, after years of unending energetic reform, there occurred a quite abrupt onset of activism fatigue that brought lawmaking and other reform endeavors to a halt. In the mid-1870s, the North is said to have lost its faith that Reconstruction might work and, hence, its activist drive.[44] Under Woodrow Wilson, World War I is said to have drained away all remaining public purpose for domestic as well as international causes; a "mood change" thus took place that in turn affected Capitol Hill.[45] A pronounced anti-New Deal "mood shift" is detected during the period 1937–1938; the economy's new downturn at that time combined with other events to sow pessimism about the New Deal enterprise in general.[46] Finally, the activism of the 1960s and 1970s is said to have lost out to a "mood shift" under Carter: the idea that society could be improved through government action gave way to pessimism, apathy, successful drives to deregulate industry, the "Sagebrush Rebellion," and the low tax ideology of California's Proposition 13.[47]

As for the beginnings of legislative surges, analysts assign prominence to a "mood change" in only one case, though there it is the leading interpretation. It involves the Progressive era, whose onset of lawmaking surges at both state and federal levels is conventionally traced to a "mood shift" toward reform activism occurring roughly in 1905. Muckraking by journalists such as Ida Tarbell and Lincoln Steffens had set the stage for it since 1902. Neither an election result nor a downturn in the economy seems to have played a role.[48] In all of American history, the beginning of the Progressive era stands out as the juncture where a "mood" account decisively outperforms competing theories.

Political Movements. Much of the dynamism of "public purpose" moods seems to be provided by political movements. The Progressive era was animated either by one long-lasting, all-embracing movement or by a variety of narrower allied ones, depending on one's interpretation. Some of that era's lawmaking can be directly traced to movement action, as Theda Skocpol has claimed for the women's movement and Congress's establishment of the Children's Bureau in 1912.[49] In the 1960s and 1970s, a sizable number of loosely allied movements—civil rights, consumer, antiwar, labor, student, women's liberation, environmental, and "public interest" groups—pursued reform campaigns. Again, particular laws enacted largely as a result can be cited: the civil rights movement, through demonstrations led by Martin Luther King, Jr. in Birmingham and Selma, was instrumental in bringing about the Civil Rights Acts of 1964 and 1965; the consumer movement, the Fair Packaging and Labeling Act of 1966 and the Consumer Product Safety Act of 1972; the environmental movement, the major clean air and water measures of 1970 and 1972; the women's movement, congressional approval of the ERA in 1972; and the public interest group Common Cause, the Federal Election Campaign Act of 1974.[50] In the case of the 1860s and 1870s, Eric Foner interprets Reconstruction as having had a movement activist base that took form as early as 1863 and lasted into the 1870s.[51] The New Deal era is least satisfactorily explicable by reference to movements. Roosevelt's "hundred days" of lawmaking in 1933 seems to have drawn on the country's obvious sense of economic emergency at that time, not movement effervescence. Still, it is becoming increasingly evident that lively movement activity by Townsendite pension advocates, share-the-wealth followers of Huey Long, labor union organizers, and even the Communist party provided an important part of the underpinning of Roosevelt's "second hundred days" in 1935.[52] Some analysts credit that session's Social Security Act, National Labor Relations Act, and Wealth Tax Act substantially to background movement pressure; members of Congress felt it and responded.[53] It was not just huge Democratic congressional majorities in Washington; there was an upwelling of the left outside.

CONCLUSION

These four accounts of legislative surges—addressing parties, elections, the economy, and public moods and movements—obviously overlap. An economic downturn, for example, may bring about an electoral upheaval or a mood shift. A mood shift may contribute to an electoral shift. An election turnover may be read by contemporaries as evidence of a mood shift. Movement activism may colonize a party and provide it dynamism, as evidently happened with the Republican party during Reconstruction (though no longer after the mid-1870s). But no one neat set of causal or correlative relations applies to all four of the prominent legislative surges of American history. Lawmaking via "party government" has occurred in some eras but not others. Economic downturns have started or stopped legislative activity at some times but not at others. Public moods and movements seem to be the most reliable factor; they somehow have figured in the dynamics of every legislative surge, though they are so elusive empirically that it is hard to get a fix on exactly when they exist or what they may be causing.

As for presidential elections—the chief concern of this essay—they play a role but not as consequentially or frequently as we imagine. In particular, "realigning elections," which are often advanced as the paramount political events of U.S. history, have not mapped all that well onto legislative surges. They have proven to be neither a necessary cause of such surges—consider the Progressive era and the 1960s–1970s period—nor a sufficient one—consider the 1890s. Beyond that, individual presidential elections can of course contribute to surges—consider 1912 and 1964—as can congressional midterms—consider 1866 and 1910. But such contributions are normally wrapped up in a multicausal package whose ingredients include events in the economy and the gyrations of public moods and movements.

At least, one might think, elections would leave a deposit of distinctive policymaking capacity whenever they elevate one party to simultaneous control of the presidency, the Senate, and the House. But there also the historical record is muddled: legislative surges have not corresponded all that neatly to times of unified party control. Consider, for example, the strenuous lawmaking during Nixon's years of divided party control, as compared with the relatively fallow legislative records under Truman, Kennedy, and Carter—all of whom enjoyed periods of one party rule.

There is a lesson here for the 1990s. At last, it was said in November 1992 when Clinton won the presidency and Democrats retained solid control of the House and Senate, we are in for another exercise of activist lawmaking. We were about to experience, to use the language of this essay, a new legislative surge. Immense programs were drawn up. The "hundred days" metaphor was dusted off.

But then, as the months elapsed during 1993 and 1994, it became increasingly clear that no such Rooseveltian surge would materialize. True, the newly ascendant Democrats enacted certain programs that a government composed of a reelected Bush administration and a Democratic Congress would most likely not have enacted—notably the Family Leave Act of 1993, the "motor voter" act of 1993, Clinton's National Service Program of 1993, and the steep tax hike on high incomes included in the Deficit Reduction Act of 1993. But this was a modest record, more like Truman's during the period 1949–1950, Kennedy's in 1961–1962, or Carter's in 1977–1978, than like Roosevelt's in 1933 and 1935 or Johnson's in 1964–1965.[54]

In terms of actual enactments, Clinton's first Congress turned out to be not all that different from the two preceding Congresses under Bush. The Family Leave Act was an innovation in the area of regulating industry, as was the Clean Air Act of 1990, the Americans with Disabilities Act of 1990, and the Civil Rights Act of 1991—all signed into law by Bush. The final version of Clinton's Deficit Reduction Act of 1993 had much in common with the Deficit Reduction Act of 1990, engineered earlier by congressional Democrats and the Bush administration—that is, a nearly $500 billion five-year bite out of the cumulative deficit (in fact, the 1993 bite ended up somewhat smaller than the 1990 one),[55] sizable cuts in defense, a hike in high-bracket income taxes (though a larger one in 1993), and increased funding for the Earned Income Tax Credit (up $12 billion in 1990 and up $20 billion in 1993).[56] The major trade agreements ratified under Clinton, the North American Free Trade Agreement (NAFTA) and the General Agreement on Tariffs and Trade (GATT), had been Bush enterprises. Campaign finance reform, an antirecession stimulus bill, and several environmental initiatives had failed to win enactment under Bush; similar measures failed under Clinton also. Health care reform, Clinton's programmatic centerpiece and his bid to rival Roosevelt and Johnson as a legislative leader, failed completely in 1994. Crime measures—the "Brady Bill," requiring a waiting period to buy handguns, and the Omnibus Act of 1994—won a new level of success under Clinton, but that was probably because opinion polls showed a significant rise in concern about crime, beginning in late 1993.[57]

What happened at the time of Clinton's election in 1992, the argument goes here, is that analysts who predicted a new legislative surge were buying too heavily into the causal power of elections. In fact, a presidential election victory, even if clothed in a claimed mandate, is not enough. Solid one party control of the government is not enough. Just about entirely lacking in the United States during the period 1993–1994 was the mix of activist public mood and movement effervescence that, in the past, has probably done more than anything else to foster legislative surges. A president or party unfortified by such public enthusiasm faces an uphill struggle.

NOTES

1. This chapter is an adapted and expanded version of "Parties, Elections, Moods, and Lawmaking Surges" by David R. Mayhew. Used by permission of Charles Scribner's Sons, a Division of Simon & Schuster, from *Encyclopedia of the American Legislative System*, Joel H. Silbey, Editor in Chief. Vol. II, pp. 885–895. Copyright © 1994 Charles Scribner's Sons.

2. (New Haven: Yale University Press, 1991).

3. John Mark Hansen, "Taxation and the Political Economy of the Tariff," *International Organization* 44 (Autumn 1990): 527–51.

4. Leonard P. Curry, *Blueprint for Modern America: Nonmilitary Legislation of the First Civil War Congress* (Nashville: Vanderbilt University Press, 1968), Chapters 2–8, 11; J. G. Randall and David Donald, *The Civil War and Reconstruction* (Boston: Little, Brown, 1969), pp. 283–92, 344–53.

5. Randall and Donald, *Civil War and Reconstruction*, pp. 284–85, 372–73, 576–86, Chapter 34, pp. 641–43; Curry, *Blueprint for Modern America*, Chapters 2, 3; William Gillette, *Retreat from Reconstruction, 1869–1879* (Baton Rouge: Louisiana State University Press, 1979), pp. 17–20.

6. Ibid., Chapters 2, 8, 11; S. G. F. Spackman, "American Federalism and the Civil Rights Act of 1875," *Journal of American Studies* 10 (1976): 313–28.

7. Richard L. McCormick, "The Discovery That Business Corrupts Politics: A Reappraisal of the Origins of Progressivism," *American Historical Review* 86 (April 1981): 266–68; George E. Mowry, *The Era of Theodore Roosevelt, 1900–1912* (New York: Harper and Brothers, 1958), pp. 71–84; David Sarasohn, *The Party of Reform: Democrats in the Progressive Era* (Jackson: University Press of Mississippi, 1989), pp. 112–18; Mayhew, *Divided We Govern*, pp. 146–48.

8. *The Rhetorical Presidency* (Princeton, N.J.: Princeton University Press, 1987), p. 101.

9. On lawmaking during Theodore Roosevelt's second administration: Mowry, *Era of Theodore Roosevelt*, Chapter 11; John Morton Blum, *The Republican Roosevelt* (Cambridge, Mass.: Harvard University Press, 1977), pp. 87–105; John Milton Cooper, Jr., *Pivotal Decades: The United States, 1900–1920* (New York: Norton, 1990), Chapter 4; Lewis L. Gould, *Reform and Regulation: American Politics, 1900–1916* (New York: Wiley, 1978), Chapter 3; Stephen Skowronek, *Building a New American State: The Expansion of National Administrative Capacities, 1877–1920* (New York: Cambridge University Press, 1982), pp. 255–59; Robert M. Crumden, *Ministers of Reform: The Progressives' Achievement in American Civilization* (New York: Basic Books, 1982), Chapter 6; Elmer E. Cornwell, Jr., *Presidential Leadership of Public Opinion* (Bloomington: Indiana University Press, 1965), pp. 24–26; Mayhew, *Divided We Govern*, pp. 118–19, 148–49, 157.

10. On lawmaking under Taft: Mowry, *Era of Theodore Roosevelt*, Chapter 12; Cooper, *Pivotal Decades*, Chapter 5; Gould, *Reform and Regulation*, Chapter 4; Paolo E. Coletta, *The Presidency of William Howard Taft* (Lawrence: University Press of Kansas, 1973), Chapters 3, 5–7, 13; Kenneth W. Hechler, *Insurgency: Personalities and Politics of the Taft Era* (New York: Columbia University Press, 1940), Chapter 8; Sarasohn, *Party of Reform*, Chapter 4; Mayhew, *Divided We Govern*, pp. 149–51; Skowronek, *Building a New American State*, pp. 261–67; Robert E. Mutch, *Campaigns, Congress, and Courts: The Making of Federal Campaign Finance Law* (New York: Praeger, 1988), pp. 1–16.

11. On lawmaking under Wilson: Arthur S. Link, *Woodrow Wilson and the Progressive Era, 1910–1917* (New York: Harper and Brothers, 1954), Chapters 2, 3, 9; Gould, *Reform and Regulation*, Chapter 6; Sarasohn, *Party of Reform*, pp. 183–89; Cooper, *Pivotal Decades*, Chapter 7; W. Elliot Brownlee, "Wilson and Financing the Modern State: The Revenue Act of 1916," *Proceedings of the American Philosophical Society* 129 (1985): 173–210; Mayhew, *Divided We Govern*, pp. 151–52.

12. William E. Leuchtenberg, *Franklin D. Roosevelt and the New Deal, 1932–1940* (New York: Harper and Row, 1963), Chapter 3 and pp. 85–86, 90–91, 135, 203–05; Arthur M. Schlesinger, Jr., *The Coming of the New Deal* (Boston: Houghton Mifflin, 1958), Chapters 2, 3, 6, 15–17, 19, 20, 26, 28; Albert U. Romasco, *The Politics of Recovery: Roosevelt's New Deal* (New York: Oxford University Press, 1983), Chapter 3.

13. Leuchtenberg, *Franklin D. Roosevelt and the New Deal*, pp. 124–33, Chapter 7, pp. 171–73; Schlesinger, *Coming of the New Deal*, Chap-

ters 18, 24; Arthur M. Schlesinger, Jr., *The Politics of Upheaval* (Boston: Houghton Mifflin, 1960), pp. 261–70, Chapters 16–18, pp. 381–84; James T. Patterson, *Congressional Conservatism and the New Deal: The Growth of the Conservative Coalition in Congress, 1933–1939* (Lexington: University Press of Kentucky, 1967), Chapter 2 and pp. 77–80.

14. Leuchtenberg, *Franklin D. Roosevelt and the New Deal*, pp. 135–42 and Chapters 10, 11; Patterson, *Congressional Conservatism*, pp. 11, 159, 233–46; James MacGregor Burns, *Roosevelt: The Lion and the Fox* (New York: Harcourt, Brace, 1956), Chapters 15–17; Barry D. Karl, *The Uneasy State: The United States from 1915 to 1945* (Chicago: University of Chicago Press, 1983), pp. 167–69.

15. John W. Jeffries, "The 'New' Deal: FDR and American Liberalism, 1937–1945," *Political Science Quarterly* 105 (Fall 1990): 397–418; Edwin Amenta and Theda Skocpol, "Redefining the New Deal: World War II and the Development of Social Provision in the United States," Chapter 2 in Margaret Weir, Ann Shola Orloff, and Theda Skocpol, eds., *The Politics of Social Policy in the United States* (Princeton, N.J.: Princeton University Press, 1988).

16. David Burner, *Herbert Hoover: A Public Life* (New York: Knopf, 1979), pp. 270–82, quotation at 282; Harris G. Warren, *Herbert Hoover and the Great Depression* (New York: Oxford University Press, 1959), Chapters 9–13; Jordan A. Schwarz, *The Interregnum of Despair: Hoover, Congress, and the Depression* (Urbana: University of Illinois Press, 1970), pp. 78–98 and Chapters 5, 6, 8; Mayhew, *Divided We Govern*, pp. 154–56. (Note that Congress traditionally held lame-duck post-election sessions—such as in early 1933—until the Twentieth Amendment abolished them, starting in 1935.)

17. Post-World War II legislative workload is discussed in Roger H. Davidson, "The New Centralization on Capitol Hill," *Review of Politics* 50 (Summer 1988): 349–50. Major statutes enacted by Congress between 1946 and 1990 are listed and discussed in Mayhew, *Divided We Govern*, Chapters 3, 4. This study is based on two sweeps through the history of those years, one using judgments rendered at the time by contemporaries (chiefly journalists) about the importance of statutes just enacted by each Congress, the other using retrospective judgments by policy specialists (writing chiefly in the 1980s) about the importance of statutes enacted in their fields during the preceding decades.

18. For analyses that explicitly compare the lawmaking record of the 1960s and 1970s (not just that of the Great Society) with those of the Progressive and New Deal eras, see Theda Skocpol, "A Society without a 'State'? Political Organization, Social Conflict, and Wel-

fare Provision in the United States," *Journal of Public Policy* 7 (1987): 364–65; and Richard A. Harris, "A Decade of Reform," Chapter 1 in Harris and Sidney M. Milkis, eds., *Remaking American Politics* (Boulder, Colo.: Westview, 1989), pp. 5, 9.

19. James L. Sundquist, *Politics and Policy: The Eisenhower, Kennedy, and Johnson Years* (Washington, D.C.: Brookings, 1968); Mayhew, *Divided We Govern*, Chapters 3, 4.

20. Robert J. Lampman, *Social Welfare Spending: Accounting for Changes from 1950 to 1978* (New York: Academic Press, 1984), pp. 8–9.

21. Christopher Howard, "The Hidden Side of the American Welfare State," *Political Science Quarterly* 108 (Fall 1993): 403–36.

22. *Politics and Social Welfare Policy in the United States* (Knoxville: University of Tennessee Press, 1986), pp. 79–83.

23. On spending initiatives under Nixon and Ford: Timothy Conlan, *New Federalism: Intergovernmental Reform from Nixon to Reagan* (Washington, D.C.: Brookings, 1988), pp. 81–82; Jodie T. Allen, "Last of the Big Spenders: Richard Nixon and the Greater Society," *Washington Post*, February 24, 1983, p. A15; Browning, *Politics and Social Welfare Policy*, pp. 79–83, 95, 110–11, 142–48, 161; James T. Patterson, *America's Struggle Against Poverty, 1900–1985* (Cambridge, Mass.: Harvard University Press, 1986), pp. 158, 165, 197–98; R. Allen Hays, *The Federal Government and Urban Housing: Ideology and Change in Public Policy* (Albany: State University of New York Press, 1985), pp. 150–53; Martha Derthick, *Policymaking for Social Security* (Washington, D.C.: Brookings, 1979), Chapter 17; Mayhew, *Divided We Govern*, pp. 81–85.

24. David Vogel, "The 'New' Social Regulation in Historical and Comparative Perspective," in Thomas K. McCraw, ed., *Regulation in Perspective: Historical Essays* (Cambridge, Mass.: Harvard University Press, 1981), p. 161.

25. Kenneth J. Meier, *Regulation: Politics, Bureaucracy, and Economics* (New York: St. Martin's Press, 1985), Chapter 4.

26. Ibid., Chapter 6.

27. Sar A. Levitan, Peter E. Carlson, and Isaac Shapiro, *Protecting American Workers: An Assessment of Government Programs* (Washington, D.C.: Bureau of National Affairs, 1986), Chapters 6, 10; Meier, *Regulation*, Chapter 8.

28. Conlan, *New Federalism*, pp. 84–89.

29. General sources on regulatory expansion in the 1960s and 1970s: Richard A. Harris, "A Decade of Reform"; David Vogel, "The Power of Business in America: A Re-appraisal," *British Journal of Political*

Science 13 (1983): 24; Robert Higgs, *Crisis and Leviathan: Critical Episodes in the Growth of American Government* (New York: Oxford University Press, 1987), pp. 246–54; Murray L. Weidenbaum, *Business, Government, and the Public* (Englewood Cliffs, N.J.: Prentice-Hall, 1977), pp. 5–10; Mayhew, *Divided We Govern*, pp. 83, 85–87. On women's rights: Jo Freeman, *The Politics of Women's Liberation: A Case Study of an Emerging Social Movement and Its Relation to the Policy Process* (New York: David McKay, 1975), Chapter 6.

30. On Carter's years: Mayhew, *Divided We Govern*, pp. 75, 76, 93–94, 98, 166–69.
31. Ibid., p. 144.
32. On state expansion during the two world wars, see Higgs, *Crisis and Leviathan*, Chapters 7, 9.
33. See, for example, Walter Dean Burnham, "Party Systems and the Political Process," Chapter 10 in William Nisbet Chambers and Burnham, eds., *The American Party Systems: Stages of Political Development* (New York: Oxford University Press, 1967), pp. 287–304. The most unqualified claim that a one-to-one correspondence has existed between "electoral realignments" and (consequent) bursts of innovative national lawmaking appears in David W. Brady, *Critical Elections and Congressional Policy Making* (Stanford, Calif.: Stanford University Press, 1988).
34. See Mayhew, *Divided We Govern*, pp. 143–44.
35. See, for example, Richard L. McCormick, "Walter Dean Burnham and 'The System of 1896,'" *Social Science History* 10 (1986): 245.
36. Brady, *Critical Elections*, Chapter 3. On the tariff: Hansen, "Taxation and the Political Economy of the Tariff," p. 540.
37. On 1977–78: Mayhew, *Divided We Govern*, pp. 107, 168–69.
38. Ibid., pp. 146–48.
39. See, for example, James L. Sundquist, "Needed: A Political Theory for the New Era of Coalition Government in the United States," *Political Science Quarterly* 103 (Winter 1988–89): 616–24.
40. Mayhew, *Divided We Govern*, pp. 146–48, 159.
41. For data on "party voting," see Jerome M. Clubb and Santa A. Traugott, "Partisan Cleavage and Cohesion in the House of Representatives, 1861–1974," *Journal of Interdisciplinary History* 7 (Winter 1977): 375–401; Patricia A. Hurley and Rick K. Wilson, "Partisan Voting Patterns in the U.S. Senate, 1877–1986," Chapter 3 in John R. Hibbing and John G. Peters, eds., *The Changing World of the U.S. Senate* (Berkeley, Calif.: IGS Press, 1990); and Samuel C. Patterson and Gregory A. Caldeira, "Party Voting in the United States Con-

gress," *British Journal of Political Science* 18 (January 1988): 111–31.

42. This conclusion may be inferred from many works on elections and the economy—for example, Gerald H. Kramer, "Short-Term Fluctuations in U.S. Voting Behavior, 1896–1964," *American Political Science Review* 65 (March 1971): 131–43.

43. Arthur M. Schlesinger, Jr., "The Cycles of American Politics," Chapter 2 in Schlesinger, *The Cycles of American History* (Boston: Houghton Mifflin, 1986).

44. Gillette, *Retreat from Reconstruction*, Chapters 7–12, 15; Eric Foner, *Reconstruction: America's Unfinished Revolution, 1863–1877* (New York: Harper and Row, 1988), pp. 524–34.

45. Richard Hofstadter, *The Age of Reform: From Bryan to F.D.R.* (New York: Vintage Books, 1955), p. 282.

46. Mayhew, *Divided We Govern*, p. 165.

47. Ibid., pp. 166–69.

48. Ibid., pp. 163–64.

49. Theda Skocpol, *Protecting Soldiers and Mothers: The Political Origins of Social Policy in the United States* (Cambridge, Mass.: Harvard University Press, 1992), Chapter 9.

50. Mayhew, *Divided We Govern*, pp. 162–63.

51. *Reconstruction: America's Unfinished Revolution.*

52. Arthur M. Schlesinger, Jr., *The Politics of Upheaval* (Boston: Houghton Mifflin, 1960), Part I.

53. Mayhew, *Divided We Govern*, pp. 161–62.

54. See the analysis in Stephen Gettinger, "View From the Ivory Tower More Rosy Than Media's," *Congressional Quarterly Weekly Report* 52 (October 8, 1994): 2850–51.

55. Data are from the Congressional Budget Office. See George Hager, "Latest CBO Figures Support Clinton Deficit Projection," *Congressional Quarterly Weekly Report* 51 (September 11, 1993): 2376; David E. Rosenbaum, "Beyond the Superlatives: Budget Bill Is Neither Biggest Deficit Cutter Nor the Biggest Tax Rise in Recent Years," *New York Times*, August 5, 1993, pp. A1, A18.

56. See George Hager, "1993 Deal: Remembrance of Things Past: With Democratic Congresses and Limited Options, New Package Is Similar to 1990 Version," *Congressional Quarterly Weekly Report* 51 (August 7, 1993): 2130–31; David Wessel, "Deficit-Cutting Bill Bears a Resemblance to 1990 Predecessor; But Differences May Be Crucial; Realistic Economic View, Increase in Taxes Are Cited," *Wall Street Journal*, August 3, 1993, pp. A3, A9; and John E. Yang, "Why Does the Budget Argument Sound So Familiar? Because

We've Heard It All Before—Three Years Ago," *Washington Post National Weekly Edition*, July 26-August 1, 1993, p. 20.

57. David Rogers, "Brady Bill's Passage Illustrates Growth of Political Concern Over Violent Crime, *Wall Street Journal*, November 26, 1993, p. A10.

CHAPTER 6

Political Parties and Presidential Elections in the Postindustrial Era

EVERETT CARLL LADD

The idea of "postindustrial" society has figured prominently in social and political analysis for well over a quarter-century. I recently had a search done of the massive collection of newspaper and magazine articles in the online NEXIS information system, and learned from it that postindustrialism has been discussed in many hundreds of stories. In recent years, the NEXIS search indicated, the idea that we are now in a postindustrial era is largely taken for granted. Authors seem to think they need do little by way of explaining the concept, or demonstrating that the United States is indeed in the midst of this era, but instead assume that "everyone knows" that it is—and then proceed to expound upon some characteristic of the economy, or politics, or some other facet of social interaction seen to follow from postindustrialism. The best theoretical work setting forth the concept remains Daniel Bell's *The Coming of Postindustrial Society*, published in 1973.[1]

I began writing about postindustrial society before Bell introduced me to the term and its systematic elaboration. In *American Political Parties*, I discussed the historical evolution of our political system, from the emergence in the infant United States during the last years of the eighteenth century of the world's first political parties to the late 1960s, when I was doing my analysis.[2] It became evident to me at the time that the United States had entered a new stage in its partisan and electoral experience, as distinctly different from that of the New Deal era as the latter is from the party system (or, in another analytical perspective, party systems) of the span from the Civil War to the 1920s. The new order was only beginning to take clear form in the late 1960s, and there were many questions regarding its final shape, but the transformation appeared to me well along and irreversible. Also, I thought the new partisan era was the product of broad, fundamental changes in social structure.

Our first party system reflected the social dynamics of a rural and agricultural nation that stood on the leading edge of the great egalitarian revolution, which Alexis de Tocqueville described so well in his brilliant exercise in social theory, *Democracy in America*. Our second system emerged from the social structural realities of a society moving from a rural and agricultural base through the extraordinary enterprise of industrial nation-building. The third system, in which political scientists of my age grew up, is often associated with the Great Depression, but its societal origins were much more profound than that. The Depression occurred as it did, with such severity, because government did not coherently respond to the host of new social and economic consequences to which industrialization had given rise. The scale and interdependence of a mature industrial society required, for example, a degree of regulation not contemplated in earlier American experience, and required as well the elaboration of a social welfare system in which government played a far larger part than it had previously. I discussed this evolution in *American Political Parties*. And, as noted, I introduced the idea that social structure had once again shifted so substantially as to require—among many other consequences—a fundamental change in the parties and elections system. Bell's book helped me—as it has helped many others—specify more precisely and with great coherence the properties of the societal change that were pushing the polity into a new era.

Since that time, I have explored the transformations of the American party system in the postindustrial era and commented on essential social structural properties of the era itself, in a great many previous publications. It is unnecessary here to revisit this analysis. I note the work for the interested reader.[3]

WHAT PARTY RESPONSE
DID POSTINDUSTRIALISM REQUIRE?

In 1974, when U.S. politics were mired in the Vietnam War anguish and the Watergate scandal, I made my first attempt to go beyond the tentative formulations of the new partisan era, which I offered in *American*

Political Parties, and enumerate specifically what I thought would be the key features of the new order. For the reader's convenience, I will repeat here that brief summary, from a November 1974 paper:

1. The Democrats have lost the presidential majority status that they enjoyed during the New Deal era, as new lines of conflict have decimated parts of the old coalition, but the Republicans have not attained presidential majority status. There is no majority party in the presidential arena.

2. There has been an inversion of the old New Deal relationship of social class to the vote. In wide sectors of public policy, high socioeconomic status (SES) groups are now more supportive of equalitarian (liberal) change than are the middle to lower SES cohorts (within White America); and, as a result, liberal (often, although not always, Democratic) candidates are finding higher measures of electoral sustenance at the top of the socioeconomic ladder than among the middle and lower rungs. This inversion follows from very basic changes in the structure of conflict in American society and is likely to be long-term.

3. The Republican coalition has experienced serious erosions and is weaker now than at any time since the days of the Great Depression, probably weaker, in fact, than at any time since the party's rise during the Civil War era.

4. A "two tier" party system has emerged, with one set of electoral dynamics operating at the presidential level and yet another in subpresidential contests.

5. The electorate is far more weakly tied to political parties now than at any time in the past century, and as it has been freed from the "anchor" of party loyalties, it has become vastly more volatile.

6. The communications function—whereby party leaders communicate with the rank and file, and the latter in turn send messages to the party leadership—has historically been a great *raison d'être* for political parties in egalitarian systems; but this function has increasingly been assumed by other structures, notably those organized around the mass media of communication.

7. A major new cohort of activists has assumed vastly increased importance in the electoral arena, a cohort whose position is closely linked to the growth of the intelligentsia in postindustrial America.[4]

Now, as I look back on these observations, I am reasonably satisfied with the effort. A few of the formulations now appear to need amendment. The second has been shown to be an overextrapolation from certain developments then evident in public opinion data. They are evident still, but the idea that there has been a full inversion of the old New Deal relationship of social class to party preferences and the vote is overstated. The United States has seen a marked decline in the salience of social class in electoral politics in the contemporary period, from what prevailed in the New Deal; and, at the same time, many social and cultural issues have intruded upon the scene, issues on which groups of higher socioeconomic status are often, even typically, more supportive of the egalitarian or the liberal side than are those of lower socioeconomic status. Nonetheless, in partisan terms, the Republicans, for the most part, do somewhat better now among voters of high income and social status than among low SES voters, and vice versa for the Democrats.

The third observation above really does not belong at all. It was a commentary on short-term developments, where the Republicans had been under siege, first in the disastrous 1964 Barry Goldwater campaign, and then in the Watergate scandal. In this environment, the party was naturally weakened. But with a few exceptions—such as the electoral loyalties of African Americans, who in the aftermath of the Goldwater election swung over massively to the Democratic party, where they have stayed—the Watergate era factors have proved to have little long-term impact. Goldwater actually helped the Republicans in sections of the South, but the sources of the GOP rise to majority status in presidential electioneering rest on a foundation far broader than anything related to Goldwater's campaign. When I wrote in 1974, I did not believe social structural factors were assigning the Republicans a permanently disadvantaged position in electoral politics, so I should not have included this observation in an effort to look long-term.

Finally, point seven above is too limited, because the changes in elite composition and outlook reached far beyond the element I identified. The new elites of the contemporary United States are far more diverse than the term *intelligentsia* can suggest.

These caveats noted, much of the formulation still seems about right to me. A new party system had emerged in the United States by the early 1970s, although it did not include the emergence of a new majority party. Voters' loyalties to parties were weaker than they had been in the past, a development with important implications all across the system's operations. The composition and philosophic stance of party elites had changed greatly from the New Deal pattern. Split electoral outcomes with, for example, one party winning the presidency and the other the Congress, were no longer accidental occurrences in the new system, as they had been in all of its predecessors back to the age of Andrew Jackson. The Democrats had lost their presidential majority, which had seemed so secure and natural in the New Deal era. Campaigning and electoral politics had indeed been transformed structurally, especially in the dramatic enlargement of the media's political communication role—played out independently of the political parties and often in opposition to them.

The linkages between the contemporary parties and elections system and the postindustrial setting are numerous. In the remainder of this essay, I will explore several of them, including the weakened party presence, more numerous political independents, an enormously expanded political role for the communications media, and a greatly transformed structure of campaigning and electoral politics.

POLITICAL INDEPENDENCE
AND THE UNANCHORED ELECTORATE

Political scientists have long noted the weakness of political parties in the United States, and they have often argued that the weakness had unfortunate consequences for U.S. political life. Woodrow Wilson advanced such arguments in 1885.[5] Writing in *Congress on Trial*, in 1949, James MacGregor Burns observed that "Many of us switch from party to party as blithely as we change fashions in clothes. We laud the statesmen who rise above party allegiances and we sneer at the faithful party hack. We pride ourselves on being 'independents.' The average American feels more loyal to the Elks or to the Legion than to his political party."[6]

If earlier eras in American electoral politics evinced a type of political party relatively weak and notably decentralized, compared to many European parties historically, and weak by the party-government model as developed by American political scientists, it is nonetheless true that parties have been weakened in several different ways, and to a notable degree, in the contemporary era. Their diminished presence sets contemporary politics off from politics in earlier times.

Vote-Switching

The growing independence of important segments of the electorate from political parties is evident in a number of kinds of behavioral and attitudinal data. In each of their presidential election year surveys from

Figure 6.1.   Vote Switching in Presidential Elections, 1952–1980*

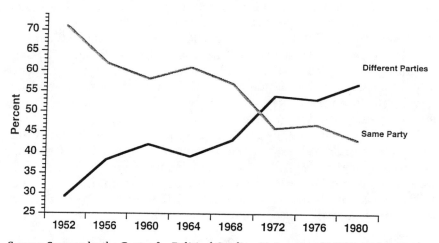

Source: Surveys by the Center for Political Studies, University of Michigan, National Elections Studies.
* Data obtained from this question: Have you always voted for the same party, or have you voted for different parties for President?

1952 to 1980, for example, researchers at the University of Michigan's Center for Political Studies asked respondents whether they "have . . . always voted for the same party or have . . . voted for different parties for President?" In 1952, 71 percent in the national sample indicated they had always or mostly voted for the same party (Figure 6.1). By 1968, however, the proportion had declined to 57 percent of the electorate and, in 1980, to just 43 percent.

This same progression even holds among people who call themselves strong partisans. In 1952, only 8 percent of self-described strong Democrats identified as vote-switchers; the proportion was 18 percent among "strong Republicans." By 1976, however, the proportion of strong Democrats saying they were vote-switchers had climbed to 30 percent and, among strong Republicans, to 33 percent. I assume this progression has continued since 1980, but the University of Michigan's Center for Political Studies stopped asking the question after the 1980 surveys.

Ticket-Splitting

The Michigan researchers in their post-election panels have continued to ask respondents how they voted for president and congressional can-

Figure 6.2   Ticket Splitting: Proportion of All Voters Who Split Their Ballot in the Year's Presidential and Congressional Contests, 1952–1992*

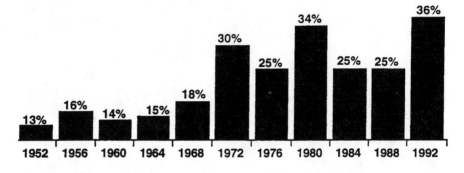

Source: Surveys by the Center for Political Studies, University of Michigan, National Elections Studies.

* Data obtained by cross-tabbing three questions from each survey: Who did you vote for: (1) for President (year); (2) for U.S. Senate (year); and (3) for U.S. House of Representatives (year)?

didates. From their findings, we can create a soft measure of ticket-splitting—voting for one party's candidate for president, and the other party's for the House or Senate. Much short-term bounce comes into this measure, to be sure, as in 1992, when independent Ross Perot was on the presidential ballot. Nonetheless, as Figure 6.2 indicates, the baseline proportion of ticket-splitters by this measure has roughly doubled over the last 40 years, to almost 30 percent of the electorate.

Independent Identification

Surveys vary as to the progression in the proportion of the public calling themselves independents in the familiar questions on party identification, but there is no doubt that a far higher proportion identify as independents now, in the postindustrial era, than did so in the 1930s, 1940s, or 1950s. Gallup has been asking the same basic party identification question since 1940: "In politics, as of today, do you consider yourself a Republican, a Democrat, or an independent?" In the surveys of the 1940s, about 20 percent of those interviewed typically put themselves in the "independent" camp. In the 1950s, the proportions were similar, though up a few points. It was not until the latter part of the 1960s that Gallup began picking up a substantial increase in the proportion who identified themselves as independents, up to the 30 to 35 percentage point range—

Figure 6.3　Party Identification, 1940–1994 (Gallup Poll)

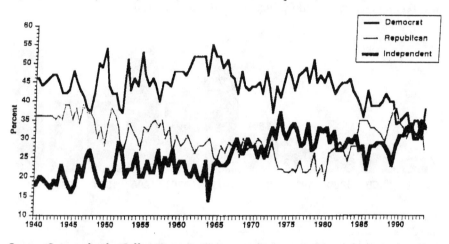

Source: Surveys by the Gallup Organization.
Note: Surveys completed from 1940–1989 were done by personal interview; surveys completed from 1990–1994 were done by telephone. Data for 1994 were taken from nine surveys conducted between January 1994 and September 1994.
* Data obtained from this question: In politics, as of today, do you consider yourself a Democrat, a Republican, or an independent?

nearly double the proportions recorded regularly in the New Deal era. Since roughly the mid-1970s, there has been no large or consistent trend. The results of the Gallup Polls are presented in Figure 6.3.

The biennial surveys taken by the University of Michigan Center for Political Studies show essentially the same thing: a big surge in the proportion calling themselves independents in the latter part of the 1960s and through the 1970s, and then modest year-to-year variations across the new plateau, which sees roughly 35 percent of the adult public identifying themselves as independents (with the Democrats modestly ahead of the Republicans among the remainder). Younger voters continue to display higher levels of professed independence than older groups in the population.

A DIMINISHED INSTITUTIONAL ROLE FOR PARTIES

As the place of political parties in voters' decision-making is markedly reduced in the contemporary party system from what it was in the predecessor systems, so, too, is the institutional presence of the political parties. As many analysts have noted, the political parties have been largely removed from presidential nominee selection—except as labels and as part of a legal structure in which nomination competition is conducted. That is, if one wants to be the presidential nominee of the Democratic party, one has to enter Democratic primaries and caucuses and lead one's supporting delegates to a convention that is run organizationally by the national Democratic party. But in contrast to the situation in all previous party systems, the institutional party has little say in who the nominee will be. Candidates decide largely on their own whether to enter the primaries; and, if they can manage in media-based campaigns to win enough rank-and-file votes, this majority choice is certain to become the party's nominee, whatever party leaders or notables think. Thus, parties provide a nominal framework for presidential nominee selection but no longer determine the outcome through their institutional processes and resources.

THE MEDIA IN THE POSTINDUSTRIAL SYSTEM

This marked weakening of the parties both in electoral loyalties and organizational vitality has occurred in large part as a direct response to social structural changes that have accompanied the postindustrial era. Postindustrialism, as Bell described it, involves the idea of the "knowledge" society. The process of creating, moving, and managing ideas figures centrally in the economic and technological dynamics of postindustrialism. Thus, the computer chip is the distinguishing technology, as Henry Ford's assembly line was in the industrial-state era. Necessarily in an idea-dependent and idea-driven society and economy, the place of communications media is enormously enlarged.

A number of scholars have ably analyzed the transformed place of the media in American electoral politics. I find the works of Thomas Patterson, Doris Graber, and Richard Rubin especially valuable.[7] As many analysts have noted, the press has increasingly taken over important facets of the communications role that were once performed by party organizations. More than two decades ago, journalist David Broder observed that news persons had begun to serve as the principal source of information about what candidates were saying and doing. They acted as talent scouts, conveying the judgment that some contenders were promising, while dismissing others as having no real talent. They operated as race callers, or handicappers, telling the public how the election contest was going and what was important in it. The press had begun to see itself as public defender, bent on exposing what it considered frailties, duplicities, and sundry other inadequacies of candidates and officeholders.[8]

The growth of a large, independent, often adversarial role by the national press in the country's electoral politics has proceeded apace since Broder wrote the above depiction. The 1992 presidential contest saw an extraordinary institutional innovation, startling even in the context of the established features of the contemporary system. For the first time in American history, a serious presidential nominee was "nominated" on television talk shows, most notably on *Larry King Live.*

The political parties are, quite simply, enormously disadvantaged with regard to communications resources in an age when communications media have such extraordinary capabilities for reaching large audiences. The early newspapers in the United States were often avowedly party papers. Today, the press is fiercely independent of party control or influence—whatever the philosophic bent of the editors may be. Most of the money spent in political communications in the United States is expended in a fashion entirely independent of party control. Partisan "spin doctors" try valiantly, of course, to get communications media to present political developments as the party would like, but they enjoy only intermittent and always highly limited success in this endeavor. Advancement in the press world is often a key to attaining influence on the parties and government side of things—as the central roles of David Gergen and George Stephanopoulos in the Clinton White House attested.

Various data give further indication of just how puny the parties' place is in the knowledge and media-based postindustrial setting. In 1990, for example, television broadcasting—the T.V. networks and the local stations—expended roughly $25.5 billion in their communications to the American public. It is estimated that roughly 25 percent of these expenditures involved news-gathering and dissemination. That is, in 1990 alone, television spent roughly $6 billion in getting out the news. In comparison, all political party and candidate expenditures for the 1989–1990 election cycle totaled about $1.1 billion. Most Americans get their views of issues and political life generally from independent news media, not from political parties or their agents. As to the future, the idea-generating and disseminating capacities of postindustrial society will only increase further, and the parties will only become more isolated and limited in their role in this area.

There is extensive argument about the press's role, compared to that of the parties—much hand-wringing in some circles. I do not wish to enter that argument here. My observation is simply that the diminished presence of the parties generally accrues in large measure from their diminished place in the political communications process, at a time when communications resources are so enormously enhanced by technological and other changes that accompany postindustrialism.

THE INDEPENDENT CITIZEN

The American public is not subscribing to a politics more independent of parties merely because it gets its political information largely from research-rich and autonomous communications media. Over the last half-century there has been an extraordinary increase in formal education, and the more educated population—with greater self-confidence in its capacity to find its way through political decision-making without guidance of political parties and with more independent sources of information—is simply less inclined than previous electorates to adhere to any party standard.

The essential character of the "knowledge society" in the United States is seen clearly in the country's increased commitment to formal education since World War II. In 1940, only 5 percent of the population age twenty-five and older had graduated from college but, by 1993, the proportion was almost 22 percent. Figure 6.4 shows that in the last two decades alone the level of formal education has increased dramatically. In 1970, about 28 percent of those age twenty-five years and older had only elementary school training; by 1993, that proportion had been cut by two-thirds, dropping to just 9.3 percent. The proportion with at least some college training climbed over this span from roughly 21 percent to about 45 percent.

If an elaborate knowledge base is a key component of the postindustrial society, the latter is required to make heavy commitments to formal education. And whatever we may conclude about the performance of America's schools and colleges, by a number of measures the United States makes a larger commitment to education than any other country. In 1987–1988, for example, when 13 million Americans attended institutions of higher education, only 1.6 million West Germans, 1.1 million British, and 1.3 million French citizens were enrolled in comparable schools. While these other countries have much smaller total populations than the United States, when one controls for population, the United States is still seen enrolling a much higher proportion of its population. Data from the Organization of Economic Cooperation and Development (OECD) show that, for 1987–1988, the last year available when this was written, 51 Americans per 1,000 population were enrolled as college or university students. The ratios were just 27 per 1,000 population in West Germany (before reunification), 24 per 1,000 in France, and 21 students per 1,000 people in Japan.[9]

Spending data show this same massive extension of formal education in the postindustrial era. In 1930, the United States spent roughly $3.4 billion for education, from elementary school through college, pri-

Figure 6.4   Educational Attainment in America, 1970 and 1993

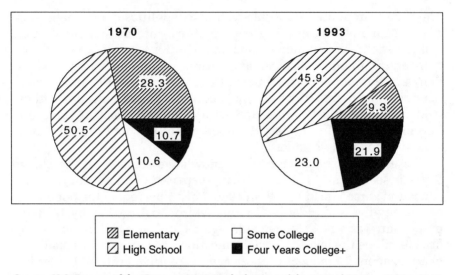

Source: U.S. Bureau of the Census, *Statistical Abstract of the United States,* 1992, p. 144;
idem, Current Population Reports, 1994, Series p. 20, No. 476, Table 1.
Note: Percentages are of those 25 years of age and older.

vate as well as public. Expenditures climbed only modestly through
1950—but at this point they took off. By 1990, U.S. spending for education had reached $358 billion, $143 billion for higher education and
$215 billion for elementary and secondary training.

The point is not, of course, that as people have become far more
highly educated in formal terms in the postindustrial setting, they have
automatically become more independent politically. Rather, it is that
the vast increases in educational commitments have added, overall, a
significant element encouraging the making of political assessments
independent of party cues and ties. It is highly unlikely that the trend
toward a weakening of party loyalties in the general citizenry and
toward an institutional diminishment of parties as well, which we have
seen over the past quarter-century, will ever be reversed, given the basic
structural properties of postindustrialism. Parties are certain to have
their political role weakened further.

ROSS PEROT AND "PEROTISM"

The big splash that independent H. Ross Perot made in the 1992 presidential election can only be understood in the context of the factors I

have been describing. More people think of themselves as independents these days, which means more people are untroubled about supporting an independent candidate. Polls have shown Perot drawing his support disproportionately from self-described independents. The 1992 Voters Research and Survey (VRS) exit poll, for example, found 43 percent of Perot voters saying they were independents. And the combined 1993 Gallup surveys, which provide the data presented in Table 6.1, indicate that 61 percent of those who recalled having voted for Perot in November 1992 put themselves in the independent column; only 18 percent called themselves Democrats and 22 percent Republicans. The national news media, especially television, are increasingly the institutional forum in which campaigns are waged; not being able to count on an established party organization is still something of a disadvantage, but not nearly so much of a disadvantage as in earlier eras.

Perot's drawing 19 percent of the popular vote in the 1992 election had other sources, to be sure, apart from a more independent electorate. A great many Americans were worried about the economy and notably dissatisfied with "politics as usual." It was a bad time to run for reelection—putting George Bush's candidacy in a hole. Democrat Bill Clinton never gained the confidence of important "swing" segments of the electorate (a weakness that contributed to his party's big setback in the 1994 "off-year" elections). This left an opening for "somebody else," into which Perot's well-financed, T.V.-savvy effort charged.

The structural changes that encouraged political efforts conducted outside the regular structure of political parties are the important things to focus on, not Perot's efforts as such. The 1992 surveys show that large proportions of those who were inclined to vote for the Texan also indicated that they were really not at all sure about him. They were using his candidacy as a means of protest. Surveys have consistently shown, since the middle of 1992, a widespread sense that Perot does not have a "democratic personality"—that he is inclined to rigidity, arrogance, and oversimplification. The weakness in Perot's political base was further indicated in 1993 during the debate over the North American Free Trade Agreement. Polls reported a sharp decline in the proportion of people who said they viewed him favorably and identified as his supporters, following the televised exchange he had with Vice President Al Gore.

Ross Perot is not without political skills and resources, but we may expect future independent candidacies that are free of his apparent deficiencies in democratic politics. The new American party system is distinguished by organizationally weak parties, strong national electronic communications media, an independent-minded citizenry, and, from these factors, continuing invitations to candidates to, in one way

Table 6.1. *Partisan Identification of the American Public, 1993 (Gallup Poll)*

	Independents (%)	Democrats (%)	Republicans (%)
EVERYONE	35	36	29
BY INCOME			
Less than $15,000	32	46	22
$15,000–$29,999	35	38	27
$30,000–$49,999	37	33	30
$50,000 and over	36	28	36
Whites Only			
Less than $15,000	34	41	26
$15,000–$29,999	37	33	31
$30,000–$49,999	37	30	33
$50,000 and over	37	26	37
BY EDUCATION			
Less than High School Graduate	32	45	24
High School Graduate	35	36	28
Some College	37	32	31
College Graduate	35	28	37
College Graduate +	36	35	30
BY AGE			
18–24 yrs. of age	41	30	29
25–29 yrs. of age	40	32	28
30–44 yrs. of age	37	34	29
45–59 yrs. of age	36	36	27
60 yrs. of age +	26	42	31
BY GENDER			
Men	39	31	30
Women	31	40	29
BY RELIGION			
Protestant	28	35	37
Catholic	33	40	27
Jewish*	47	23	30
None	47	35	25
GROUPS DEFINED BY RACE, REGION, RELIGION, AND ETHNICITY			
Whites and Blacks, South and Non-South			
Whites, Outside South	38	31	31
Southern Whites	33	33	34
Blacks, Outside South	24	70	6
Southern Blacks	25	68	7

Table 6.1　(continued)

	Independents (%)	Democrats (%)	Republicans (%)
Whites, by Region			
East	37	32	31
Midwest	41	30	29
South	33	33	34
West	35	30	35
Whites, by Religion and South/Non-South			
Non-Southern Protestants	34	25	41
Southern Protestants	24	34	42
Non-Southern Catholics	34	39	26
Southern Catholics	26	38	36
Northeastern White Protestants	34	24	42
Northeastern White Catholics	34	36	30
Born in the United States	35	35	30
Born outside the United States	40	36	24
POLITICAL GROUPINGS			
Conservative	28	25	47
Moderate	40	37	23
Liberal	36	53	11
Those who voted in the 1992 elections	36	35	30
Those who did not vote in the 1992 elections	35	28	37
Those who voted for Bush	25	8	68
Those who voted for Clinton	24	70	6
Those who voted for Perot	61	18	22

Source: These data are from a data set made up of all interviews in the twenty-eight Gallup surveys, taken from January through December of 1993. The total number of cases of this combined data set is 31,178.

*These numbers are from eight Gallup surveys, taken between October 1991 and May 1992, which were combined. There were insufficient cases in the 1993 surveys because religion was asked in only five of them.

or another, "end-around" the traditional mechanisms of the country's two-party system.

I am not among those who have concluded that these developments necessarily pose a threat to the quality of American democracy. Elsewhere I have developed my disagreement with the "more responsible two-party system" literature and argument.[10] I do agree, nonetheless, that a successful American democracy requires both a vigorously participating citizenry and well-functioning representative institutions. The nurturing and "peer reviewing" of presidential nominees by political parties has much to commend it, even to those of us who are far from unsympathetic to direct democracy ideals. If political parties are not going to play this important role with any vigor or coherence in the postindustrial setting, we need to think carefully about how the function is to be performed. A situation where candidates come from nowhere, bursting on the political stage, lightly reviewed by a press often more interested in stirring the pot than in careful, sustained scrutiny, is not going to be at all satisfactory in the long run. I am afraid that I see prospects of contenders emerging from this process who are stronger than H. Ross Perot and yet, in their own way, as profoundly unsuited to the demands of the presidency as he is.

THE COLLAPSE OF TRADITIONAL CLASS POLITICS

The United States has never had class politics in the grand European style: bourgeoisie against aristocracy; working class against bourgeoisie; and so on. It is true, nonetheless, that in the third era of American political party experience, the era of the mature industrial state, class divisions were relatively sharp and salient. Under the new or expanded government programs of Franklin Roosevelt's administration, working-class Americans received important recognition and support: national legislation guaranteeing the right to organize and bargain collectively, minimum-wage laws, Social Security, guarantees of occupational health and safety and of humane working conditions, for example. During the New Deal, the labor union movement gained strength. The political climate that followed the outbreak of the Great Depression, including the encouragement of unionism given by FDR's administration, legislation supporting unionism, and the vigorous initiatives of a new generation of labor leaders, resulted in a surge in union membership, from 3.5 million in 1931 to 10 million on the eve of World War II, to more than 14 million when the war ended. By 1955, 33 percent of all workers in non-agricultural pursuits were in labor unions.

Today, only about 16 percent of the workforce is unionized. The one area where unionism is growing is among government employees.[11] Studies show that in the private sector, only 12 percent of workers are in trade unions, down from 23 percent just fifteen years ago.[12]

What has been happening, of course, in the postindustrial setting is that the traditional working class—urban, blue-collar, and trade union—has lost ground numerically, while at the same time it has seen its socioeconomic position strengthened. Most of the urban working class of the 1930s were economic have-nots; if they were not necessarily poor, they were right on the margin, economically. As such, they supported government-directed efforts to change the economic order. The trade union movement organized this working class and pushed effectively for its economic betterment and security. In the decades that followed, however, unions achieved many of their objectives through collective bargaining and as a result of the overall growth of the American economy. The unionized labor force moved up the socioeconomic ladder. In 1989, according to data from seven national surveys taken by the Gallup Organization, over 76 percent of union families—those in which at least one of the principal wage earners belongs to a union—owned their homes rather than rented them. Only about 4 percent of union members had less than a high school education, and 19 percent were college graduates. Just 5 percent of these union families reported incomes of under $10,000, compared to 16 percent of non-union families. At the same time, 58 percent of union households, compared to 38 percent of non-union households, had incomes of $30,000 a year or more. In recent years, sectors of the American workforce, including some that are unionized, have experienced real economic distress in a changing economy characterized by sharp international competition. Nonetheless, the generalization holds that much of the working class of the 1930s has moved up the economic ladder.

In short, the basis for the relatively robust class politics of the New Deal years has eroded in the postindustrial setting. African Americans as a group rank low in socioeconomic position and look overwhelmingly to the Democratic party as the principal political instrument for redressing their grievances. But with this single exception—where dissatisfactions derive not just from traditional class factors, but from ones rooted in racial experience, as well—class politics of a traditional sort simply does not exist in postindustrial America. Controlling for race, low-income people are somewhat more likely to be Democrats, while upper-income people are more likely to be Republicans. But, as the Gallup Poll data in Table 6.1 indicate, these differences are modest. According to the VRS election day survey in November 1992, among Whites, 52 percent of those with family incomes of under $15,000 voted for Democrat Clinton, compared to 40 percent of those earning between $15,000 and $30,000, 37 percent of those in the $30,000 to $50,000 income range, 37 percent in the $50,000 to $75,000 range, and 34 percent of persons with family incomes of $75,000 a year and higher.

In short, except for the very lowest income group (under $15,000 per year in this VRS survey), there simply were no significant differences in voting among the various income strata in the last presidential contest. The dynamic of postindustrial society, especially as it accrues from historically unprecedented affluence and an intense emphasis on ideas and symbols, defines lines of political cleavage markedly different from those that became familiar in the industrial era.

CULTURAL POLITICS

Its population fed by great streams of immigration from many different countries, the United States has historically been a nation of great ethnic and cultural diversity. It has followed naturally, then, that ethnic and cultural divisions—between Protestants and Catholics, "wets" and "drys," Blacks and Whites, etc.—have often impressed themselves on the vote and on political party preference. The New Deal era stands out in American history as an exception to the general rule that, in the United States, "cultural politics"—understood in the sense just enumerated—has predominated over "class politics." The renewed importance of cultural cleavages in the elections of the contemporary era represents a return to what has been historically familiar. Still, many of the cultural splits now evident are new ones. The now-familiar "gender gap" is, for example, one that has apparently no precedent in earlier eras. In elections of the last fifteen years or so, however, it has been a staple.

In many, though by no means all, contests for high office, women now give more support to Democratic candidates than do men; and, in contests between a man and a woman, female voters are more inclined to back the woman than are male voters, especially if the contest pits a Democratic woman against a Republican man. In the latter instances, the gender gap is often large. For example, in the 1992, full term U.S. Senate race in California between Democrat Barbara Boxer and Republican Bruce Herschensohn, women voted for Boxer by a landslide 57 to 37 percent margin, while men backed Herschensohn by a 51 to 43 percent margin.[13]

Typically, the gender gap is larger among young voters than among their elders, and larger between college-educated men and women than between those with high school educations. In the 1992 presidential balloting, for example, just 39 percent of men eighteen to twenty-four years of age backed Clinton, compared to 52 percent of women in that age bracket. Among those sixty-five years and older, in contrast, Clinton received the same 50 percent support among women and men alike.

Religious group differences have often been large in American voting, but now the "religious factor" evinces a new twist. Contemporary voting displays a strong connection between frequency of church attendance and partisan choice. All groups of African Americans, including churchgoers, are heavily Democratic. Among Whites, though, Republicans do far better with the "churched" part of the electorate than with the "unchurched." The VRS election day poll in 1992 found, for example, that Whites who attend religious service weekly (roughly one-third of the national electorate) voted for George Bush over Bill Clinton by 53 percent to 31 percent, with 15 percent backing Ross Perot. In contrast, all White voters gave Bush 40 percent support, while 39 percent backed challenger Clinton, and 20 percent backed Perot. Fifteen percent of voters interviewed by VRS on Election Day in 1992 checked off the questionnaire category, "born-again Christian/fundamentalist" as applying to them. Among this group, Bush was strong indeed, winning the support of nearly two-thirds of the total. On the other hand, he was supported by fewer than one in five of those who said they had no religious ties (7 percent of all voters).

In the present system, the religious factor involves *religiosity*, not *denomination,* as it did historically. Differences separating Protestants and Catholics in voting patterns in recent elections are easily the smallest they have been at any time since the 1830s. They are, in fact, virtually inconsequential. But variables such as frequency of church attendance, the sense of the importance of religion in one's life, holding to traditional religious views about such matters as belief in Heaven and Hell and the inerrancy of the Bible (or conversely rejecting these beliefs) have become key correlates or predictors of voting choice. While it certainly is not the case that all or even most religious conservatives or traditionalists are political conservatives and Republicans, the GOP does in fact significantly better now among such groups than in the rest of the electorate.

The exceptional resources for communication, a distinguishing feature of postindustrial society, allow groups to define themselves far more readily and extensively than was possible in any other era in the country's history and to establish links to people of like mind without regard to geographic distance. Postindustrialism by itself does not create gender differences on policies and candidates, although the huge increase in the proportion of women in the workforce, which is one key element of the occupational setting today, has undoubtedly brought women distinctive new opportunities and new problems. Nonetheless, postindustrial society's emphasis on ideas and symbols and their elaborate communication does enhance the prospects of cultural cleavages, such as those surrounding gender, becoming more salient. A relatively affluent population, relatively leisured, operating in a communications-rich environment, will inevitably partake heavily of cultural splits of all kinds and will introduce them prominently into its voting choices.

ENVOI

There will undoubtedly be some curves in the road ahead, but the general course of elections and party competition in the postindustrial era seems evident enough. The group basis of voting bears little resemblance to that of the New Deal years, with "cultural groups" dominating the scene. Most important, the postindustrial electorate is increasingly cut loose from party organizational influences and partisan loyalties and seeks to navigate independently through media-centered campaigns and elections.

For anyone who came of age politically in the preceding party system, the new one is, at the least, jarring. Whether it poses greater challenge to the quality of democratic life remains to be seen. We need careful, systematic inquiry—as free of nostalgia as it possibly can be—to explore those possible challenges and their remedies.

NOTES

1. Bell clearly deserves to be credited with introducing and developing the idea of "postindustrial society," although, as he has noted, the term actually appeared earlier than his first usage of it, with a quite different meaning. David Reisman wrote on "Leisure and Work in Postindustrial Society," an essay printed in the compendium *Mass Leisure* (Glencoe, Ill.: The Free Press, 1958). In the twenty-three years since *The Coming of Postindustrial Society* (New York: Basic Books) was published, no one has matched Bell's theoretic richness in treating the idea.
2. Everett Carll Ladd, *American Political Parties: Social Change and Political Response* (New York: Norton, 1970).
3. Everett Carll Ladd, *Where Have All The Voters Gone?: The Fracturing of America's Political Parties* (New York: Norton, 1978, 1982); *The American Polity: The People and Their Government*, 5th ed. (New York: Norton, 1993); with Charles D. Hadley, *Transformations of the American Party System: Political Coalitions from the New Deal to the 1970s* (New York: Norton, 1975, 1978); "Pursuing American Voters: V. O. Key, Jr., and a Modern Political Science Odyssey," paper delivered at the Annual Meeting of the Southern

Political Science Association, New Orleans, La., 1974; "Political Parties and Governance in the Eighties," in *Politics and the Oval Office*, A. Meltsner, ed. (San Francisco: Institute for Contemporary Studies, 1981), Chapter 4; "The Brittle Mandate: Electoral Dealignment and the 1980 Presidential Election," *Political Science Quarterly* 96 (Spring 1981): 1–25; "The 1986 Election and Its Aftermath," *Public Opinion* 9 (January/February 1987): 21; "Party Reform and the Public Interest," in *Elections American Style*, A. James Reichley, ed. (Washington, D.C.: Brookings, 1987), pp. 222–239; "The 1986 Elections," Issue No. 5 of the *Ladd Report* (Norton, 1987); *The Ladd 1988 Election Update*, published in May, September, and October, 1988 (New York: Norton); "A Confirming Election," *Public Opinion* 11 (January/February 1989): 2–3; "The 1988 Elections: Continuation of the Post-New Deal System," *Political Science Quarterly* 104 (Spring 1989): 1–18; "The Big Shift in Party Strength in the '80s," *The Public Perspective* 1 (November/December 1990): 11–12; "Like Waiting for Godot: The Uselessness of 'Realignment' for Understanding Change in Contemporary American Politics," *Polity* 22 (Spring 1990): 511–25; a similar version of the proceeding was published in Byron E. Shafer, ed., *The End of Realignment? Interpreting American Electoral Eras* (Madison: University of Wisconsin Press, 1991), Chapter 2; "Republicans and Democrats: As the New Decade Begins," *The World and I* 5 (February 1990); "The 1990 Elections: A Clear Message, Unclear Results," *The World and I* 6 (January 1991); "The 1992 Vote for President Clinton: Another Brittle Mandate?," *Political Science Quarterly* 108 (Spring 1993): 1–28; "The 'New' American Party System Really Isn't New Anymore: Like It or Not, It Rests on a Firm Foundation," *Cosmos Journal* 4 (Spring 1994): 71–75.

4. From "Pursuing American Voters," mimeo (November 1974), pp. 16–17. I reiterated this summary a year later in *Transformations of the American Party System*.

5. Woodrow Wilson, *Congressional Government* (Boston: Houghton-Mifflin, 1885). As a result of the parties' weakness, Wilson wrote, "The average citizen may be excused for esteeming government at best but a haphazard affair upon which his vote and all his influence can have but little effect. How is his choice of a representative in Congress to affect the policy of the country as regards the questions in which he is most interested . . . ? It seems almost a thing of despair to get any assurance that any vote he may cast that even in an infinitessimal degree affect the essential course of administration" (pp. 331–32).

6. James MacGregor Burns, *Congress on Trial: The Legislative Process and the Administrative State* (New York: Gordian Press, 1966; first published 1949), p. 193.

7. Thomas E. Patterson, *The Mass Media Election: How Americans Choose Their President* (New York: Praeger, 1980); and idem, *Out of Order* (New York: Knopf, 1993); Doris A. Graber, *Mass Media and American Politics* 4th ed. (Washington, D.C.: CQ Press, 1993); and Richard L. Rubin, *Press, Party, and Presidency* (New York: Norton, 1981), especially pp. 147–80.

8. David S. Broder, "Political Reporters in Presidential Politics," in Charles Peters and Timothy J. Adams, eds., *Inside the System: A Washington Monthly Reader* (New York: Praeger, 1970), pp. 3–22.

9. OECD, "Education in OECD Countries," 1987–1988 (Paris: OECD, 1990), p. 104; *OECD in Figures*, 1991, pp. 48–49.

10. Ladd, "Political Parties, 'Reform,' and American Democracy," in John Kenneth White and Jerome M. Mileur, eds., *Challenges to Party Government* (Carbondale, Ill.: Southern Illinois University Press, 1992), pp. 22–39.

11. Indeed, the author of this chapter is a trade unionist. The University of Connecticut faculty voted in 1976 to be represented by the American Association of University Professors in collective bargaining, and the AAUP remains the faculty's union in the full, formal bargaining sense. Government workers' unions have, in general, been growing, even as trade unionism at large has been shrinking.

12. Dina Milbank, "Union Woes Suggest How the Labor Force in U.S. is Shifting," *Wall Street Journal*, May 5, 1992, p. 1.

13. Data on the gender gap in the 1992 elections have been brought together in *The Public Perspective* 4 (January/February 1993). See the "Public Opinion and Demographic Report" of that issue, especially pages 98–101.

CHAPTER 7

Conclusion

HARVEY L. SCHANTZ

In the Conclusion, I would like to inventory and extend some of what has already been said in order to underscore central themes and facts. To organize the discussion, I will return to the three questions that I posed in the Introduction. My goal is not to offer an original comprehensive statement, but rather to reexamine the chapters that have gone before and to systematize the answers to our lines of inquiry.

ARE PRESIDENTIAL ELECTIONS A SET OF FIFTY-TWO DISCRETE EVENTS, OR ARE THERE PATTERNS AMONG THEM?

Although every presidential election has its unique aspects, the thrust of this book has been to point out similarities and patterns among them.

Process

Candidate Pool. Throughout U.S. history, presidential hopefuls and winners have emerged from a select group of high national offices—state governorships, U.S. Senate, vice presidency, Cabinet, and military. All presidents, and virtually all presidential contenders, have been male, White, and Christian. These informal rules of presidential prominence are mutually reinforcing, since the Congress, Cabinet, and military are dominated by White males.

211

Nomination Process.   The dominant mechanism for deciding the party nomination has been the congressional caucus (1800–1824); a party leader controlled national convention (1832–1908); a mixed system of delegate selection (1912–1968); and a primary dominated system (since 1972).[1] The overall thrust of these changes has been to open up influence in the nomination process to more and more people.

While the party convention retains its structure, its nominating function has changed. Since the 1950s, and especially since the 1970s and the rise of presidential primaries, its function has been to ratify or confirm a consensus leader rather than to independently choose a nominee.

General Election Campaigns.   American presidential elections have always been dominated by a two-party system. In individual presidential elections, the two major political parties have regularly received 96 percent or more of the total vote.[2] Only five political parties have ever elected presidents (Table 1.3). The last thirty-six elections, beginning with 1852, have all been won by the Democrats and Republicans. Since 1856, the Democrats and Republicans have finished first or second in all presidential elections, except in 1912 when former President Theodore Roosevelt finished second as the candidate of the Progressive party, winning 27.4 percent of the total vote.

Ross Perot's 18.9 percent of the total vote is the third highest vote for a third-place finisher in an American presidential election. Perot's finish ranks behind, as Milton Cummings points out, two former presidents; Roosevelt's 1912 showing, which was accompanied by Republican President Taft's 23.2 percent of the total vote; and former President Millard Fillmore's 21.5 percent of the total vote, as the 1856 candidate of the Whig-American party. (Fillmore was a nonelected Whig president who had been denied party renomination in 1852.)

In 1992, Bill Clinton won with 43.0 percent of the total vote. This was the sixteenth time in U.S. history and the sixth time this century that a president was elected with less than one-half of the total vote.[3] The previous time this happened was in 1968, when Richard Nixon received 43.4 percent of the total vote.

The presidency is decided by electoral votes, not by popular balloting. To win the presidency, a candidate needs a majority of the electoral votes. With only four exceptions—in election years 1800, 1824, 1876, and 1888—the electoral vote process has reflected the popular vote choice. Through the years, and especially in recent decades, though, the electoral vote margin has tended to magnify the popular vote victory.

The election of 1976 ushered in two important changes in the election process. Televised presidential debates, which highlighted the

1960 Kennedy-Nixon contest, became the more or less permanent central events of presidential campaigns. And second, public finance of major party campaigns and matching funds for the nomination process replaced large contributors as the most direct funding source.

Voting. Voter turnout was generally higher in the nineteenth century than in the twentieth. From 1840 to 1900, turnout of the voting age population was never less than 69.5 percent. Between 1904 and 1916, turnout was in the 60 percent range. In 1920 and 1924, turnout was just below 50 percent. From 1928 to 1984, turnout varied between 53.4 percent to 65.4 percent, peaking in 1960.[4] Turnout bottomed out at 50.2 percent of the voting age population in 1988, recovering to 55.2 percent in 1992.

A number of changes instigated the decline of turnout around the turn of the century. These included the beginning of voter registration requirements, the dampening of party loyalties, the spread of one-party domains, and the disenfranchisement of Blacks and many Whites in the South by the poll tax and literacy tests.[5] Turnout reached its nadir during the period 1920–1924, the two first elections with female suffrage. Many new voters were simply not accustomed to voting and were not yet registered. Today, though, women have a slightly higher turnout rate than men. Since 1960, turnout has declined due to a general weakening of party loyalties and falling efficacy levels among the electorate. This decline is especially noteworthy when one considers that education levels, the best predictor of turnout on the individual level, have risen in the general population (Figure 6.4).

Throughout U.S. history, incumbent presidents have done very well in general elections. However, in recent years, incumbents have not fared as well, losing in 1976, 1980, and 1992.

Perhaps the trend toward greater incumbent risks in presidential elections is tied to two changes I previously mentioned: the rise of televised debates and government finance. Challengers have much more to gain from televised debates. The debates are opportunities for the challenger to act presidential and are a potential minefield for incumbents. In all three recent incumbent losses, the challenger gained valuable ground in the debates.

The financing of presidential elections probably also works to the disadvantage of incumbents. The government money allows the challenger to spend enough to run a first-class campaign and to gain name recognition among the electorate. Challengers do not have to go through the demeaning and time-consuming process of raising funds. Thus, both the televised debates and the government money level the playing field between challenger and incumbent; and the incumbent then has to defend the administration's record.

The Michigan model of voting behavior focuses on the long-term attitude of party identification and short-term attitudes toward current candidates and issues.[6] In his chapter, Cummings classifies the short-term factors into situational and strategic factors. Situational factors, according to Cummings, are "changes in the total environment within which the election campaign ha(s) to be fought." Strategic factors are actions taken or not taken by the candidates. According to Cummings, the situational and strategic factors in 1992 favored the Democrats and helped reverse the recent string of Republican presidential victories.

In other chapters of this book we have seen that, through the years, the long-term factor of party identification has generally been less relevant to voters. More and more, voters are casting their votes based on their issue preferences and on evaluations of the candidates.

Policy

The voting behavior literature, as we just saw, finds that policy considerations are now more important to voters than they were in the 1950s. Everett Carll Ladd argues that while economics, or "class politics," was the most important policy consideration during the New Deal era, voters in the postindustrial age are more concerned with "cultural politics" and social issues. Indeed, according to Ladd, the New Deal was the only extended time frame in U.S. history when economic issues were most important in voters' minds.

Throughout the twentieth century, but especially since the New Deal, the Democrats have been the more liberal party and Republicans have been more conservative. These policy and ideological differences, argues Gerald Pomper, are clearer now than they were in many earlier elections. In the 1992 election, though, Cummings argues that the Democrats benefitted greatly by moderating their message; they followed Downsian logic and moved toward the center of the ideological continuum.[7]

In his chapter, David Mayhew points out that midterm elections have policy effects. According to Mayhew's analysis, midterm elections—in the years 1918, 1938, 1966—often deauthorize the policy thrust of the preceding presidential election. The midterm loss of seats for the party in the White House is thus an institutionalization of the president's decline of popularity. The recent 1994 congressional midterm election appears to be a rather stark example of this. Moreover, the 1994 midterm election authorized a new policy agenda as specified in the Republican Contract with America. Due to the midterm loss of seats, presidential influence on public policy is generally greatest in the first two years of a term.

Political Change

Partisan Stability and Change. A fundamental electoral pattern is the substantial election-to-election correlation of the state presidential vote distribution. This is typical of, and in this research strategy defines, stable electoral eras. Stable eras are periodically interrupted by a period of coalitional change, indicated by a drop-off in these correlations.

In Figure 4.1, Gerald Pomper presents these correlations for the years 1956 to 1992. As he explains, the high correlation for 1956 reflects the end of the stable New Deal coalition era. Thereafter, the election-to-election correlation of the vote falls dramatically, bottoming out in 1968. The 1980 vote correlates very highly with 1976, and there continues to be high election-to-election correlations, indicative of a current stable era.

Partisan stability and change also are often viewed as change in voting coalitions.[8] A voting coalition is composed of various groupings of voters who support a party or candidate; for example, the Democratic coalition is often said to be composed of minorities, union households, Jewish voters, and lower-income groups. From this perspective, Ladd points out that since 1980, women have trended Democratic and men Republican—the so-called gender gap. Lower-income groups have remained supportive of the Democratic party. Our analysts single out many coalitional changes over the years. There have been so many voter coalition changes since the 1930s, that Cummings concludes that today's "voting patterns would have startled an electoral analyst in the days of Franklin Roosevelt."

One may also measure political change by comparing the total national vote distribution across a series of elections. This is the basis of Burnham's analysis of critical elections.[9]

However one measures change—redistribution of state votes, coalition change, or total vote change—elections or eras of electoral change are frequently called realignments. A beginning definition of realignment is a persistent, widespread change in voting behavior. Between the occasional elections of change are the much more frequent elections that do not disturb the prevailing voting patterns. A party system may be viewed as a set of elections with a stable alignment, bounded by elections of change.[10]

CARNEGIE LIBRARY
LIVINGSTONE COLLEGE
SALISBURY, NC 28144

Party Eras. There have been many attempts to group together presidential elections. The simplest way is to demarcate consecutive party wins (Table 1.4).

The most frequent way of presenting electoral eras is the party systems approach, developed by Walter Dean Burnham.[11] According to Burnham, the U.S. party system has gone through six eras or party systems: (1) the experimental system, 1789–1820; (2) the democratizing system, 1828–1860; (3) the Civil War system, 1860–1893; (4) the industrialist system, 1894–1932; (5) the New Deal system, 1932–1968; and (6) the era of the "permanent campaign and interregnum state." According to Burnham, change from one era to another is fueled by party realignment elections.

Everett Carll Ladd has developed the major alternative conceptualization of party history.[12] Ladd feels that changes in party eras "are the product of broad, fundamental changes in social structure." As we have seen, Ladd asserts that the U.S. party system has gone through four eras, each one reflecting a distinct "sociopolitical period" and its attendant "agenda." These periods are the rural Republic, industrializing nation, industrial state, and postindustrial era.

Sectionalism. A sectional voting pattern is one in which there are great differences between the regions. A national voting pattern is one in which there is relative uniformity in voting. The examination in chapter 3, by Harvey Schantz, finds that presidential elections group together into alternating extended periods of sectional and national voting patterns. Sectional patterns are very often related to Burnham's party systems. Thus, the industrializing era is known for its sectionalism—east versus west versus south. The New Deal era and our current times are characterized by national voting patterns.

It is often argued that the conditions of postindustrialism—national communications, rapid transportation—lead to an erosion of sectionalism. But sectional voting patterns may still be found in contemporary Western democracies. One scholar, for example, adopting the research design used in chapter 3, found an increase in sectional voting in Canadian elections over the last century.[13] The political issue agenda probably accounts for the degree of sectional voting. The saliency of sectional issues in an election reflect both the societal setting and the strategies of the political parties.

Divided Government. Divided government is a partisan alignment in which control of the White House and one or both chambers of Congress are held by different political parties. During the first six Reagan

CARNEGIE LIBRARY
LIVINGSTONE COLLEGE
SALISBURY, NC 28144

years, from 1981 to 1986, divided government prevailed with a Republican president, a Republican Senate majority, and a Democratic House majority. From 1987 to 1992, divided government consisted of a Republican president, Reagan and Bush, and Democratic majorities in the House and Senate. In 1994, voters once again chose divided government, electing a Republican House and Senate.

Unified government is a partisan alignment in which the president and majorities in the House and Senate are of the same party. As Milton Cummings points out, the 1992 election ended twelve years of divided government and ushered in two years of unified government as Democratic candidate Bill Clinton won the presidency and the Democrats retained control of the House and Senate. For most of U.S. history, unified government has been the norm, but over the last forty years, it has been rare.

ARE PRESIDENTIAL ELECTIONS EQUAL IN IMPORTANCE, OR ARE SOME MORE IMPORTANT THAN OTHERS?

In a constitutional sense, presidential elections are equal. Each one results in the selection of a president for four years. But specific elections have deeper or longer lasting effects—impacts that extend beyond four years—on process, policy, and political change.

Process

Nominations.   In 1824, the failure of the Democratic-Republican party to unify around the candidate nominated by their congressional caucus led to the demise of that nominating system and to the growth of the convention system. The unhappiness with the 1968 Democratic National Convention led to subsequent reform of the nominating process. Since 1972, the primary election gauntlet has been the only way for a candidate to capture a party nomination.

General Elections.   In 1800, the electoral college result was deadlocked between the two Democratic-Republican candidates, Thomas Jefferson and Aaron Burr. This deadlock led to the Twelfth Amendment to the Constitution (1804), which provides for separate electoral vote balloting for president and vice president. The 1972 election stands out because of the Watergate scandal. As a result of this "third-rate burglary," the campaign finance laws for presidential elections were greatly strengthened.

"Traumatic Elections."   A. James Reichley has identified five "traumatic elections" in which "the national political order approached or reached constitutional crisis: 1860, 1876, 1888, 1912, and 1968."[14] These coincide with the Civil War, the end of Reconstruction, the electoral vote victory of a popular vote loser, Progressivism, and the Wallace challenge.

Policy

Authorizing Elections.   Elections that induce policy change (whether realigning in voting patterns or not) are important. Mayhew has termed these policy change contests "authorizing" elections.[15] He singles out 1964 as such an election. The 1980 election also probably fits in this category.

Deauthorizing Elections. Elections that close out a period of policy change (whether realigning in voting patterns or not) are also important. Mayhew calls these "deauthorizing" elections. I would place into this category the 1952 election, which ended five Democratic victories and marked the end of the New Deal era.

Political Change

Turnover Elections.   One type of election that has been identified as more crucial than others is the election that results in a turnover of the party in office. At a minimum, these elections signal the ascendancy of a new president and partisan leadership team. The challenging party takes control of the White House and the top appointments in the executive branch. There also is possibly a major new direction in policy.

In Table 1.4, Harvey Schantz lists the twenty party turnovers in U.S. history. Milton Cummings, in chapter 2, points out that the 1992 Clinton victory is the ninth such turnover in the twentieth century. All of these represent a leadership change and some of these, no doubt, instigated major policy changes.

Realigning Elections.   Realigning elections are important, by definition, because they signal the beginning of new voting alignments. The list of party realignments usually includes the years 1800, 1860, 1896, and 1932, and probably should include 1968.

Many political scientists feel realigning elections are crucial because, along with changed voting patterns, they usher in massive policy change. Burnham, for example, wrote that "critical realignments . . . are intimately associated with and followed by transformations in large clusters of policy."[16] New directions in governance are said to ride the wave of electoral change. In fact, realignment theory in its most developed form asserts that realigning elections include changed voting patterns, changed partisan control of government, and a new direction to public policy. In his chapter, David Mayhew undermines the importance of realigning elections by questioning their causal link to policy change.

Status Quo Elections. Some elections are important for what did *not* happen. The 1896 loss of Bryan, for example, prevented the capturing of the White House by a candidate committed to a radical course of action. The 1964 and 1972 presidential elections may be similarly thought of as status quo elections, as voters rejected the bids of nominees advocating nonincremental policy change.

A stable electoral pattern, on the other hand, may mask major policy change. The election of 1876, for example, appears to be a status quo one in that a Republican was elected for the fifth straight time. But the dealings that allowed Rutherford Hayes to win an electoral vote majority included the end of Reconstruction in the South—a very marked policy change.

WHAT ARE THE RELATIONSHIPS OF PRESIDENTIAL ELECTIONS TO THE POLITICAL PARTIES, PUBLIC POLICY, AND SOCIETY?

Political Parties

The political parties are vitally involved in all aspects of the presidential selection process. Elections are possible without parties, but the United States does not have much experience in this regard.

Parties and the Nomination Process. Many of the contributors to this book examine the role of the party organization in presidential nominations. In chapter 1, Schantz views the presidential nominee as emerging from an interactive process involving candidates, voters, and the press, with only a minor independent role for party leaders. This is essentially the process described by Cummings, in his outline of the dynamics of the 1992 contest. In 1992, according to Cummings, Clinton won the nomination through his success in the presidential primaries, especially those held on Super Tuesday, March 10, in the South. Likewise, President Bush had to repel Buchanan's challenge by defeating him in the primaries in order to be renominated. Ladd agrees with the foregoing descriptions and adds that this attenuated role for the party organizations is "in contrast to the situation in all previous party systems. . . ."

Pomper heartily dissents from this shared perspective. He argues that "recent nominations, particularly in 1992, evidence a trend toward increased party influence in the selection of national leadership." Although the nominations of Republican Barry Goldwater in 1964 and Democrat George McGovern in 1972 illustrate the weakness of party organization, in more recent years insurgent candidates have not been successful in their bids for party nomination. Presidential nominees since 1980, according to Pomper, have been party organization leaders, factional leaders, or incumbent presidents. Clinton's power base was the Democratic Leadership Council. "Clinton's success," writes Pomper, "is a testament to the influence of that faction, far more than evidence of the decline of party and the substitution of unmediated access to the voters."

Parties and Voters. Ladd describes an electorate that is much less anchored to party labels than in previous eras. He finds that voters in the postindustrial era are more likely to switch their presidential vote between the parties from one election to the next and also finds a trend towards more frequent ticket-splitting by voters. Ladd, as well as Schantz and Cummings, in the first two chapters of this book, all find an increase in the proportion of voters who identify themselves as independent of party.

For the most part, Pomper has agreed with these views.[17] But in this book, he cites trends of increasing party relevance to voters. These changes include an increase in strong party identifiers, stability in state-level voting coalitions between 1976 and 1992, and a decline in congressional districts won by a representative and presidential candidate of different parties. Pomper also emphasizes that voters demonstrated strong party loyalty in the 1992 presidential election.

Parties and Policy. The political parties deal with policy in all of the processes that we have been describing. The political parties promote distinct policy messages to appeal to their distinctive coalitions. Pomper emphasizes these policy messages with respect to the party platforms. Schantz discusses them within the context of campaign appeals. These propositions are in contrast to the belief, widely-held before the 1964 Johnson-Goldwater contest, that the Democrats and Republicans were without major policy differences and that they both sought the safety of the political middle.

The political parties, though, have some leeway to tailor their message for political exigencies. Thus, Cummings describes how the Democratic party, led by the Democratic Leadership Council, moderated its campaign message between 1988 and 1992. On the other hand, both Cummings and Schantz point out that the Republicans became more strident in their conservatism between the two Bush elections and that this change may have hurt them at the ballot box.

Years ago, E. E. Schattschneider argued that the party that defines the preeminent issue in an election will be the victor.[18] "The effort in all political struggle is to exploit cracks in the opposition while attempting to consolidate one's own side." Picking up on this theme (but without citing Schattschneider), William Safire last year argued that the "crack" in the Republican party centers on abortion, and the Democratic fault line is affirmative action.[19] Both parties are currently trying to exploit these cracks in 1996. They seek to drive a "wedge" into the opposition and "split off a great segment of the other party's vote."

Accounting for Public Policy

In his chapter, David Mayhew is concerned with the correlates or instigators of major legislative surges—of which he counts four—in U.S. history. He finds that the best predictor of these surges is public moods, rather than the economy, political parties, or elections.

Party Government. To be sure, Mayhew does find some support for "party government" lawmaking. The Republican party and the legislation from 1861 to 1875 is, according to Mayhew, "the leading instance of a surge driven by one party. . . ." The New Deal of Franklin Roosevelt "is a good case." And many "initiatives" of Lyndon Johnson's Great Society, continues Mayhew, "unquestionably offer a leading instance of party-based lawmaking."

Not all policymaking is by "party government," however. According to Mayhew, Democrats and progressive Republicans passed the Progressive era legislation and such a cross-party coalition passed key legislation in the last Hoover Congress. The civil rights laws of the Great Society era were supported by Northerners of both parties. And many laws and regulations from 1969 to 1974 benefited from President Richard Nixon's support. I would add that during much of the last half-century, the conservative coalition, made up of southern Democrats and Republicans, has been a cross-party alliance of great significance to congressional policy making.

In a recent examination of congressional legislation, from 1946 to 1990, Mayhew showed that there were as many major bills passed during years of divided party control as there were during periods of unified control of government.[20] In his chapter here, Mayhew finds that the four legislative surges were not the sole domain of the unified years. Unified control was the setting for the legislative surge of the Civil War and Reconstruction era. But important elements of the three other legislative surges occurred during times of split party control of government.

Cross-party alliances and partisan accommodation during divided control raise some questions about American democracy and the workings of our party system. On the one hand, these policy making processes may be a breach with voters as the two parties behave in "collusion and mutual evasions of responsibility on a large scale."[21] On the other hand, though, these policy making processes may reflect the "partisan divergence and ideological convergence" of the electoral verdict.[22] In other words, "bipartisan government" may very well reflect the popular "consensus on many issues."[23]

Elections and Mandates. Mayhew's scheme assigns relatively little independent influence to elections in the policy making process. He does feel, however, that electoral realignments were instrumental in the legislative surge of the Civil War-Reconstruction era and Roosevelt's New Deal. But, as we have seen, he does not believe that all electoral realignments induce great policy change. He finds that some elections authorize or deauthorize policy making. But such elections are relatively few.

The attenuated influence of elections on public policy results from the difficulty of implementing mandates. First, policy making by mandate requires that voters choose candidates based on policy promises. Second, leaders must discern the precise issue preferences of voters. And last, elected leaders must pass their party programs into law once in office. As Pomper and Lederman concluded, "In the United States at least, none of these three conditions is substantially satisfied."[24]

When all is said and done, perhaps the most a newly elected president wins is a "permissive consensus,"[25] within which to operate during a short "honeymoon" period.

Society

The relationship between society and presidential elections is reciprocal; each has considerable influence on the other.

Society As the Independent Variable. The society is the major "mold" into which the political parties and elections system fits.[26] The environment of the parties—the American mold—includes public ambivalence toward political parties, as well as constitutional arrangements, statutes, and judicial doctrine: the separation of powers and the regulation of nominating and electoral processes, for example. The electoral vote system is probably the most significant constitutional feature of the presidential selection process. Federal campaign finance laws are a significant statutory aspect of presidential selection.

Society also determines the possible lines of conflict in our elections. In other words, the agenda of politics reflects class and group interests. As society changes, the premier conflicts change.[27] Thus, the agenda of politics in the rural Republic—a local versus a national politics—differs from the political agenda during the era of the industrial state—the creation of a managerial state to police industry.

Society also determines the texture of political campaigns. The technologies of television, polling, and jet travel were not available to the politicians of the rural Republic. A highly educated and, for the most part, affluent electorate is not as dependent on political parties for information and material benefits. Television media blitzes, independent voting, and candidate-centered campaigns reflect the wider societal setting.

The Effects of Elections on Society. Elections have considerable influence on American society. Voters gain indirect control over policy through the ballot box. "Initiatives in a democratic system lie not with the voters but with politicians."[28] And, in our political system, voters determine who these politicians will be.

Elections also offer general policy guidance to our officials. Most times, mandates offer precious little detail. James L. Sundquist's description of the 1960 Kennedy mandate is illuminating: "But, as in other years—like 1932 and 1952—when the people changed party tenure in the White House, the mandate of the voters was clear only in its general outlines, obscure in its particulars."[29] Sometimes—not too often—a mandate may be precise, however. The 1988 "election results," wrote Pomper in early 1989, "provide no policy mandate for the new President other than the confining promise of no increase in taxes."[30]

Elections also lend stability to the political system. They provide an outlet for political dissent while legitimizing the government. Mass politics is changed by elections "from a means of asserting demands to a collective statement of permission."[31]

Most important, elections help to fulfill the societal function of conflict resolution. Elections provide a means for selecting particular leaders and a basis for a peaceful, scheduled transition of power.[32] In other words, the wars of domestic politics are recorded in the fifty-two American presidential elections.

NOTES

1. Leon D. Epstein, *Political Parties in the American Mold* (Madison: University of Wisconsin Press, 1986), pp. 88–102.
2. Calculated from Congressional Quarterly Inc., *Guide to U.S. Elections*, 2nd ed. (Washington, D.C. 1985), pp. 329–366; *Congressional Quarterly Weekly Report* 47 (January 21, 1989): 139 and 51 (January 30, 1993): 233.
3. Congressional Quarterly, *Guide to U.S. Elections*, p. 321.
4. Walter Dean Burnham, "The Turnout Problem," in *Elections American Style*, ed. A. James Reichley (Washington, D.C.: Brookings, 1987), pp. 97–133, at 113–114. The Burnham turnout percentages are based on the population of eligible voters, and are thus slightly higher than the turnout percentages cited in chapter 1, which are based on the voting age population.
5. See the research reports by Walter Dean Burnham, Philip E. Converse, and Jerrold G. Rusk in the *American Political Science Review* 68 (September 1974): 1002–1057.
6. Norman R. Luttbeg and Michael M. Gant, *American Electoral Behavior 1952–1992* (Itasca, Ill.: Peacock, 1995), pp. 12–20.
7. Anthony Downs, *An Economic Theory of Democracy* (New York: Harper and Row, 1957), Chapter 8; Richard Scammon and Ben J. Wattenberg, *The Real Majority: An Extraordinary Examination of the American Electorate* (New York: Coward, McCann, and Geoghesan, 1970).
8. Everett Carll Ladd, with Charles D. Hadley, *Transformations of the American Party System: Political Coalitions from the New Deal to the 1970s*, 2nd ed. (New York, Norton, 1978).
9. Walter Dean Burnham, *Critical Elections and the Mainsprings of American Politics* (New York: Norton, 1970), Chapters 1–2.
10. Paul Kleppner, "Critical Realignments and Electoral Systems," in *The Evolution of American Electoral Systems*, Kleppner et al. (Westport, Conn.: Greenwood, 1981), chapter 1.
11. Walter Dean Burnham, "Party Systems and the Political Process," in *The American Party Systems: Stages of Political Development*, ed. Burnham and William Nisbet Chambers (New York: Oxford University Press, 1967), Chapter 10; and idem, "Critical Realignment: Dead or Alive?" in *The End of Realignment?: Interpreting American Electoral Eras*, ed. Byron E. Shafer (Madison: University of Wisconsin Press, 1991), Chapter 5, esp. p. 117.
12. Everett Carll Ladd, *American Political Parties: Social Change and Political Response* (New York: Norton, 1970); and Ladd, with Had-

ley, *Transformations of the American Party System.*

13. Mark Stern, "The Persistence of Regionalism in Canadian Federal Elections," paper presented at Second Biennial Conference on Canadian Studies, Moscow, Russia, July 7–10, 1993.

14. A. James Reichley, "The Electoral System," in *Elections American Style*, ed. Reichley (Washington, D.C.: Brookings, 1987), pp. 1–26, at 12–17.

15. David R. Mayhew, "Congressional Representation: Theory and Practice in Drawing the Districts," in *Reapportionment in the 1970s*, ed. Nelson W. Polsby (Berkeley: University of California Press, 1971), pp. 249–285, esp. pp. 260–269; and see Hanna Fenichel Pitkin, *The Concept of Representation* (Berkeley: University of California Press, 1967).

16. Burnham, *Critical Elections*, p. 9.

17. Gerald M. Pomper, *Passions and Interests: Political Party Concepts of American Democracy* (Lawrence: University Press of Kansas, 1992), pp. 101–115.

18. E. E. Schattschneider, *The Semisovereign People: A Realist's View of Democracy in America* (Hinsdale, Ill.: Dryden Press, 1960), pp. 62–77, quotation, pp. 69–70.

19. William Safire, "The Double Wedge," *New York Times*, February 23, 1995, p. A23.

20. David R. Mayhew, *Divided We Govern: Party Control, Lawmaking, and Investigations: 1946–1990* (New Haven: Yale University Press, 1991).

21. Walter Dean Burnham, "The Legacy of George Bush: Travails of an Understudy," in *The Election of 1992*, ed. Gerald M. Pomper (Chatham, N.J.: Chatham House, 1993), pp. 1–38, quotation, p. 22.

22. Milton C. Cummings, Jr., *Congressmen and the Electorate: Elections for the U.S. House and the President, 1920–1964* (New York: The Free Press, 1966), p. 109.

23. Paul Frymer, "Ideological Consensus within Divided Party Government," *Political Science Quarterly* 109 (Summer 1994): 287–311, quotation at 310.

24. Gerald M. Pomper, with Susan S. Lederman, *Elections in America: Control and Influence in Democratic Politics*, 2nd ed. (New York: Longman, 1980), p. 212.

25. V. O. Key, Jr., *Public Opinion and American Democracy* (New York: Knopf, 1961), pp. 32–35.

26. Epstein, *Political Parties in the American Mold.*

27. Ladd, *American Political Parties: Social Change and Political Response.*

28. Pomper, with Lederman, *Elections in America*, p. 216.

29. James L. Sundquist, *Politics and Policy: The Eisenhower, Kennedy, and Johnson Years* (Washington, D.C.: Brookings, 1968), p. 467.
30. Gerald M. Pomper, "The Presidential Election," in *The Election of 1988: Reports and Interpretations* (Chatham, N.J.: Chatham House, 1989), pp. 129–152, at 150.
31. Benjamin Ginsberg, *The Captive Public: How Mass Opinion Promotes State Power* (New York: Basic Books, 1986), p. 185.
32. V. O. Key, Jr., *Politics, Parties, and Pressure Groups*, 5th ed. (New York: Crowell, 1964), pp. 5–6, 10.

Appendix

Presidential Election Results, 1789–1992

No.	Year	Candidate[a]	Political Party[b]	Percent of Total Popular Vote	Electoral Votes
1[c]	1789	George Washington			69
		John Adams			34
		John Jay			9
		Nine others			26
2[c]	1792	George Washington			132
		John Adams			77
		George Clinton			50
		Two others			5
3[c]	1796	John Adams	F		71
		Thomas Jefferson	D-R		68
		Thomas Pinckney	F		59
		Aaron Burr	D-R		30
		Nine others			48
4[c]	1800	Thomas Jefferson	D-R		73[d]
		Aaron Burr	D-R		73
		John Adams	F		65
		Charles C. Pinckney	F		64
		John Jay	F		1
5	1804	Thomas Jefferson	D-R		162
		Charles C. Pinckney	F		14
6	1808	James Madison	D-R		122
		Charles C. Pinckney	F		47
		George Clinton	I D-R		6
7	1812	James Madison	D-R		128
		DeWitt Clinton	F, I D-R		89

No.	Year	Candidate[a]	Political Party[b]	Percent of Total Popular Vote	Electoral Votes
8	1816	James Monroe	D-R		183
		Rufus King	F		34
9	1820	James Monroe	D-R		231
		John Quincy Adams	I D-R		1
10	1824	John Quincy Adams	D-R	30.9	84[d]
		Andrew Jackson	D-R	41.3	99
		Henry Clay	D-R	13.0	37
		William H. Crawford	D-R	11.2	41
11	1828	Andrew Jackson	D	56.0	178
		John Quincy Adams	N-R	43.6	83
12	1832	Andrew Jackson	D	54.2	219
		Henry Clay	N-R	37.4	49
		William Wirt	A-M	7.8	7
		John Floyd	I D	0.0[e]	11
13	1836	Martin Van Buren	D	50.8	170
		William H. Harrison	W	36.6	73
		Hugh L. White	W	9.7	26
		Daniel Webster	W	2.7	14
		Willie Person Mangum	I D	0.0[e]	11
14	1840	William H. Harrison	W	52.9	234
		Martin Van Buren	D	46.8	60
15	1844	James K. Polk	D	49.5	170
		Henry Clay	W	48.1	105
		James G. Birney	L	2.3	0
16	1848	Zachary Taylor	W	47.3	163
		Lewis Cass	D	42.5	127
		Martin Van Buren	FS	10.1	0
17	1852	Franklin Pierce	D	50.8	254
		Winfield Scott	W	43.9	42
		John P. Hale	FS	4.9	0
18	1856	James Buchanan	D	45.3	174
		John C. Fremont	R	33.1	114
		Millard Fillmore	W-A	21.5	8
19	1860	Abraham Lincoln	R	39.8	180
		Stephen A. Douglas	D	29.5	12
		John C. Breckinridge	SD	18.1	72
		John Bell	CU	12.6	39
20	1864	Abraham Lincoln	R	55.0	212

No.	Year	Candidate[a]	Political Party[b]	Percent of Total Popular Vote	Electoral Votes
		George B. McClellan	D	45.0	21
21	1868	Ulysses S. Grant	R	52.7	214
		Horatio Seymour	D	47.3	80
22	1872	Ulysses S. Grant	R	55.6	286
		Horace Greeley	D,LR	43.8	66[f]
23	1876	Rutherford B. Hayes	R	48.0	185[g]
		Samuel J. Tilden	D	51.0	184
24	1880	James A. Garfield	R	48.27	214
		Winfield S. Hancock	D	48.25	155
		James B. Weaver	GB	3.3	0
25	1884	Grover Cleveland	D	48.5	219
		James G. Blaine	R	48.3	182
26	1888	Benjamin Harrison	R	47.8	233[g]
		Grover Cleveland	D	48.6	168
		Clinton B. Fisk	PROH	2.2	0
27	1892	Grover Cleveland	D	46.1	277
		Benjamin Harrison	R	43.0	145
		James B. Weaver	POP	8.5	22
		John Bidwell	PROH	2.3	0
28	1896	William McKinley	R	51.0	271
		William J. Bryan	D, POP	46.7	176
29	1900	William McKinley	R	51.7	292
		William J. Bryan	D	45.5	155
30	1904	Theodore Roosevelt	R	56.4	336
		Alton Parker	D	37.6	140
		Eugene V. Debs	SOC	3.0	0
31	1908	William H. Taft	R	51.6	321
		William J. Bryan	D	43.1	162
		Eugene V. Debs	SOC	2.8	0
32	1912	Woodrow Wilson	D	41.8	435
		Theodore Roosevelt	PROG	27.4	88
		William H. Taft	R	23.2	8
		Eugene V. Debs	SOC	6.0	0
33	1916	Woodrow Wilson	D	49.2	277
		Charles E. Hughes	R	46.1	254
		Allan L. Benson	SOC	3.2	0
34	1920	Warren G. Harding	R	60.3	404

No.	Year	Candidate[a]	Political Party[b]	Percent of Total Popular Vote	Electoral Votes
		James M. Cox	D	34.2	127
		Eugene V. Debs	SOC	3.4	0
35	1924	Calvin Coolidge	R	54.1	382
		John W. Davis	D	28.8	136
		Robert M. La Follette	PROG	16.6	13
36	1928	Herbert C. Hoover	R	58.2	444
		Alfred E. Smith	D	40.8	87
37	1932	Franklin D. Roosevelt	D	57.4	472
		Herbert C. Hoover	R	39.6	59
		Norman M. Thomas	SOC	2.2	0
38	1936	Franklin D. Roosevelt	D	60.8	523
		Alfred M. Landon	R	36.5	8
		William Lemke	U	2.0	0
39	1940	Franklin D. Roosevelt	D	54.7	449
		Wendell Willkie	R	44.8	82
40	1944	Franklin D. Roosevelt	D	53.4	432
		Thomas E. Dewey	R	45.9	99
41	1948	Harry S Truman	D	49.5	303
		Thomas E. Dewey	R	45.1	189
		J. Strom Thurmond	SRD	2.40	39
		Henry A. Wallace	PROG	2.38	0
42	1952	Dwight D. Eisenhower	R	55.1	442
		Adlai E. Stevenson	D	44.4	89
43	1956	Dwight D. Eisenhower	R	57.4	457
		Adlai E. Stevenson	D	42.0	73
44	1960	John F. Kennedy	D	49.7	303
		Richard M. Nixon	R	49.6	219
		Harry F. Byrd	D	0.2	15
45	1964	Lyndon B. Johnson	D	61.1	486
		Barry M. Goldwater	R	38.5	52
46	1968	Richard M. Nixon	R	43.4	301
		Hubert H. Humphrey	D	42.7	191
		George C. Wallace	AI	13.5	46
47	1972	Richard M. Nixon	R	60.7	520
		George S. McGovern	D	37.5	17
48	1976	Jimmy Carter	D	50.1	297

No.	Year	Candidate[a]	Political Party[b]	Percent of Total Popular Vote	Electoral Votes
		Gerald R. Ford	R	48.0	240
49	1980	Ronald Reagan	R	50.7	489
		Jimmy Carter	D	41.0	49
		John B. Anderson	I	6.6	0
50	1984	Ronald Reagan	R	58.8	525
		Walter Mondale	D	40.6	13
51	1988	George Bush	R	53.4	426
		Michael S. Dukakis	D	45.6	111
52	1992	Bill Clinton	D	43.0	370
		George Bush	R	37.4	168
		Ross Perot	I	18.9	0

Source: Congressional Quarterly, Inc., *Guide to U.S. Elections,* 2nd ed. (Washington, D.C., 1985), pp. 269–313 and 329–366; updated for 1988 and 1992.

[a] This listing of candidates includes all candidates receiving 2 percent or more of the popular vote and, beginning with 1804, all candidates receiving two or more electoral votes.

[b] Political party abbreviations are: AI (American Independent) A-M (Anti-Masonic); CU (Constitutional Union); D (Democrat); D-R (Democratic-Republican); F (Federalist); FS (Free Soil); GB (Greenback); I (Independent); L (Liberty); LR (Liberal Republican); N-R (National-Republican); POP (Populist); PROG (Progressive); PROH (Prohibition); R (Republican); SD (Southern Democrat); SOC (Socialist); SRD (States' Rights Democrat); U (Union); W (Whig); W-A (Whig-American).

[c] In the first four elections, the runner-up in the electoral vote became vice president. The Twelfth Amendment, ratified in 1804, provides for separate electoral votes for president and vice president.

[d] The House chooses the president if no candidate receives an electoral vote majority. This occurred twice, in 1800 and 1824. Since 1804, as outlined in the Twelfth Amendment, the House chooses from among the three leading candidates.

[e] South Carolina did not have popular voting for electors until 1868.

[f] Greeley died before the electoral vote balloting; his electoral votes were split among four candidates.

[g] Twice, in 1876 and 1888, the popular vote winner lost the electoral vote.

Suggested Reading

1. OVERVIEWS

A. The Presidential Selection Process

Asher, Herbert B. *Presidential Elections and American Politics: Voters, Candidates, and Campaigns Since 1952*, 5th ed. Pacific Grove, Calif.: Brooks/Cole Publishing, 1992.

Polsby, Nelson W. and Aaron Wildavsky. *Presidential Elections: Strategies and Structures in American Politics*, 9th ed. Chatham, N.J.: Chatham House, 1996.

Rose, Gary L., ed. *Controversial Issues in Presidential Selection*, 2nd ed. Albany: State University of New York Press, 1994.

Wayne, Stephen J. *The Road to the White House 1996: The Politics of Presidential Elections*. New York: St. Martin's Press, 1996.

B. The American Party System

Beck, Paul Allen and Frank J. Sorauf. *Party Politics in America*, 7th ed. New York: HarperCollins, 1992.

Epstein, Leon D. *Political Parties in the American Mold*. Madison: University of Wisconsin Press, 1986.

Keefe, William J. *Parties, Politics, and Public Policy in America*, 7th ed. Washington, D.C.: CQ Press, 1994.

C. The American Presidency

Edwards, George C., III, and Stephen J. Wayne. *Presidential Leadership: Politics and Policy Making*, 3rd ed. New York: St. Martin's Press, 1994.

Koenig, Louis W. *The Chief Executive*, 6th ed. Orlando: Harcourt Brace Jovanovich, 1996.

Thomas, Norman C., Joseph A. Pika, and Richard A. Watson. *The Politics of the Presidency*, 3rd ed. Washington, D.C.: CQ Press, 1993.

2. THE PRESIDENTIAL SELECTION PROCESS

A. The Pool of Candidates

Abramson, Paul R., John H. Aldrich, and David W. Rohde. "Progressive Ambition Among United States Senators: 1972–1988." *Journal of Politics* 49 (February 1987): 3–35.

Aldrich, John H. *Before the Convention: Strategies and Choices in Presidential Nomination Campaigns*. Chicago: University of Chicago Press, 1980, Chapters 1–2.

Hargrove, Erwin C. and Michael Nelson. *Presidents, Politics, and Policy*. Baltimore: Johns Hopkins University Press, 1984, Chapter 5.

Hess, Stephen. "'Why Great Men are Not Chosen Presidents': Lord Bryce Revisited." In *Elections American Style*, ed. A. James Reichley. Washington, D.C.: Brookings, 1987, Chapter 4.

Peabody, Robert L., Norman J. Ornstein, and David W. Rohde. "The United States Senate as a Presidential Incubator: Many Are Called but Few Are Chosen." *Political Science Quarterly* 91 (Summer 1976): 237–258.

B. The Nomination Process

Bartels, Larry M. *Presidential Primaries and the Dynamics of Public Choice*. Princeton, N.J.: Princeton University Press, 1988.

Buell, Emmett H., Jr., and Lee Sigelman, eds. *Nominating the President*. Knoxville: University of Tennessee Press, 1991.

Keech, William R. and Donald R. Matthews. *The Party's Choice*. Washington, D.C.: Brookings, 1976.

Orren, Gary R. and Nelson W. Polsby, eds. *Media and Momentum: The New Hampshire Primary and Nomination Politics*. Chatham, N.J.: Chatham House, 1987.

Shafer, Byron E. *Bifurcated Politics: Evolution and Reform in the National Party Convention*. Cambridge, Mass.: Harvard University Press, 1988.

C. The General Election

Alexander, Herbert E. *Financing Politics: Money, Elections, and Political Reform*, 4th ed. Washington, D.C.: CQ Press, 1992.

Hess, Stephen. *The Presidential Campaign*, 3rd ed. Washington, D.C.: Brookings, 1988.

Jamieson, Kathleen Hall. *Packaging the Presidency: A History and Criticism of Presidential Campaign Advertising*, 2nd ed. New York: Oxford University Press, 1992.

Jamieson, Kathleen Hall and David S. Birdsell. *Presidential Debates: The Challenge of Creating an Informed Electorate*. New York: Oxford University Press, 1988.

Patterson, Thomas E. *Out of Order*. New York: Knopf, 1993.

Peirce, Neal R. and Lawrence D. Longley. *The People's President: The Electoral College in American History and the Direct Vote Alternative*, rev. ed. New Haven: Yale University Press, 1981.

Rosenstone, Steven J., Roy L. Behr, and Edward H. Lazarus. *Third Parties in America*. Princeton, N.J.: Princeton University Press, 1984.

D. Voting: Behavior, Forecasting, History

Flanigan, William H. and Nancy H. Zingale. *Political Behavior of the American Electorate*, 8th ed. Washington, D.C.: CQ Press, 1994.

Lewis-Beck, Michael S. and Tom W. Rice. *Forecasting Elections*. Washington, D.C.: CQ Press, 1992.

Lichtman, Allan J. and Ken DeCell. *The Thirteen Keys to the Presidency*. Lanham, Md.: Madison Books, 1990.

Luttbeg, Norman R. and Michael M. Gant. *American Electoral Behavior 1952–1992*, 2nd ed. Itasca, Ill.: Peacock, 1995.

Miller, Warren E. and Teresa E. Levitin. *Leadership and Change: Presidential Elections from 1952 to 1976*. Cambridge, Mass.: Winthrop, 1976.

Nie, Norman H., Sidney Verba, and John R. Petrocik. *The Changing American Voter*, rev ed. Cambridge, Mass.: Harvard University Press, 1979.

Reichley, A. James. *The Life of the Parties: A History of American Political Parties*. New York: The Free Press, 1992.

Tufte, Edward R. *Political Control of the Economy*. Princeton, N.J.: Princeton University Press, 1978.

Wattenberg, Martin P. *The Decline of American Political Parties, 1952–1988*. Cambridge, Mass.: Harvard University Press, 1990.

3. ELECTIONS AND PUBLIC POLICY

A. The Role and Function of Elections

Burnham, Walter Dean. "Elections As Democratic Institutions." In *Elections in America*, ed. Kay Lehman Schlozman. Boston: Allen and Unwin, 1987, Chapter 2.

Dahl, Robert A. "Myth of the Presidential Mandate." *Political Science Quarterly* 105 (Fall 1990): 355–372.

Ginsberg, Benjamin. *The Consequences of Consent: Elections, Citizen Control and Popular Acquiescence.* Reading, Mass.: Addison-Wesley, 1982.

Ginsberg, Benjamin. *The Captive Public: How Mass Opinion Promotes State Power.* New York: Basic Books, 1986.

Kelley, Stanley, Jr. *Interpreting Elections.* Princeton, N.J.: Princeton University Press, 1983.

Pomper, Gerald M., with Susan S. Lederman. *Elections in America: Control and Influence in Democratic Politics,* 2nd. ed. New York: Longman, 1980.

B. Policy Making

Brady, David W. *Critical Elections and Congressional Policy Making.* Stanford, Calif.: Stanford University Press, 1988.

Chubb, John E. and Paul E. Peterson, eds. *The New Direction in American Politics.* Washington, D.C.: Brookings, 1985.

Mayhew, David R. *Divided We Govern: Party Control, Lawmaking, and Investigations, 1946–1990.* New Haven: Yale University Press, 1991.

Sinclair, Barbara. *Congressional Realignment, 1925–1978.* Austin: University of Texas Press, 1982.

Sinclair, Barbara. "Agenda Control and Policy Success: Ronald Reagan and the 97th House." *Legislative Studies Quarterly* 10 (August 1985): 291–314.

Sundquist, James L. *Politics and Policy: The Eisenhower, Kennedy, and Johnson Years.* Washington, D.C.: Brookings, 1968.

4. POLITICAL CHANGE

A. Social and Agenda Change

Carmines, Edward G. and James A. Stimson. *Issue Evolution: Race and the Transformation of American Politics.* Princeton, N.J.: Princeton University Press, 1989.

Edsall, Thomas Byrne, with Mary D. Edsall. *Chain Reaction: The Impact of Race, Rights, and Taxes on American Politics.* New York: Norton, 1991, 1992.

Ladd, Everett Carll. *American Political Parties: Social Change and Political Response.* New York: Norton, 1970.

Ladd, Everett Carll, with Charles D. Hadley. *Transformations of the American Party System,* 2nd ed. New York, Norton, 1978.

Scammon, Richard M. and Ben J. Wattenberg. *The Real Majority: An Extraordinary Examination of the American Electorate.* New York: Coward, McCann, and Geoghegan, 1970, 1971.

B. Realignment

Burnham, Water Dean. *Critical Elections and the Mainsprings of American Politics.* New York: Norton, 1970.

Campbell, Bruce A. and Richard J. Trilling, eds. *Realignment in American Politics: Toward a Theory.* Austin: University of Texas Press, 1980.

Clubb, Jerome M., William H. Flanigan, and Nancy H. Zingale. *Partisan Realignment: Voters, Parties, and Government in American History.* Beverly Hills, Calif.: Sage, 1980; reissued 1990, Boulder, Colo.: Westview Press.

Sundquist James L. *Dynamics of the Party System: Alignment and Realignment of Political Parties in the United States,* rev. ed. Washington, D.C.: Brookings, 1983.

C. Party Systems

Chambers, William Nisbet and Walter Dean Burnham, eds. *The American Party Systems: Stages of Political Development.* New York: Oxford University Press, 1967, 1975.

Kleppner, Paul, et al. *The Evolution of American Electoral Systems.* Westport, Conn.: Greenwood, 1981.

Shafer, Byron E., ed. *The End of Realignment? Interpreting American Electoral Eras.* Madison: University of Wisconsin Press, 1991.

D. Classifying Elections

Campbell, Angus, Philip E. Converse, Warren E. Miller, and Donald E. Stokes. *The American Voter.* New York: Wiley, 1960, pp. 531–538.

Campbell, Angus. "A Classification of the Presidential Elections." In *Elections and the Political Order,* eds. Campbell, Philip E. Converse, Warren E. Miller, and Donald E. Stokes. New York: Wiley, 1966, Chapter 4.

Key, V. O., Jr. *Politics, Parties, and Pressure Groups,* 5th ed. New York: Crowell, 1964, Chapter 19.

Kleppner, Paul. "Critical Realignments and Electoral Systems." In *The Evolution of American Electoral Systems,* Kleppner et al. Westport, Conn.: Greenwood, 1981, Chapter 1.

Nardulli, Peter F. and Jon K. Dalager. "The Presidential Election of 1992 in Historical Perspective." In *America's Choice: The Election of*

1992, ed. William Crotty. Guilford, Conn.: Dushkin, 1993, Chapter 13.

Pomper, Gerald M. "Classification of Presidential Elections." *Journal of Politics* 29 (August 1967): 535–566.

Pomper, Gerald M., with Susan S. Lederman. *Elections in America: Control and Influence in Democratic Politics*, 2nd ed. New York: Longman, 1980, Chapter 5.

E. Sectionalism

Ewing, Cortez A. M. *Presidential Elections: From Abraham Lincoln to Franklin D. Roosevelt.* Norman: University of Oklahoma Press, 1940.

Hagstrom, Jerry. *Beyond Reagan: The New Landscape of American Politics*, rev. ed. New York: Penguin Books, 1989.

Holcombe, Arthur N. *The Political Parties of To-Day: A Study in Republican and Democratic Politics*, 2nd ed. New York: Harper and Brothers, 1925.

Key, V. O., Jr. *Politics, Parties, and Pressure Groups*, 5th ed. New York: Crowell, 1964, Chapter 9.

Mileur, Jerome M. "The General Election Campaign: Strategy and Support." In *America's Choice: The Election of 1992*, ed. William Crotty. Guilford, Conn.: Dushkin, 1993, Chapter 4.

Peirce, Neal R. and Jerry Hagstrom. *The Book of America: Inside Fifty States Today*, rev. ed. New York: Warner Books, 1984.

Phillips, Kevin P. *The Emerging Republican Majority.* Garden City, N.Y.: Anchor, 1970; Arlington House, 1969.

Schattschneider, E. E. *The Semisovereign People: A Realist's View of Democracy in America.* Hinsdale, Ill.: Dryden Press, 1960, 1975, Chapter 5.

F. Divided Government

Cox, Gary W. and Samuel Kernell, eds. *The Politics of Divided Government.* Boulder, Colo.: Westview, 1991.

Fiorina, Morris P. *Divided Government.* New York: Macmillan, 1992.

Mayhew, David R. *Divided We Govern: Party Control, Lawmaking, and Investigations, 1946–1990.* New Haven: Yale University Press, 1991.

Sundquist, James L. "Needed: A Political Theory for the New Era of Coalition Government in the United States." *Political Science Quarterly* 103 (Winter 1988–89): 613–635.

G. Party Theory and Renewal

Baer, Denise L. and David A. Bositis. *Politics and Linkage in a Democratic Society*. Englewood Cliffs, N.J.: Prentice-Hall, 1993.

Cotter, Cornelius P. and John F. Bibby. "Institutional Development of Parties and the Thesis of Party Decline." *Political Science Quarterly* 95 (Spring 1980): 1–27.

Kayden, Xandra and Eddie Mahe, Jr. *The Party Goes On: The Persistence of the Two-Party System in the United States*. New York: Basic Books, 1985.

Pomper, Gerald M. *Passions and Interests: Political Party Concepts of American Democracy*. Lawrence: University Press of Kansas, 1992.

Pomper, Gerald M., ed. *Party Renewal in America: Theory and Practice*. New York: Praeger, 1980.

Price, David E. *Bringing Back the Parties*. Washington, D.C.: CQ Press, 1984.

Sabato, Larry J. *The Party's Just Begun: Shaping Political Parties for America's Future*. Glenview, Ill.: Scott, Foresman, 1988.

Schlesinger, Joseph A. "On the Theory of Party Organization." *Journal of Politics* 46 (May 1984): 369–400.

Schlesinger, Joseph A. "The New American Political Party." *American Political Science Review* 79 (December 1985): 1152–1169.

Schlesinger, Joseph A. *Political Parties and the Winning of Office*. Ann Arbor: University of Michigan Press, 1991, 1994.

White, John Kenneth and Jerome M. Mileur, eds. *Challenges to Party Government*. Carbondale: Southern Illinois University Press, 1992.

H. Political Cycles

Huntington, Samuel P. *American Politics: The Promise of Disharmony*. Cambridge, Mass.: Harvard University Press, 1981.

Resnick, David and Norman C. Thomas. "Cycling Through American Politics." *Polity* 23 (Fall 1990): 1–21.

Schantz, Harvey L. "The Changed Landscape of United States Politics 1960 to 1993." In *Re-Naming the Landscape*, ed. Jurgen Kleist and Bruce A. Butterfield. New York: Peter Lang, 1994, pp. 203–225.

Schlesinger, Arthur M., Jr. "The Cycles of American Politics." In *The Cycles of American History*. Boston: Houghton Mifflin, 1986, Chapter 2.

I. Postindustrial Society

Bell, Daniel. *The Coming of Post-Industrial Society: A Venture in Social Forecasting.* New York: Basic Books, 1973, 1976.

Brick, Howard. "Optimism of the Mind: Imagining Postindustrial Society in the 1960s and 1970s." *American Quarterly* 44 (September 1992): 348–380.

Inglehart, Ronald. *Culture Shift in Advanced Industrial Society.* Princeton, N.J.: Princeton University Press, 1990.

Kassiola, Joel Jay. *The Death of Industrial Civilization: The Limits to Economic Growth and the Repoliticization of Advanced Industrial Society.* Albany: State University of New York Press, 1990.

Phillips, Kevin P. *Mediacracy: American Parties and Politics in the Communication Age.* Garden City, N.Y.: Doubleday, 1975.

5. CLASSICS

Burns, James MacGregor. *The Deadlock of Democracy: Four-Party Politics in America.* Englewood Cliffs, N.J.: Prentice-Hall, 1963.

Burns, James MacGregor. *Presidential Government: The Crucible of Leadership.* Boston: Houghton Mifflin, 1965, 1973.

Campbell, Angus, Philip E. Converse, Warren E. Miller, and Donald E. Stokes. *The American Voter.* New York: Wiley, 1960.

Campbell, Angus, Philip E. Converse, Warren E. Miller, and Donald E. Stokes, eds. *Elections and the Political Order.* New York: Wiley, 1966.

Chamberlain, Lawrence H. *The President, Congress, and Legislation.* New York: Columbia University Press, 1946.

Cummings, Milton C., Jr. *Congressmen and the Electorate: Elections for the U.S. House and the President, 1920–1964.* New York: The Free Press, 1966.

Cummings, Milton C., Jr., ed. *The National Election of 1964.* Washington, D.C.: Brookings, 1966.

David, Paul T., ed. *The Presidential Election and Transition 1960–1961.* Washington, D.C.: Brookings, 1961.

Downs, Anthony. *An Economic Theory of Democracy.* New York: Harper and Row, 1957.

Ewing, Cortez A. M. *Presidential Elections: From Abraham Lincoln to Franklin D. Roosevelt.* Norman: University of Oklahoma Press, 1940.

Holcombe, Arthur N. *The Political Parties of To-Day: A Study in Republican and Democratic Politics*, 2nd ed. New York: Harper and Brothers, 1925.

Key, V. O., Jr. *Politics, Parties, and Pressure Groups*, 5th ed. New York: Crowell, 1964.

Key, V. O., Jr., with the assistance of Milton C. Cummings, Jr. *The Responsible Electorate: Rationality in Presidential Voting, 1936–1960.* Cambridge, Mass.: Harvard University Press, 1966.

Mayhew, David R. *Party Loyalty Among Congressmen: The Difference Between Democrats and Republicans, 1947–1962.* Cambridge, Mass.: Harvard University Press, 1966.

Pomper, Gerald M. *Nominating the President: The Politics of Convention Choice.* Evanston, Ill.: Northwestern University Press, 1963; rev. ed. New York: Norton, 1966.

Rossister, Clinton. *The American Presidency*, rev. ed. New York: Mentor Books, 1960.

Schattschneider, E. E. *Party Government.* New York: Holt, Rinehart and Winston, 1942.

Schattschneider, E. E. *The Semisovereign People: A Realist's View of Democracy in America.* Hinsdale, Ill.: Dryden Press, 1960, 1975.

6. RECENT ELECTIONS

Abramson, Paul R., John H. Aldrich, and David W. Rohde. *Change and Continuity in the 1980 Elections.* Washington, D.C.: CQ Press, 1982, 1983.

Abramson, Paul R., John H. Aldrich, and David W. Rohde. *Change and Continuity in the 1984 Elections.* Washington, D.C.: CQ Press, 1986, 1987.

Abramson, Paul R., John H. Aldrich, and David W. Rohde. *Change and Continuity in the 1988 Elections.* Washington, D.C.: CQ Press, 1990, 1991.

Abramson, Paul R., John H. Aldrich, and David W. Rohde. *Change and Continuity in the 1992 Elections.* Washington, D.C.: CQ Press, 1994, 1995.

Ceaser, James and Andrew Busch. *Upside Down and Inside Out: The 1992 Elections and American Politics.* Lanham: Md.: Rowman and Littlefield, 1993.

Crotty, William, ed. *America's Choice: The Election of 1992.* Guilford, Conn.: Dushkin, 1993.

Ladd, Everett Carll. "The Brittle Mandate: Electoral Dealignment and the 1980 Presidential Election." *Political Science Quarterly* 96 (Spring 1981): 1–25.

Ladd, Everett Carll. "On Mandates, Realignments, and the 1984 Presidential Election." *Political Science Quarterly* 100 (Spring 1985): 1–25.

Ladd, Everett Carll. "The 1988 Elections: Continuation of the Post-New Deal System." *Political Science Quarterly* 104 (Spring 1989): 1–18.

Ladd, Everett Carll. "The 1992 Vote for President Clinton: Another Brittle Mandate?" *Political Science Quarterly* 108 (Spring 1993): 1–28.

Loevy, Robert D. *The Flawed Path to the Presidency 1992: Unfairness and Inequality in the Presidential Selection Process*. Albany: State University of New York Press, 1994.

Nelson, Michael, ed. *The Elections of 1984*. Washington, D.C.: CQ Press, 1985.

Nelson, Michael, ed. *The Elections of 1988*. Washington, D.C.: CQ Press, 1989.

Nelson, Michael, ed. *The Elections of 1992*. Washington, D.C.: CQ Press, 1993.

Pomper, Gerald M., with colleagues. *The Election of 1976: Reports and Interpretations*. New York: David McKay, 1977.

Pomper, Gerald M., with colleagues. *The Election of 1980: Reports and Interpretations*. Chatham, N.J.: Chatham House, 1981.

Pomper, Gerald M., with colleagues. *The Election of 1984: Reports and Interpretations* Chatham, N.J.: Chatham House, 1985.

Pomper, Gerald M., with colleagues. *The Election of 1988: Reports and Interpretations*. Chatham, N.J.: Chatham House, 1989.

Pomper, Gerald M., with colleagues. *The Election of 1992: Reports and Interpretations*. Chatham, N.J.: Chatham House, 1993.

Sandoz, Ellis and Cecil V. Crabb, Jr., eds. *A Tide of Discontent: The 1980 Elections and Their Meaning*. Washington, D.C.: CQ Press, 1981.

7. REFERENCE

Congressional Quarterly, Inc. *Guide to U.S. Elections*, 3rd ed. Washington, D.C., 1994.

Nelson, Michael, ed. *Guide to the Presidency*. Washington, D.C.: Congressional Quarterly, Inc., 1989.

Scammon, Richard M., comp. and ed. *America Votes: A Handbook of Contemporary American Election Statistics*, Vols. 1–11. Vols. 1–2, New York: Macmillan, 1956, 1958. Vols. 3–5, Pittsburgh: University of Pittsburgh Press, 1959, 1962, 1964. Vols. 6–11, Washington, D.C.: Congressional Quarterly, Inc., 1966–1975, various years.

Scammon, Richard M. and Alice V. McGilivray, comps. and eds. *America Votes: A Handbook of Contemporary American Election Statistics*, Vols. 12–20 Washington, D.C.: Congressional Quarterly, Inc. 1977–1993, various years.

Schlesinger, Arthur M., Jr., ed., and Fred L. Israel and David J. Frent, assoc. eds. *Running for President: The Candidates and Their Images, 1789–1992*, two volumes. New York: Simon and Schuster, 1994.

About the Authors

Milton C. Cummings, Jr. is a professor of political science at The Johns Hopkins University, Baltimore, Maryland. He received his doctorate from Harvard University and has been a Rhodes Scholar and Guggenheim Fellow. His many books include *Congressmen and the Electorate: Elections for the U.S. House and the President, 1920–1964*, *The National Election of 1964*, and *Democracy Under Pressure: An Introduction to the American Political System*, 7th edition.

Everett Carll Ladd is a professor of political science at the University of Connecticut and executive director and president of The Roper Center for Public Opinion Research, Storrs, Connecticut. He received his doctorate from Cornell University and has served as a Woodrow Wilson Fellow and as a Guggenheim Fellow. He is the author of numerous articles in scholarly and learned journals. His many books include *American Political Parties: Social Change and Political Response*, *Transformations of the American Party System: Political Coalitions from the New Deal to the 1970s*, and *The American Polity: The People and Their Government*, 5th edition.

David R. Mayhew is Alfred Cowles Professor of Government, Department of Political Science, Yale University, New Haven, Connecticut. He received his doctorate from Harvard University and has served as a Congressional Fellow of the American Political Science Association and as a Guggenheim Fellow. His books and articles include, "Congressional Elections: The Case of the Vanishing Marginals," *Congress: The Electoral Connection*, and *Divided We Govern: Party Control, Lawmaking, and Investigations, 1946–1990*.

Gerald M. Pomper is a professor of political science at the Eagleton Institute of Politics, Rutgers University, New Brunswick, New Jersey. He received his doctorate from Princeton University and has served as a Fulbright-Hays Visiting Professor at Tel Aviv University and as a Tip O'Neill Fellow at Northeastern University. His numerous scholarly articles and books include "From Confusion to Clarity: Issues and American Voters, 1956–1968," "Classification of Presidential Elections," *Passions and Interests: Political Party Concepts of American Democracy,* and *The Election of 1992.*

Harvey L. Schantz is a professor and department chair of political science at the State University of New York, Plattsburgh. He received his doctorate from The Johns Hopkins University and has served as a Congressional Fellow of the American Political Science Association and as a Visiting Fellow at Yale University. His articles on American national politics include, "Contested and Uncontested Primaries for the U.S. House," "Inter-Party Competition for Congressional Seats: The 1960s and 1970s," and "The Erosion of Sectionalism in Presidential Elections."

Index

A

Abramson, Paul R., 31, 47, 48
Adams, John, 35, 37
Adams, John Quincy, 37, 98, 101–103
Adams, Timothy J., 210
Adamson Act, 161
Affluence, 6, 206, 223
African Americans, 3, 11–12, 27, 30, 52, 67–69, 70, 74, 76, 77, 79, 83, 84–85, 88, 159–60, 192, 202, 205, 206, 207, 213
Age and Politics, 10, 52–53, 70, 74, 196, 202
Agricultural Adjustment Acts, 162, 163
Agriculture, 6, 37, 38, 94, 96, 120, 190
Alabama, 63, 125, 126
Alaska, 59, 63, 90, 126
Aldrich, John H., 13, 31, 44, 47, 48
Aldrich, Nelson, 171
Alexander, Herbert E., 46
Allen, Jodie T., 184
Ambition, Presidential, 12, 13
Amenta, Edwin, 183
American Voter, The, 35
Americans with Disabilities Act, 180
Anderson, John B., 26, 170
Arizona, 63, 90, 126
Arkansas, 63, 73, 75, 85, 125, 126
Arterton, F. Christopher, 46
Asher, Herbert B., 34, 35, 43, 45–49
Availability, Presidential, 10

B

Baer, Denise L., 154
Bailey, Stephen, 155
Balz, Dan, 91

Bank of the United States, 37, 102, 167
Banking Act of 1935, 162
Barber, James David, 43
Barnard, Chester I., 142, 154
Bayh, Birch, 172
Beck, Paul Allen, 45, 125–27, 129, 154
Bell, Daniel, 7, 189, 190, 197, 208
Bentsen, Lloyd, 10, 61, 62, 80, 90
Berelson, Bernard, 47
Berke, Richard, 155
Bibby, John F., 155
Billington, Ray Allen, 123
Black Americans. *See* African Americans.
Blau, Peter, 154
Blum, John Morton, 182
Border States, 18, 69, 95, 97, 100–102, 105–108, 110, 113–14, 116–19, 126, 129
Bositis, David A., 154
Boxer, Barbara, 206
Bradley, Bill, 67
Brady, David W., 147, 185
Brams, Steven J., 46
Brassil, Margaret, 89
Braun, Carol Mosely, 79
Brodbeck, Arthur J., 47
Broder, David S., 91, 133, 136, 148, 197, 198, 210
Brown, Jerry, 69, 70, 144
Browning, Robert X., 165, 184
Brownlee, W. Elliot, 182
Bruzios, Christopher, 152, 155
Bryan, William Jennings, 27, 38, 108, 118, 168, 219
   cross of gold, 119

Buchanan, Patrick J., 21, 64, 66–67, 71, 86, 88, 144, 219

Buckley v. Valeo, 26

Bull Moose Party, 74. *See also* Progressive Era.

Burdick, Eugene, 47

Burner, David, 183

Burnham, Walter Dean, 31, 47, 49, 128, 129, 152–53, 185, 215, 216, 218–19, 224, 225

Burns, James MacGregor, 133, 183, 193, 210

Burr, Aaron, 217

Busch, Andrew E., 44

Bush, George, 72, 87, 137, 144, 217
 Approval Ratings, 62, 64, 65, 86–87, 88, 89
 Campaign and Election of 1988, 28, 31, 61, 73, 75, 82, 86, 123, 136, 138, 144
 Campaign and Election of 1992,
  defeat of, 41, 51, 80–89, 201, 221
  Democratic field of candidates, influence on, 67
  general election campaign, 20, 27, 29, 68, 70–72
  nomination of, 15, 21, 62, 64–66, 71, 86, 88, 144, 150, 219–20
  and Perot Spring campaign, 67
  vote for, 31, 34, 72–78, 82, 89, 119, 203, 207
 Legislation and, 180

Business, 27, 39, 109, 142

Butler, David, 131

Butterfield, Bruce A., 50

C

Cabinet Positions, 11, 211

Caldeira, Gregory A., 185–86

Calhoun, John C., 70, 85

California, 18, 20, 23, 24, 27, 62, 63, 66, 76, 86, 90, 100, 107, 113, 117, 120, 126, 160, 174

Campaign Finance. *See* Finance, Campaign.

Campaign Organization, 25, 26

Campaigns. *See* General Election Campaigns.

Campbell, Angus, 47, 49, 90, 92

Campbell, Ben Nighthorse, 79

Candidates,
 campaigns by, 15, 19, 24–29, 31, 136, 200–201, 203–204, 223
 media and, 18–19
 pool of, 9, 10–13, 211
 voter evaluation of, 32, 34–35

Cannon, Joseph G., 171

Carlson, Peter E., 184

Carmines, Edward G., 153

Carter, Jimmy,
 campaign and election of 1976, 17, 56, 61, 85, 119, 120, 123, 138, 140
 campaign and election of 1980, 21, 29, 41, 56, 64, 140, 144
 legislative record as president, 166, 167, 169–70, 177, 179, 180

Catholic Americans, 3, 11, 27, 38, 52, 75, 77, 108, 202–203, 207

Caucus-Convention System, 13–17. *See also* Nomination Process.

Chambers, William Nisbet, 49, 128, 185, 224

Chicago, 14, 20

Children's Bureau, 161, 178

Chiles, Lawton, 83

Christian Americans, 11, 77, 207, 211

Civil Rights Acts, 55, 159, 160, 164, 166, 172, 178, 180, 221

Civil Rights Movement, 109, 160, 178

Civil War and Reconstruction, 4, 5–6, 38, 39, 93, 95, 104, 118, 218
 Legislative Surge, 5, 159–60, 177, 178, 221, 222
 Political Legacy, 56–57, 93, 103, 105, 108–109, 118, 122, 216

Civilian Conservation Corps, 162

Clagget, William, 125, 127

Class Politics, 27, 31, 95, 96, 191, 192, 214
 Collapse of, 6, 204–206

Clay, Henry, 98, 101, 129, 159

Clayton Antitrust Act, 161

Clean Air Acts, 165, 166, 172, 178, 180

Cleveland, Grover, 38, 42, 159, 168

Clinton, Bill, 92, 150
 administration of, 80, 146, 150, 179–81, 198, 201, 217
 character and scandals, 12, 69, 76, 135
 congressional relations and support, 146–49, 150–51, 179–81
 and DLC, 83–84, 145

general election campaign, 24, 68, 70–72, 146, 201
and midterm of 1994, 201
nomination of, 15, 18, 21, 67–70, 144–45, 150, 219–20
and Perot spring campaign, 67
victory of, 24, 51, 79, 80–89, 123, 212, 217, 218
vote for, 24, 31, 34, 52–53, 62, 72–78, 82, 85, 119, 123, 138, 140, 151–52, 153, 203, 205–207, 212
Clinton, Hillary Rodham, 69, 150
Clubb, Jerome M., 127–28, 153, 185
CNN (Cable News Network), 20
Coal Mine Health and Safety Act, 165
Cold War, end of, 82, 88
Coletta, Paolo E., 182
Colorado, 62, 63, 76, 90, 126
Common Cause, 178
Communist Party, 178
Comprehensive Employment and Training Act (CETA), 165
Congress, U.S., 10, 19, 23, 53–54, 80, 94, 136, 146–49, 174–75, 214–15. *See also* House, U.S.; Senate, U.S.; Lawmaking Surges.
Congressional Caucus, 19, 212, 217
Conlan, Timothy, 184
Connecticut, 63, 70, 126
Conservative Coalition in Congress, 147, 169, 172, 221
Constitution, U.S., 9, 37, 94
  Amendments,
    Eighteenth, 162
    Fifteenth, 160
    Fourteenth, 159
    Nineteenth, 162
    Seventeenth, 161
    Sixteenth, 161
    Thirteenth, 159
    Twelfth, 10, 217
    Twentieth, 183
    Twenty-First, 167
    Twenty-Second, 10, 42
    Twenty-Third, 23
  Eligibility for presidency (Article I and II), 9, 10, 11, 12, 13
Constitutional Union Party, 130, 132
Consumer Movement, 178
Consumer Product Safety Act, 165, 178

Consumer Protection Agency, 166, 170
Contract with America, 169, 214–15
Conventions, Party. *See* National Party Conventions.
Converse, Philip E., 47, 49, 92, 224
Cook, Rhodes, 44, 45, 47, 49, 133
Coolidge, Calvin, 108
Cooper, John Milton, Jr., 182
Cooper, Joseph, 6–7
Cornwell, Elmer E., Jr., 182
Corrado, Anthony, 154
Cotter, Cornelius P., 154, 155
Cox, James, M., 171
Crawford, William H., 129
Crime Legislation, 147, 148, 180
Cronin, Thomas E., 12, 43, 44
C-SPAN (Cable Satellite Public Affairs Network), 20
Crotty, William, 46, 133, 135–36, 152
Crumden, Robert M., 182
Cultural Politics, 6, 71, 192, 206–208, 214
Cummings, Milton, C., Jr., 1, 2, 3, 6, 43, 46, 47, 51, 89, 90, 212, 214, 215, 217, 218, 219, 220, 221, 225
Cuomo, Mario, 67
Curry, Leonard P., 181

D
Dallas, 71
Davidson, Roger H., 183
Davis, Morton D., 46
Death Penalty, 84
Debates, Presidential, 25, 28–29, 68, 71, 212–14 *passim*
DeCell, Ken, 49
Deficit Reduction Acts, 180
Delaware, 63, 126
Delegate Selection, 13–19. *See also* Nomination Process.
Democracy, 4, 9, 31, 37, 141, 157, 201, 203–204, 208, 222, 223
Democratic Leadership Council (DLC), 82–84, 145, 220
Democratic National Committee, 13, 14, 15–16, 143, 146
Democratic National Convention, 13, 14, 19–22, 68, 70, 145, 197, 217
Democratic Party, 3, 37–38, 53–54, 78–80, 136, 137, 142, 149–51, 214, 216–17, 220, 221

Democratic Party *(continued)*
  and congressional elections, 56–57, 58–
    59, 79–80, 91, 206
  and congressional policy making, 146–
    49, 157–87 *passim*, 221–22
  and presidential general elections, 24,
    26–27, 35–40, 54–56, 61–62, 63, 67,
    68, 70–72, 80–89 *passim*, 90, 137–
    41, 145–46, 153, 212, 214, 218, 220–
    21
  and presidential nominations, 11–22
    passim, 67–70, 143–45, 197, 217,
    219–20
  and sectionalism, 4, 54–59, 74–76, 93–
    133 *passim*
  and voting behavior, 6, 31–40, 52, 57,
    60–61, 72–78, 137–41, 153, 191–96
    passim, 201–203, 205–207, 214, 215
*Democratic Party of the U.S. v. Wisconsin
    ex. rel La Follettte,* 16
Democratic-Republican Party (Jeffersonian
    Democrats)
  congressional caucus, 19, 217
  electoral college deadlock, 217
  message of, 37
  record in presidential elections, 35, 36,
    37, 40
  sectionalism in presidential voting, 93,
    94, 97, 98–103, 111–14, 122, 128–
    29,
  all southern ticket in 1828, 70, 85
  support for, 37
Dennis, Jack, 35, 48
Dependent Pension Act, 167
Derthick, Martha, 184
Dewey, Thomas E., 39
Dingley Tariff Act, 168
District of Columbia, 13, 15, 23, 26, 61, 62,
    63, 67, 73, 90, 126, 153, 159
Divided and Unified Government, 5, 53–
    54, 80, 146–49, 173–74, 179, 181,
    191, 192–93, 216–17, 221–22
Dixiecrats, 54
Dole, Robert, 86
Donald, David, 181
Donovan, Beth, 45, 46
Downs, Anthony, 141, 154, 214, 224
Dukakis, Michael, 62
  as candidate, 29, 61, 82, 84, 123, 144, 146
  vote for, 61–62, 63, 73, 75, 90, 140

his voters of 1988 in 1992, 75, 84, 151–52
Duke, Lois Lovelace, 133

E
Earned Income Tax Credits, 165, 172, 180
East, 27, 38, 62, 95, 123
Economic Opportunity Act, 164, 172
Economic Stabilization Act, 166
Economy, 95
  as campaign issue, 27, 64, 65, 66, 84, 105
  and legislative surges, 5, 175–77, 178
  performance of, 64, 65, 66, 80–82, 87, 88
  as voting issue, 34, 73, 75, 80–82, 204–
    206, 214
Edsall, Mary D., 85, 92
Edsall, Thomas Byrne, 85, 92
Education Levels and Politics, 6, 30, 74,
    199–200, 202, 205, 213, 223
Edwards, George C. III, 46
Eisenhower, Dwight,
  and elections, 39, 49, 56, 104, 120
  as legislative leader, 147
  as military candidate, 11
  and Twenty-Second Amendment, 10, 42
Electoral Coalitions. *See* New Deal, as
    voter coalition; and Voting Coali-
    tions in Presidential Elections.
Electoral Vote System (College), 9, 20, 23–
    24, 26–27, 62, 73, 95, 122, 128, 130,
    212, 217, 218, 223
Electorate, 51–53, 223. *See also* Indepen-
    dents, electorate.
Elementary and Secondary Education Act,
    164
Eligibility for Presidency, 9, 10
Elving, Ronald D., 45
Emancipation Proclamation, 159
Emergency Banking Act, 162
Emergency Petroleum Allocation Act, 166
Emergency Relief and Construction Act,
    163, 171
Emergency Relief Appropriation Act, 162
Employee Retirement Income Security Act
    (ERISA), 165
Endangered Species Act, 165
Enforcement Acts, 160
Environmental Movement, 178
Epstein, Leon D., 14, 44, 45, 135, 143, 154,
    224, 225
Equal Employment Opportunity Act, 166

Equal Rights Amendment, 166, 172, 178
Era of Good Feelings, 37
Ewing, Cortez A. M., 94–95, 122, 124

F
Fair Labor Standards Act, 163
Fair Packaging and Labeling Act, 165, 178
Family Leave Act, 147, 150, 180
Farm Tenancy Act, 163
Federal Communications Commission, 162
Federal Deposit Insurance Corporation, 162
Federal Election Campaign Act. *See* Finance, Campaign.
Federal Emergency Relief Act, 162
Federal Farm Loan Act, 161
Federal Housing Administration, 162
Federal Reserve Act, 161
Federal Trade Commission, 161
Federalist Party, 19, 35, 36, 37, 38, 40, 93, 151
Females. *See* Women.
Fillmore, Millard, 212
Finance, Campaign, 213–14
    Buckley v. Valeo, 26
    and campaign organization, 25
    candidate fund-raising ability, 12
    for general election, 25–26
    legislation, 15, 20, 25–26, 145, 147, 148, 161, 166, 178, 180, 223
    qualifying for matching funds, 12–13
    and national conventions, 20
    as party resource, 145–46
Finifter, Ada W., 48, 152
Flanigan, William H., 125, 127–28, 153
Florida, 63, 75, 85, 125, 126
Flowers, Gennifer, 69
Foner, Eric, 178, 186
Food Stamp Acts, 164, 165, 172
Ford, Gerald R., 15, 21, 29, 41, 42, 61, 164–66, 173
Ford, Henry, 197
Foreign Policy and Defense Issues, 29, 34, 39, 64, 65, 82, 83, 86, 87, 88, 94, 102
Frankovic, Kathleen A., 48
Freeman, Jo, 185
Frontloading, 18
Frymer, Paul, 225

G
Gallup Poll, 11, 12, 60, 61, 64, 65, 68, 70, 71, 72, 195–96, 201, 202–03, 205
Gans, Daniel J., 49
Gant, Michael M., 224
Gaudet, Hazel, 47
Gender Gap, 6, 11, 77, 206, 207, 208, 215. *See also* Men, Women.
General Agreement on Tariffs and Trade (GATT), 149, 180
General Election Campaign, 22–29, 41–42, 70–72, 85–86, 88, 212–13, 217
Georgia, 63, 69, 75, 85, 91, 125, 126, 160
Gephardt, Richard, 67
Gergen, David, 198
Gerth, H. H., 154
Gettinger, Stephen, 186
Gillette, William, 181, 186
Gingrich, Newt, 169
Ginsberg, Benjamin, 43, 226
Glass-Steagall Act, 163
Gold Standard Act, 168
Goldwater, Barry, 14, 55, 78, 144, 192, 220
Gorbachev, Mikhail, 87
Gore, Al, 92
    Bush attacks on, 72
    Clinton-Gore ticket, 24, 62, 68, 70, 71, 75, 83, 86
    debate with Perot in 1993, 201
    did not run for president in 1992, 67
    DLC, ties to, 83
    as presidential candidate in 1988, 67, 83
    southern strategy and, 70, 75, 85
    as vice-president, 147
Gould, Lewis L., 182
Governorships, 11, 13, 19, 79, 144–45, 211
Graber, Doris A., 197, 210
Gramm, Phil, 12, 21, 147
Grant, Ulysses S., 39, 41
Great Britain, 144–45, 199
Great Depression, 6, 53, 132, 163, 171, 176, 190, 191, 204
Great Society, 164, 169, 172, 173, 221
    Legislation, 164
Greenstein, Fred I., 49–50
Grenada Invasion, 87
Guffey-Snyder Coal Act, 162
Gulf War, 12, 64, 65, 86
Gulliver, Hal, 132

H

Hadley, Charles D., 7, 90, 130, 132, 208, 224–25
Hager, George, 186
Haggerty, Brian A., 46
Hagstrom, Jerry H., 132
Hamilton, Alexander, 167
Hansen, John Mark, 155, 181, 185
Hargrove, Erwin C., 12, 43
Harkin, Tom, 69, 70
Harris, Douglas B., 83, 92
Harris, Richard A., 184
Harrison, Benjamin, 167, 168
Harrison, William Henry, 38, 99, 102, 128, 131
Hart, Gary, 12, 144
Hartwig, Frederick, 48
Hawaii, 59, 63, 90, 126
Hayes, Rutherford, 219
Hays, R. Allen, 184
Hechler, Kenneth W., 182
Hepburn Act, 160
Herrera, Richard, 149
Herrnson, Paul, 154
Herschensohn, Bruce, 206
Hess, Stephen, 13, 44
Hibbing, John R., 185
Higher Education Act, 165
Higher Education Facilities Act, 164
Higgs, Robert, 185
Hispanic Americans, 52, 74, 76, 79
Hoffman, Paul J., 155
Hofstadter, Richard, 186
Holcombe, Arthur N., 48, 94, 95, 122, 124
Holman, C. B., 133
Home Owners' Loan Act, 162
Homestead Act, 159
Hoover, Herbert, 121, 163, 173, 221
Hopkins, Harry, 162
House of Representatives, U.S.,
  diversity in, 79
  elections to, 3, 54, 56–57, 58–59, 78–79, 194–95, 214–15
  party voting in, 146–49, 174–75
  and presidential selection, 19, 23
Housing Measures (Johnson-Nixon years), 165
Houston, 71
Howard, Christopher, 184
Hughes, Charles Evans, 171, 174

Humphrey, Hubert H., 14, 20, 62
Hurley, Patricia A., 185
Hussein, Saddam, 64, 86
Hutchison, Kay Bailey, 91

I

Idaho, 63, 90, 126
Ideology
  and party leaders, 17, 82–84, 86, 102, 149–51
  and voting, 75, 203
Illinois, 62, 63, 70, 126
Income and Politics, 3, 27, 31, 37, 52, 73, 75, 80–82, 83, 192, 202, 204–206, 215
Income Tax, 161, 163, 171, 180
Incumbency, 25, 27–29, 34, 41–42, 51, 64, 118, 213–14
  and policy conversion, 5, 170
Independents, 79
  candidates, 22–23, 26, 73–74, 126, 136, 151, 200–201, 203–204
  electorate, 6, 27, 32, 33, 52, 61, 71, 75, 78, 136, 151, 191, 193–196, 199–200, 208. *See also* Party Identification; Third Parties.
Indian Reorganization Act, 162
Indiana, 63, 76, 126
Industrialization, 5–6, 38, 39, 95, 103, 109, 122, 190, 216
Iowa, 17, 18, 63, 86, 100, 107, 113, 117, 126
Iran-Contra Affair, 72, 87
Issues and Voting, 34–35. *See also* Economy, as voting issue; Foreign Policy and Defense Issues; Ideology and Voting; and Social Issues.
Ivacko, Thomas M., 48

J

Jackson, Andrew, 37, 193
  Bank Veto, 167
  electoral record, 36, 37–38, 41, 98, 100, 113,
  executive authority, idea of, 38
  Sectionalism and Voting, 101, 102, 103, 114, 129
  all southern ticket in 1828, 70, 85
  Whig dislike for, 38
Jackson, Henry, 172
Jackson, Jesse, 17, 67, 70, 84–85, 88, 144

Jacksonian Democrats. *See* Democratic Party.
Jacobson, Gary, 152
Jefferson, Thomas, 37, 167, 217
Jeffersonian Party. *See* Democratic-Republic Party.
Jeffries, John W., 183
Jenkins, William R., 48
Jewell, Malcolm, 152
Jewish Americans, 3, 11, 27, 52, 75, 76, 202, 215
Johnson, Andrew, 40, 49, 159, 169, 170, 172, 173
Johnson, Hiram, 174
Johnson, Lyndon B., 180
  Campaign and election of 1960, 10, 54, 61,
  Campaign and election of 1964, 55, 78, 123, 138, 169, 220
  legislative record as president, 55, 147, 164–65, 169, 172, 173, 176, 180, 221
  Withdrew from 1968 election, 42, 64
Johnson-Nixon-Ford Legislative Surge, 5, 164–66, 177, 221–22
Jones, Charles O., 90,

K

Kansas, 63, 126
Karl, Barry D., 183
Katz, Jeffrey L., 45
Keech, William R., 44, 48
Keefe, William J., 46, 136, 152
Keith, Bruce, 152
Kennedy, Edward M., 21, 144, 170
Kennedy, John F., 53, 150, 164
  Catholic presidential candidate, 11
  campaign and election of 1960, 24, 28–29, 30, 53, 54, 55, 61, 110, 120, 138, 140, 212–13, 223
  legislative record under, 164, 179, 180
Kentucky, 63, 85, 126,
Kerrey, Bob, 69, 70
Key, V. O., Jr., 6, 35, 42, 44, 45, 47, 48, 88–89, 92, 95–96, 108, 109, 111, 121–27, 130–33, 137, 140, 154, 225, 226
Keynesian Economic Measures, 163, 164
Keynote Address, 20–21
King, Anthony, 50, 141
King, Martin Luther, Jr., 178
Kinnock, Neil, 145

Kleist, Jurgen, 50
Kleppner, Paul, 125–27, 130, 224
Klu Klux Klan Act, 160
Koenig, Louis W., 43
Kolbe, Richard L., 44
Kramer, Gerald H., 186

L

Labor Legislation, 160, 161, 162–63, 204. *See also* particular laws.
Labor Unions, 3, 27, 38, 75, 76, 178, 204–05, 210
Ladd, Everett Carll, 1, 2, 5–6, 7, 17, 45, 48, 49, 77, 90, 91, 108, 125–30, 132, 189, 208–210, 214–16, 219, 220, 224, 225
La Follette, Robert, 160, 171, 174
La Follette Seamen's Act, 161
LaGuardia, Fiorello, 172
Lampman, Robert J., 184
Land Management Measures, 110, 166
Larry King Live, 67, 198
Lawmaking Surges, 5, 158–81
  Causes, 167–181, 221–22
    Economy, The, 175–77
    Elections, 168–70
    Moods and Movements, 177–79
    Political Parties, 170–75
  Content, 159–67
    Civil War and Reconstruction Era, 93, 159–60
    Johnson-Nixon-Ford Era, 164–66
    New Deal Era, 162–63
    Progressive Era, 160–62
  Defined, 158–59
Lazarsfeld, Paul F., 47
Lederman, Susan S., 39, 43, 46, 49, 125, 127, 153, 225
Legal Tender Act, 159
Leuchtenberg, William E., 182, 183
Levitan, Sar A., 184
Lichtman, Allan J., 49
Lincoln, Abraham, 39, 40, 41, 49, 159
Link, Arthur S., 182
Long, Huey, 178
Long, Russell, 172
Longley, Lawrence D., 133
Louisiana, 63, 75, 85, 125, 126
Luttbeg, Norman R., 224

M

Madison, James, 37

Magnuson-Moss Act, 165

Maine, 24, 63, 74, 126

Maisel, Louis Sandy, 6–7, 46, 92, 155

Major, John, 144

Males. *See* Men.

Mandates, Electoral, 5, 89, 169, 180–81, 222, 223

Mann-Elkins Act, 161

Manufacturing, 6, 94, 96

March, James, 154

Maryland, 62, 63, 74, 126

Mass Media. *See* Media.

Mass Transit Measures, 164, 165

Massachusetts, 24, 61, 63, 126, 128, 160, 171, 174

Matthews, Donald R., 43, 44

Mayer, William, 140, 152–54, 156

Mayhew, David R., 1, 2, 5, 7, 109, 125–27, 129, 130, 155, 157, 159, 181–86, 214, 218, 219, 221, 222, 225

McClosky, Herbert, 149, 155

McCormick, Richard L., 181, 185

McCormick, Richard P., 99, 102, 128, 129

McCraw, Thomas K., 184

McGillivray, Alice V., 55, 63, 91, 126

McGovern, George, 17, 144, 220

McGovern-Fraser Commission, 14, 143

McKinley, William, 39, 118, 138, 168

McKinley Tariff Act, 167, 168

McWilliams, Wilson Carey, 123, 133

Meat Inspection Act, 161

Media of Communication, 6, 12, 15, 18–22 *passim*, 25, 26, 41, 66, 67, 70, 71, 84, 191, 193, 197–98, 201, 207, 223. *See also* debates, presidential

Medicare and Medicaid, 164, 172

Meier, Kenneth J., 184

Mellon, Andrew, 167

Meltsner, A., 209

Men, 6, 11, 27, 52, 74, 77, 202, 206, 211, 213, 215

Michels, Robert, 141

Michigan, 24, 62, 63, 126

Michigan, University of, 32, 33, 87, 88, 194, 195, 196, 214

Middle Atlantic, 97, 100–102, 106–109, 111, 113, 114, 116–17, 119, 122, 126

Middle Class, 6, 27, 83

Midwest, 24, 62, 74, 79, 95, 97, 106–111 *passim*, 116–17, 119, 126

Milbank, Dina, 210

Mileur, Jerome M., 123, 133, 210

Military Careers, 10–11, 12, 76, 211

Milkis, Sidney M., 184

Miller, Warren E., 47, 49, 92, 153

Mills, C. Wright, 154

Mills, Wilbur, 172

Mining, 94, 165. *See also* particular laws.

Minnesota, 61, 63, 126, 160, 174

Minor Parties. *See* Third Parties.

Minorities. *See* African Americans.

Miranda, Patricia A., 82, 91

Mississippi, 63, 126

Missouri, 24, 62, 63, 126

Momentum, 18

Mondale, Walter, 18, 61, 82, 140, 144

Monroe, James, 37

Montana, 16, 62, 63, 76, 90, 126

Moods. *See* Public Moods.

Morehouse, Sarah, 152

Morrill Land-Grant College Act, 159, 171

Morrill Tariff Act, 159, 171

Movements, Political, 5, 14, 178

Mowry, George E., 181, 182

Moynihan, Charles A., 45

Muckraking, 178

Munger, Frank, 47

Murphy, Reg, 132

Muskie, Edmund, 172

Mutch, Robert E., 182

N

Nader, Ralph, 165, 170

National Association for the Advancement of Colored People (NAACP), 67

National Banking Act, 159

National Environmental Policy Act, 165, 172

National Health Insurance, 150–51, 166, 180

National Health Planning and Resources Development Act, 166

National Industry Recovery Act, 162

National Labor Relations Act, 162, 171, 178

National Party Conventions, 14, 17, 19–22, 145, 212. *See also* Democratic National Convention; Republican

National Convention; and Nomination Process.
National-Republican Party, 98, 101
National Service Program, 147, 180
Nationalization of Politics, 95–96, 97, 121–22
Native Americans, 79
Naval Act, 167
Nebraska, 24, 63, 126
Nelson, Candice J., 46
Nelson, Michael, 12, 43
Neumann, Sigmund, 124
Nevada, 63, 76, 90, 126
New Deal, 150, 177
    as legislative surge, 5, 38, 158, 162–63, 168, 169, 171–72, 173, 174, 175, 176, 177, 178, 204, 218, 221, 222
    political change since, 3, 4, 51, 53, 54–61, 77–78, 95, 96, 111, 118, 122, 123, 138, 140, 190, 191, 192–93, 195–96, 205, 206, 208, 214, 215, 216, 218
    as voter coalition, 3, 38, 53, 54–61, 95, 96, 103, 104, 120–22, 138, 140, 206, 214, 216, 218
New England, 26, 37, 93, 97, 100–103, 105–11, 113, 114, 116–17, 118, 120, 121, 122, 126
New Frontier, 164
New Hampshire, 15, 18, 63, 64, 66, 69, 86, 126
New Jersey, 18, 24, 63, 126, 160, 171, 174
New Mexico, 63, 76, 90, 126
Newspapers. *See* Media of Communication.
New York City, 20, 70
New York State, 18, 23, 24, 27, 63, 70, 101, 126, 160, 171, 173–74
Nixon, Richard M., 64
    campaign and election of 1960, 28, 29, 30, 53, 212–13
    electoral victories, 39, 73, 123, 212
    legislative record as president, 164–66, 172, 173, 174, 175, 176, 179, 221
    nomination of 1972, 15
    southern strategy, 27, 123
Nomination Process, 13–22, 41–42, 84–85, 86, 143–45, 196–97, 204, 212, 217, 219–21. *See also* Democratic Party and presidential nominations;

Republican Party and presidential nominations.
Norris, George, 171
Norris-LaGuardia Act, 163, 171
North American Free Trade Agreement (NAFTA), 147, 180, 201
North (non-South), 18, 54–57, 58–59, 61–62, 70, 76, 90, 121
North Carolina, 63, 75, 85, 125, 126
North Dakota, 63, 91, 126, 160, 171, 174
Northeast, 24, 74, 79, 93, 108, 122
Northern Tier Strategy, 123
Nunn, Sam, 83

O

Occupational Changes, 6, 191, 192, 204–205
Occupational Safety and Health Act (OSHA), 165
O'Hara, Rosemary, 155
Ohio, 63, 126, 171, 173
Oklahoma, 63, 126
Old Northwest (1824–1852), 97, 100, 102, 113, 114, 126, 129
Open Housing Act, 166
Oregon, 63, 76, 90, 126
Orloff, Ann Shola, 183
Ornstein, Norman J., 43
Ostrogorski, Moisei, 141

P

Pacific Coast States, 76, 97, 106–107, 108, 109, 116–17, 120, 123, 126
Pacific Railroad Act, 159, 171
Parties, 1, 4–6, 25, 26, 27, 135–56, 193, 219–21
    Character of, 140–43
    as competing organizations, 5
    decline thesis, 4–5, 15, 135–36, 140–41, 144, 145, 146, 149, 151
    and legislative surges, 5, 170–75
    in marketplace, 142, 151–52
    organizational developments, 5, 15, 143–46, 196–97
    in postindustrial era, 189–210, 223
    programs of, 146–51
    as purposive organizations, 151
    renewal of, 5
    turnovers in presidential elections, 39–40, 49, 51

Parties *(continued)*
  voting coalitions in presidential elections, 137–40, 141, 151
  winning parties in presidential elections, 35–39
Party Control, Divided. *See* Divided and Unified Government.
Party Eras, 39–40, 216
Party Government, 146–49, 170–73, 193, 203–204, 221–22,
Party Identification, 3, 27–31 *passim*, 32, 33, 34–35, 52, 57, 60–61, 75, 78, 88, 94, 136, 151–52, 195–196, 202–203, 213
Party Systems, 49, 53–54, 103, 129, 168, 190, 216
Party Voting in Congress, 146–49, 174–75
Patterson, James T., 183, 184
Patterson, Orlando, 155
Patterson, Samuel C., 185–86
Patterson, Thomas E., 197, 210
Peabody, Robert L., 43
Pennsylvania, 62, 63, 126
Perot, H. Ross, 6, 87, 152, 195
  and Bush, George, 67, 84
  campaign and candidacy, 26, 67, 68, 70, 71–72, 88, 145
  election outcome, impact on, 84, 88, 89, 140
  and independence of electorate, 75, 78, 136, 151, 200–201, 203–204
  vote for, 30, 31, 34, 52–53, 72–78, 82, 84, 136, 140, 152, 203, 207, 212
Perotism, 6, 200–201, 203–204
Persian Gulf War, 12, 64, 65, 86
Peters, Charles, 210
Peters, John G., 185
Phillips, Kevin P., 111, 131, 132, 153
Pierce, Franklin, 41
Pika, Joseph A., 43, 46
Pious, Richard M., 49
Pitkin, Hanna, 225
Plains States, 97, 105, 106–07, 108, 110, 116–17, 119, 120, 126
Platforms, Party, 14, 19, 21, 82–84, 150
Policy. *See* Public Policy.
Policy Change, 5, 157–187, 218
Political Change, 2, 3, 51–92, 215–217, 218–219
Political Efficacy, 31, 213

Political Parties. *See* Parties.
"Political Prominence." *See* Pool of Candidates.
Polsby, Nelson W., 18, 22, 26, 44, 45, 46, 47, 49, 143, 154, 225
Pomper, Gerald M., 1, 2, 4–7, 10, 21, 39, 43, 46–49, 90, 125, 127, 133, 135, 152–54, 156, 214, 215, 220, 222, 223, 225, 226
Pool of Candidates, 9, 10–13, 211
Population Movements, 30, 93, 105, 109–110, 206
Populist Party, 108, 119
Postal Savings System, 161
Postindustrial U.S., 5–6, 189–210, 214, 216
Powell, Colin, 11, 12
Presidency, 38, 41–42, 53–54, 80, 94
Presidential Elections,
  comparative importance, 1, 217–19
  factors in, 3, 87–88, 214
  functions of, 5, 9, 223
  and legislative surges, 5, 168–70
  patterns in, 1, 54–56, 211–17
  time dimension, 1, 35, 53
  trends, 35–42
  types of
    authorizing, 169–70, 218
    deauthorizing, 169–70, 218
    deviating, 49, 88
    maintaining, 88
    reaffirmations of support, 39, 88, 89
    realigning, 4, 5, 56, 88, 137–140, 157, 168, 215, 216, 218–19, 222
    status quo, 219
    traumatic, 218
    turnover and reelections, party, 39–40, 49, 51, 218
    votes of lack of confidence, 3, 88–89
Presidential Selection Process, 2, 9–50, 211–14, 217–18
Press. *See* Media of Communication.
Price, David E., 136, 152
Primary Election System (presidential), 13–17. *See also* Nomination Process.
Process. *See* Presidential Selection Process.
Progressive Era, 177, 178, 218
  legislative surge, 5, 108, 160–62, 169, 171, 173–74, 177–78, 221–22

Progressive Party vote, 74, 108, 120, 212
Prohibition, 38, 108, 167
Prospective Voting, 34
Protestant Americans, 27, 52, 75, 77, 202–203, 207
Public Interest Groups, 178
Public Moods, 5, 177–78
Public Policy, 1, 2, 5, 9, 17, 34, 218, 221–22. *See also* Lawmaking Surges.
Public Utilities Holding Company Act, 162
Pure Food and Drug Act, 161

Q
Quayle, Dan, 12, 68, 71

R
Race and Politics, 11, 84–85, 137. *See also* particular races.
Randall, J. G., 181
Ranney, Austin, 44, 143, 154, 155
Reagan, Ronald, 21, 39, 61, 62, 75, 82, 137, 144, 150
  Administration of, 53, 64, 216–17
  Approval ratings, 87
  campaign and election of 1980, 15, 29, 76, 78, 136, 138, 144, 170
  campaign and election of 1984, 15, 24, 29, 60, 61, 76, 86, 87, 136, 138, 144
  legislative record, 147, 166, 167
  personal characteristics, 12
  and Twenty-Second Amendment, 10, 42
Realignment. *See* Elections, Types of.
Reciprocal Trade Agreements Act, 162
Reconstruction Acts, 159–160
Reconstruction Era. *See* Civil War and Reconstruction Era.
Reconstruction Finance Corporation, 163
Regionalism. *See* Sectionalism.
Registration, Voter, 16, 147, 180, 213
Regulation and Deregulation of Industry, 165, 166, 167, 170, 172, 180, 190, 223
Reichley, A. James, 44, 48, 49, 209, 218, 224, 225
Reisman, David, 208
Religion and Politics, 11, 52, 77, 202–203, 207. *See also* particular religions.
Republican National Committee, 13, 15–16, 18, 45, 146

Republican National Convention, 13, 14, 19–22, 68, 71, 86, 145
Republican Party, 3, 38–39, 53–54, 78–80, 142, 149–51, 214, 216–17, 220, 221
  and congressional elections, 56–57, 58–59, 79–80, 91, 206, 214–15
  and congressinal policy making, 146–49, 157–87, *passim*, 221–22
  and presidential general elections, 26–27, 35–40, 61–62, 63, 65, 68, 70–72, 80–89 *passim*, 138, 145–46, 212, 219, 220–21
  and presidential nominations, 11–22 *passim*, 64, 66–67, 144–45, 219–20
  and sectionalism, 4, 56–59, 74–76, 93–133 *passim*
  and voting behavior, 31–40, 52, 57, 60–61, 72–78, 138, 191–96 *passim*, 201–203, 205–207, 214, 215
Responsible Parties. *See* Party Government.
Retrospective Voting, 34
Revenue Acts, 161, 163, 171
Revenue Sharing, 165
Rhode Island, 63, 126
Robertson, Pat, 17, 86
Robinson-Patman Act, 163
Rockefeller, Jay, 67
Rocky Mountain States, 76, 90, 97, 106–111, 116–119, 122, 126
Rohde, David W., 31, 43, 47, 48, 155
Rogers, David, 187
Roman Catholics. *See* Catholic Americans.
Romasco, Albert U., 182
Roosevelt, Franklin D., 180
  congressional support and opposition, 162–63, 169, 172
  electoral record, 10, 38, 41, 54, 73, 74, 108–09, 110, 118, 168
  and New Deal electoral era, 3, 53, 54, 57, 60, 77–78, 108–09, 110, 118, 121, 138, 139–40, 162, 168, 169, 215, 222
  presidential administration and public policy, 162–63, 167, 168, 169, 171, 172, 176, 178, 180, 204, 221, 222
  and Twenty-Second Amendment, 10
Roosevelt, Theodore, 74, 160–61, 169, 171, 173–74, 212
Rose, Richard, 131
Rosenbaum, David E., 186

Rosenstone, Steven J., 155
Rossiter, Clinton, 11, 12, 43
Rubin, Richard L., 197, 210
Rural Electrification Administration, 162
Rusk, Jerrold G., 224

S
Safire, William, 221, 225
San Diego, 20
Sarasohn, David, 181, 182
Scammon, Richard M., 55, 63, 91, 126, 153, 224
Schantz, Harvey L., 1–4, 6, 9, 50, 90, 93, 211, 216, 218–21
Schattschneider, E. E., 2, 6, 31, 47, 95–96, 109, 111, 120–25, 127, 132, 141, 154, 156, 221, 225
Schlesinger, Arthur M., Jr., 177, 182, 183, 186
Schlesinger, Joseph A., 141, 142, 154
Schulman, Mark A., 47, 48,
Schumpeter, Joseph, 141
Schwarz, Jordan A, 183
Scott, W. Richard, 154
Secretary of State, 11
Sectionalism, 3–4, 93–133, 216
  and electoral college, 122, 123
  erosion of, 95–96, 97, 109, 111, 118, 120, 121, 122, 123, 216
  measurement of, 3–4, 97, 125–28
  and New Deal Transition, 120–22
  in presidential vote, 97–111
    1824–1852, 98–103
    1856–1992, 103–111
  in 1992, 74–76
  in presidential vote swing, 111–120
    1824–1852, 111–14
    1856–1992, 114–20
  South v. Rest of U.S.
    House Elections, 1950–1994, 56–57, 58–59
    Presidential Elections, 1932–1992, 54–56
  Strategies, electoral, 123
  Theory of, 93–96
Securities Measures, 162
Sedition Act, 37
Senate, U.S.,
  as delegates, 19
  diversity in, 79

elections to, 3, 10, 53–54, 79–80, 91, 161, 194–95, 206
Party Voting in, 146–49, 174–75
as Source of presidential candidates, 11, 13, 211
as Source of vice-presidential nominees, 11
and vice-president selection, 23
Shade, William G., 97, 99, 126, 128, 129
Shafer, Byron E., 49, 129, 153, 209, 224
Shapiro, Isaac, 184
Shelby, Richard C., 80
Sherman Antitrust Act, 167
Sherman Silver Purchase Act, 167
Sherwood, Tom, 91
Silbey, Joel H., 128, 129, 181
Simon, Herbert, 154
Sinclair, Barbara, 155
Skocpol, Theda, 178, 183–84, 186
Skowronek, Stephen, 182
Slavery, 38, 39, 95, 102, 159–60, 171
Smith, Al, 11, 120, 121
Smith, John, 145
Social Issues, 34, 39, 71, 83, 84, 137, 192, 221
Social Security Legislation, 162, 165, 172, 178, 204
Social Welfare Spending, 38, 83, 150, 165
Society, 1, 5–6
  and elections, 222–23
  Postindustrial, 5–6
  Socioeconomic Eras, 5–6, 189–90, 216
Soil Conservation and Domestic Allotment Act, 162
Sorauf, Frank J., 45, 125, 126, 127, 129, 146, 154, 155
South, 72, 213
  in Congress, 172
  as convention site, 20
  and Democratic party, 38, 82
  and Democratic-Republican party, 37
  and electoral votes, 24, 26
  and House, U.S. elections, 56–57, 58–59, 79
  and New Deal voter coalition, 3, 54–57, 60
  and presidential election tickets, 70, 75, 85, 88
  Presidential elections, voting in, 30, 54–56, 57, 61, 75–76, 77, 85

Republican rise in, 3, 192
and sectionalism in presidential elections, 93, 95, 97, 102–111, 116–23
Super Tuesday and frontloading, 18, 66, 69. *See Also* Civil War and Reconstruction Era.
South Atlantic States (1824–1852), 93, 97, 100–103, 113, 114, 125, 129
South Carolina, 63, 125, 126
South Dakota, 24, 62, 63, 86, 126
Southern Democratic Party, 130, 132
Southern Strategy, 27, 85, 123
Southwest States (1824–1852), 93, 97, 100–103, 113, 114, 125–26, 129
Soviet Union, 65, 82, 88
Spackman, S. G. F., 181
Stacks, John F., 43
States,
Presidential Election of 1988, 63
Progressive Era Policy Making, 160, 171, 173–74
Sections, Classified by, 21–22
Voting Coalitions in Presidential Elections, 4, 137–140, 151. *See also* particular states and persons.
States' Rights Party, 54
Steffens, Lincoln, 178
Stenholm, Charles, 147
Stephanopoulos, George, 198
Stern, Mark, 225
Stevenson, Adlai E., 38
Stimson, James A., 153
Stockdale, James, 68
Stokes, Donald E., 47, 49, 92, 224
Sumner, Charles, 160
Sundquist, James L., 48, 49, 56, 90, 130, 153, 173, 184, 185, 223, 226
Super Delegates, 19, 144
Super Tuesdays, 18, 66, 69, 86, 219
Supplementary Security Income, 165
Supreme Court, U.S., 16, 26, 161, 163, 172

T

Taft, William Howard, 161, 171, 174, 212
Tarbell, Ida, 178
Tariffs, 94, 95, 102, 159. *See also* particular laws.
Taylor Grazing Act, 162
Taylor, Paul, 133
Taylor, Zachary, 38

Television. *See* Media of Communication; debates, presidential
Temchin, Earl M., 48
Tennessee, 63, 75, 85, 126
Tennessee Valley Authority, (TVA), 162, 163, 172
Texas, 10, 23, 24, 61, 63, 76, 126
Thatcher, Margaret, 144
Third Parties, 22–23, 26, 73–74, 119–20, 123, 126, 129–31 *passim*, 212. *See also* particular candidates, parties, and independents.
Thomas, Norman C., 43, 46
Thurmond, J. Strom, 119–20, 147
Ticket Splitting, 136, 152, 194–95. *See also* Two-Tiered Party System.
Tillman Act, 161
Tocqueville, Alexis de, 190
Townsend Movement, 178
Traffic Safety Act, 165
Traugott, Santa A., 185
Truman, Harry S, 42, 55, 64, 73, 77, 138, 139–140, 179, 180
Truth in Lending Act, 165
Tsongas, Paul, 66, 68, 69, 70, 144
Tugwell, Rexford G., 44
Tulis, Jeffrey K., 161
Turner, Frederick Jackson, 93–94, 95, 123, 124
Turnout. *See* Voter Turnout.
Turnover, Incumbent and Party, 39–40, 42, 49, 51
Two Party System, 9, 13, 212
Two Term Tradition, 10
Two-Tiered Party System, 53–54, 152, 191, 192–93. *See also* Ticket Splitting.

U

Unemployment Insurance, 165
Underwood Tariff Act, 161
Unified Party Control. *See* Divided and Unified Party Control.
Urbanization 95, 95
Utah, 62, 63, 90, 126

V

Van Beek, Stephen D., 131
Van Buren, Martin, 28, 101–102, 114, 128, 129
Vermont, 63, 79, 126

Vice-President, 10, 11, 13, 14, 19, 22, 23, 28, 49, 61, 70, 71, 211
Vietnam War, 12, 164, 178, 190
Virginia, 63, 125, 126, 129
Vogel, David, 165, 184–85
Vote Switching, 193–94
Voter Choice, 31–35, 207, 214
Voter Research and Surveys Exit Polls, 52–53, 74–75, 81, 82, 201, 205–206, 207
Voter Turnout, 17, 27, 29–31, 51–53, 72, 73, 213, 224
Voting, 6, 29–35, 213–14
Voting Coalitions in Presidential Elections, 3, 4, 9, 27, 84–85, 95, 137–140, 141, 151, 215
Voting Rights Act of 1965, 164, 172, 178, 221

W

Wagner, Robert F., 171
Wagner-Steagall Housing Act, 163, 171
Wallace, George, 120, 218
Walsh, Lawrence E., 72
War Mobilization Enactments, 167
Warren, Harris G., 183
Washington, George, 9, 35, 36,
Washington State, 63, 76, 90, 126
Water Pollution Legislation, 165, 166, 178
Watergate Scandal, 164, 190, 192, 217
Watson, Richard A., 43, 46
Wattenberg, Ben J., 153, 224
Wattenberg, Martin P., 152, 155
Wayne, Stephen J., 45, 46, 49
Wealth Tax Act, 162, 178
Weber, Max, 143
Webster, Daniel, 99, 128
Weidenbaum, Murray L., 185
Weinberger, Casper W., 72
Weir, Margaret, 183

Wessel, David, 186
West, 24, 26, 62, 76, 79, 90, 93, 95, 166
West Virginia, 63, 90, 126
Wheeler, Burton, 172
Whig-American Party, 212
Whig Party, 4, 19, 35, 36, 38, 40, 98, 99, 102, 105, 111, 114, 121, 122, 128, 130, 131, 151, 159, 171, 212
White, Hugh L., 99, 102, 128, 129
White, John Kenneth, 153, 210
White, Theodore H., 44, 89
White Americans, 11, 27, 52, 74, 77, 85, 160, 191, 202–03, 205, 207, 211, 213
Wildavsky, Aaron, 18, 22, 26, 45, 46, 47, 49
Wilder, Douglas, 68–69, 70, 84–85, 88
Wilderness Act, 164
Will, George F., 110, 131
Wilson, Rick K., 185
Wilson, Woodrow, 193, 209
   and elections, 38, 49, 73, 169, 171
   as governor, 171, 174
   presidential administration and public policy, 38, 159, 161–62, 167, 169, 171, 173, 177
Winnowing, 12–13, 18
Winston, Pamela, 89
Wisconsin, 16, 63, 126, 160, 171, 174
Wise, David, 43, 46, 47, 90
Women, 6, 11, 27, 30, 52, 74, 77, 79, 162, 166, 202, 206–208, 213, 215
Women's Movements, 178
Workforce, 6, 27, 191, 192, 204–205
Wyoming, 63, 90, 126

Y

Yang, John E., 186–87

Z

Zingale, Nancy H., 125, 127–28, 153

50,28

128204